Management for Professionals

More information about this series at http://www.springer.com/series/10101

Jim Austin • Judith Bentkover
Laurence Chait
Editors

Leading Strategic Change in an Era of Healthcare Transformation

Springer

Editors
Jim Austin
Executive Master of Healthcare Leadership
Brown University
Providence, RI, USA

Judith Bentkover
Executive Master of Healthcare Leadership
Brown University
Providence, RI, USA

Laurence Chait
Executive Master of Healthcare Leadership
Brown University
Providence, RI, USA

ISSN 2192-8096 ISSN 2192-810X (electronic)
Management for Professionals
ISBN 978-3-319-30775-6 ISBN 978-3-319-30776-3 (eBook)
DOI 10.1007/978-3-319-30776-3

Library of Congress Control Number: 2016939220

Printed on acid-free paper

This Springer imprint is published by Springer Nature
The registered company is Springer International Publishing AG Switzerland

To our spouses, Susan Conger-Austin,
Peter Allaman, and Ann Chait.

Preface

Healthcare is personal. Healthcare is local. And healthcare is one of the greatest challenges faced by countries around the world. The magnitude of these challenges calls for fundamental change to address inherent problems in the healthcare system and ensure sustainable access to healthcare for generations to come.

As authors, educators, practitioners, and participants in the healthcare system, we find ourselves in the midst of these challenges and their solutions. Certainly, change is occurring, but not nearly as broadly and rapidly as we believe is necessary. Today's mindsets and methods are inappropriate and/or insufficient to enable the level of needed change.

Our observations lead us to ask four simple questions (some with not-so-simple answers):

- **Why change?** Given history and ongoing challenges, why call for transformational change?
- **What to change?** What areas for change are most promising—areas with the greatest potential to yield significant benefits?
- **How to change?** What is the balance between incremental change and more fundamental, longer-term, transformational change?
- **When to change?** What is the speed and timing of suggested changes?

Part I provides frameworks for answering these questions. Parts II, III, and IV—Case Studies—utilize these frameworks to outline examples of transformational change in multiple healthcare settings. Together, this book provides both a guide for healthcare leadership teams grappling with change and real-world examples that emphasize lessons learned from comparable efforts.

We are all faculty members in Brown University's Executive Master of Healthcare Leadership (EMHL) program, preparing leaders to transform healthcare. EMHL is designed for clinicians, executives, and senior administrators with significant responsibility in the healthcare industry. The program seeks to create and effect real, lasting change in moving towards a healthcare system centered on the patient, replacing traditional silos with innovative, collaborative efforts to truly transform healthcare. Participants identify a critical challenge they face in their role in healthcare that requires transformative change. Throughout the program, students gather advice, resources, and support to identify and implement creative solutions to their chosen challenges. As indicated, this book outlines our various frameworks to transform healthcare (Part I), complemented by examples primarily provided by our students of the transformational changes they realized utilizing these frameworks (Parts II, III, and IV). The book balances theory with real-world examples, so healthcare leaders can utilize it as a guide for driving transformational change in their own organizations.

We, the authors, come from a variety of academic and professional backgrounds: a former senior healthcare executive at an international medical products company who teaches management and marketing; a healthcare strategy consultant teaching value creation as a means of attaining high performance; and a health economist with a career split between international healthcare consulting and academe, lecturing on healthcare policy and data-driven decision-making.

This book is for current healthcare leaders, grappling with how to transform their organization to meet the evolving, often contradictory needs of changing local healthcare systems. A fundamental assumption of this book is that healthcare transformation is possible. But what do we mean by "*transformational*" change? Definitions abound from the *incremental* aimed at reducing the *rate* of healthcare cost increases to *improving population health.* And does transformational change mean working *within or outside* of existing institutions and relationships?

The frameworks outlined in Part I are meant to aid healthcare leaders and their teams in undertaking *either of these, ideally related journeys—transforming within or beyond existing healthcare institutions.* The case studies in Parts II, III, and IV are examples of institutional improvement *and* expansion.

Through this book, we hope to share an effective "treatment plan" with healthcare leaders around the world who understand the need for transformational change and are seeking the tools and processes to achieve it.

Providence, RI, USA

Jim Austin
Judith Bentkover
Laurence Chait

Acknowledgement

The authors wish to thank Angela Sherwin, our cheerful colleague, whose organizational skills and support throughout was instrumental in keeping us motivated and on track.

Contents

1 **Introduction** 1
Jim Austin, Judith Bentkover, and Laurence Chait

Part I Strategic Issues and Frameworks

2 **Setting the Stage: Today's Healthcare Challenges** 15
Jim Austin, Judith Bentkover, and Laurence Chait

3 **Building Blocks for Strategic Planning** 25
Jim Austin, Judith Bentkover, and Laurence Chait

4 **Tools for Transformational Strategic Planning** 47
Jim Austin, Judith Bentkover, and Laurence Chait

5 **Driving Successful Implementation** 71
Jim Austin, Judith Bentkover, and Laurence Chait

Part II Case Examples of Institutional Change: Hospitals, Treatment Centers, and Provider Groups

6 **The Pursuit of the Integrated Multidisciplinary Service Line** 93
James Andrews

7 **Creating Ever Better Ways to Provide Cost-Effective Care for Our Community: The Coastal Medical Journey** 107
Meryl Moss

8 **Transforming the Facility Master Planning Process: How to Manage Risk in Times of Uncertainty** 119
David H. Deininger

Part III Case Examples of Population Health Change

9 **Buprenorphine Integrated Care Delivery Project: Genesis of the Howard University Urban Health Initiative** 139
Chile Ahaghotu

10 Transforming Cancer Survivorship Care 151
Doreen Wiggins

Part IV Case Examples of Market Transformation

11 Importance of a Vision: Licensure of Medical Dosimetrists 161
Brian Napolitano

12 Transforming Health Information Management: AHIMA and Scenario Planning 169
Linda Kloss

13 Transformation of Brand Planning to Embrace Future Uncertainties: A Pharmaceutical Company's Voyage 181
Brendan O'Brien

Part V Concluding Remarks

14 Conclusion 193
Jim Austin, Judith Bentkover, and Laurence Chait

Index 201

Editor Bios

Jim Austin a former senior executive at Baxter Healthcare, combines business strategy and organizational development theory with extensive industry experience. In 2013, Brown University appointed Jim an Adjunct Senior Lecturer in the Executive Master of Healthcare Leadership program where he leads the graduate Management & Marketing course. He also lectures at the Wharton Business School and Duke CE where he tailors and delivers senior-level seminars on Strategy, Strategic Execution, Scenario Planning, and Critical Thinking for a number of leading companies including Boston Scientific, Coca-Cola, Lincoln Financial, JP Morgan Chase, Roche China, General Electric, Boston Scientific, McKesson, and Hitachi.

From 2005 to 2016, Mr. Austin worked at Decision Strategies International, leaving as a Senior Principal. There he led numerous projects including scenarios of the future for a Medical Devices firm; R&D priorities for a major consumer products company; a strategic plan for the American College of Radiology; scenarios of the future for the League of Southeastern Credit Unions; and a new vision/priorities at RAND Health. Today, he heads his own consulting/executive development firm, JH Austin Associates, Inc.

Jim holds a BA in Economics and Politics from Yale University. He was a Special Student at the Massachusetts Institute of Technology in the Urban Studies Department and received a joint Masters in Public Affairs (MPA) and a Masters in Urban and Regional Planning (MURP) from the Woodrow Wilson School, Princeton University.

Judith Bentkover is the Executive and Academic Director in Brown University's Executive Master of Healthcare Leadership program. She is a Professor of the Practice in the Department of Health Services, Policy and Practice at Brown and also a Professor of the Practice in the Economics Department at Tufts University.

As the former President and Chief Executive Officer (CEO) of Innovative Health Solutions, a consulting firm providing research and strategic analysis to healthcare manufacturers, providers, and payers, Dr. Bentkover led international multidisciplinary teams in projects focused on applied economic and decision analysis associated with the use of pharmaceuticals, devices, biotechnology products, procedures, and diagnostic, therapeutic, and preventive regimens. As Partner-in-Charge of KPMG's global

Strategic Health Solutions practice, she helped life sciences companies bring products to market, obtain reimbursement, and maximize revenues associated with their sale. Earlier in her career, she was a faculty member at Harvard University and taught in the School of Public Health and Kennedy School of Government. She also served as the Deputy Director of the Boston Health Care Coalition, which she helped start. In this capacity, she worked with employers, hospitals, labor unions, patient organizations, and insurers collectively to address the issues of rising healthcare costs and disparities in access to healthcare.

Dr. Bentkover has authored approximately 100 research articles, chapters, monographs, books, and reports. She has testified before Congress, explaining the drivers of hospital costs. Dr. Bentkover is a reviewer for several pharmacoeconomics, medical, and health policy journals. She was included on Health Care 500's list of the most influential health policy makers in the USA and is recognized as a developer of therapy economics, translating cost-benefit methodology into innovative strategic management tools. She often is invited as a guest lecturer at universities, executive workshops, and conferences.

Laurence Chait Mr. Chait is an Adjunct Senior Lecturer at Brown University, where he teaches a Masters-level course in Strategy. He is also Managing Director of Chait & Associates, Inc., a consultancy that advises senior management and their teams on achieving and sustaining high performance—and helps them keep their strategic initiatives on track. He has over forty years of experience in business management and information technology.

In his consulting work, Mr. Chait has helped executives and organizations across industries manage change. His focus is on strategic business planning, change management, process improvement, and knowledge leverage. In addition, Mr. Chait supports clients as an executive and team coach.

Prior to Chait and Associates, Mr. Chait was Vice President and Director of Arthur D. Little, Inc. He held positions including Chief Knowledge Officer and Principal. While at ADL, Mr. Chait developed the firm's Business Process Improvement methodology and built its practice in that area.

Introduction

1

Jim Austin, Judith Bentkover, and Laurence Chait

Abstract

The US healthcare system faces upheaval ranging from incremental efforts to improve operating efficiencies to more transformational changes to care delivery and payment systems. Interestingly, all major economies confront similar issues: "demand-side" growth for care driven primarily by aging populations and "supply-side" resource constraints from the ever-increasing costs of providing such care. While cultural, historical, and political differences among nations will yield different solutions pertaining to the "correct" allocation and financing of healthcare products and services, leaders across the globe must deal with ever-increasing uncertainty as to the scope and speed of their healthcare systems' evolutions. What to do? This book will provide healthcare leaders with the tools, processes, and examples/case studies to lead strategic change in their organizations.

The US healthcare system faces upheaval ranging from incremental efforts to improve operating efficiencies to more transformational changes to care delivery and payment systems. Interestingly, all major economies confront similar issues: "demand-side" growth for care driven primarily by aging populations and "supply-side" resource constraints from the ever-increasing costs of providing such care.

J. Austin (✉) • J. Bentkover • L. Chait
Executive Master of Healthcare Leadership, Brown University, Providence, RI, USA
e-mail: james_austin@brown.edu; judith_bentkover@brown.edu; Lpchait-ca@chait.net

J. Austin et al. (eds.), *Leading Strategic Change in an Era of Healthcare Transformation*, Management for Professionals,
DOI 10.1007/978-3-319-30776-3_1

While cultural, historical, and political differences among nations will yield different solutions pertaining to the "correct" allocation and financing of healthcare products and services, leaders across the globe must deal with ever-increasing uncertainty as to the scope and speed of their healthcare systems' evolutions. What to do? This book will provide healthcare leaders with the tools, processes, and examples/case studies to lead strategic change in their organizations.

All healthcare leaders struggle to define their path forward in these times of high uncertainty. The theme of this book is:

> Incremental change is essential—organizations need to focus on the short-term to remain stable, efficient, effective, and well financed. But, this is not enough. Organizations that will succeed in the longer-term must also pursue transformational change to expand the way healthcare is delivered and financed—as well as each organization's role in a newer, more enduring system.

Written for senior healthcare executives, this book focuses on how to lead transformative, strategic change in times of great uncertainty. While organizations must change to meet the evolving needs of their healthcare systems, the problem is understanding where and how to change. Failures of strategy are often failures to anticipate a reality different than what an organization is willing to see.

While each country's healthcare system will evolve differently, two interrelated themes extend across nations: the need to improve outcomes and quality while lowering costs and the need to improve population health, not just treat the sick. For example, in 2012 the US Centers for Medicare and Medicaid Services (CMS) began rewarding and penalizing hospitals based on patient satisfaction scores and outcomes measures. And in 2015, CMS announced a goal of tying 85 % of all traditional Medicare payments to quality or value by 2016, and 90 % by 2018 (CMS 2015). Payment for volume of healthcare delivered is *morphing* into payment for value of healthcare delivered and *shifting* focus to capitated, risk-based "per-member-per-month" payment schemes. Physicians who were once viewed as independent contractors are *moving into* the role of hospital employees or developing affiliations with integrated care systems. Personal doctor–patient relationships are *expanding* to include multidisciplinary care teams.

But such issues are not unique to developed markets. In January 2014, Indonesia launched a broad healthcare coverage plan for its 250 million citizens. Over 133 million signed up for a plan that included everything from maternity checkups to expensive cancer operations. According to an independent survey, 81 % of Indonesians were satisfied with the program. Unfortunately, costs are rising dramatically:

> Last year, the program cost 3.3 trillion rupiah ($224 million) more than it took in from participants and from a government fund that pays the premiums for more than 97 million poor Indonesians. This year's shortfall could deepen to 13.5 trillion rupiah, the health ministry has projected. As a result, Indonesia is undertaking a costly overhaul… [including the need to raise] healthcare premiums by year-end… (Rachman 2015).

Neal Halfon (2014) outlines a three-stage evolution of any health-delivery system. In summary:

1. Stage 1: Acute Care System, characterized by episodic, nonintegrated, fee-for-service care interventions.
2. Stage 2: Coordinated Healthcare, focusing on outcomes, preventative care, with cost/quality metrics supported by strong information technology (IT) networks.
3. Stage 3: Community-Based, Integrated Care centered on population health, integrated networks and risk-based, capitated payment systems emphasizing outcomes.

More recently, the Health Care Advisory Board argued what healthcare systems are facing is the shift from a "traditional market" to a "retail market," specifically:

- **Buyers**: From passive employer, price-insulated employee to activist employer, price-sensitive individuals
- **Networks**: From proliferation of product options to narrow, custom networks
- **Plan Comparisons**: From minimal transparency to clear plan comparisons
- **Employer Role**: From reduced switching costs to ease of annual plan switching
- **Premiums**: From cost exposure to high deductibles and variable contributions based on individual situation (Daniel and Kupper 2015)

Healthcare leaders should ask themselves: where is my group or institution in this progression, or how does my organization relate to healthcare organizations in this progression? Where could we be in the future? How should I, as a healthcare leader, drive strategic changes in my organizations to meet the evolving needs of my healthcare environment? What short-term, incremental changes should we be putting in place … and what transformational, longer-term initiatives should we be focusing on?

A fundamental assumption of this book is that healthcare transformation is possible. But what do we mean by "*transformational*" change? Definitions abound from the *incremental* aimed at reducing the *rate* of healthcare cost increases to "*global health*" focusing on "*improving health and achieving equity* in health for all people worldwide" (Marušić 2013). In-between these extremes are multiple gradations of "transformational." Clayton Christensen, for example, argues for "disruptive innovations to revitalize the healthcare industry," meaning low cost, readily available technologies that will "provide sophisticated service in affordable settings" (Christensen et al. 2000; Ulwick et al. 2003).[1]

This book is for current healthcare leaders, grappling with how to transform their organization to meet the evolving, often contradictory needs of changing local healthcare systems. Does that mean working within or outside of existing institutions and relationships?

---

[1] Interestingly, the recently announced partnership between IBM and Novo Nordisk A/S "to create a so-called virtual doctor for diabetes patients that could dispense treatment advice such as insulin dosage" (Roland 2015) is an example of such innovations.

Dr. Karen Hein writes to improve access, raise quality and lower overall costs, leaders must redefine their role in health to "understand the notion of population health by providing a coordinated array of services across the entire continuum of care and especially by focusing on wellness/prevention and post-acute care. Geisinger is indeed one example, but… there are growing examples of 'Accountable Health Communities.'"[2] Such institution-expanding experiments are beginning. Chapter 9 and Chapter 10 are examples of Population Health initiatives indicative of broader institutional reform efforts. The Coastal Medical and AHIMA cases (Chapters 7 and 12, respectively) are examples of institutional improvement *and* expansion; the remaining cases focus on transformational change within current institutions. Thus, the frameworks outlined in the case studies (Chapters 6-13) are meant to aid health-care leaders and their teams in undertaking *either of these, ideally related journeys—transforming within or beyond existing healthcare institutions.*

Structure of the Book

This book addresses these questions and more, as described in the roadmap to the book chapters below.

Part I—Strategic Issues and Frameworks

Part I comprises four chapters outlining strategic issues facing healthcare leaders paired with recommended frameworks to drive transformational change from concept to execution.

Chapter 2—Setting the Stage: Today's Healthcare Challenges

This chapter provides an overview of the healthcare system's evolution over the last century and the rapidly growing challenges that exist today. Healthcare leaders, seeking ways through these challenges, must answer four simple questions:

- Why change?
- What to change?
- How to change?
- When to change?

The chapter focuses on these questions, explaining why change is necessary today and prime targets for change. The chapter then discusses how to change and

[2] Personal communication with Dr. Karen Hein, who is an Adjunct Professor of Family & Community Medicine at Dartmouth Medical School, a past member of the Green Mountain Care Board (VT), and immediate past president of the William T. Grant Foundation.

whether the changes can be incremental or need to be transformational. Finally, the reader can grapple with the question, "when to change?" The answer is simple: *now*.

Chapter 3—Building Blocks for Strategic Planning

Successful strategic planning requires several building blocks. The foundation includes an appropriate "mindset," a relevant methodology, a focused team, and a holistic approach. This chapter explores these building blocks and how they can be best used.

Mindset. Strategic planning is only as good as the decision-making process that leads to strategic choices. One difficulty in times of uncertainty is how individuals process information—what they are willing to consider. Healthcare leaders must help their teams overcome their tendencies to be "predictably irrational" and open to new, innovative, potentially disruptive opportunities. Good decisions involve three distinct steps that help overcome all-too-common "decision traps"—framing issues far too narrowly, being overconfident in the information that's gathered, and falling into groupthink to make decisions. This chapter outlines multiple examples and frameworks that should help teams and decision makers to increase their objectivity and creativity when approaching difficult strategic choices.

Effective Methodology. Successful strategic planning builds on a set of interlinked steps and resulting outcomes. Leaders design a strategic planning process to develop a set of action plans that will achieve an organization's mission and vision. Leaders must utilize appropriate, effective methodologies, or processes in designing a transformational strategic plan.

Appropriate and Focused Team. To develop an optimum strategic plan, people from across an organization, representing all organizational levels, should be involved in some way in the process. Such involvement is important not only to develop the plan itself but also to help ensure a supportive culture for its implementation.

Holistic Approach. While leaders are often aware of and concerned about "silos" in their organization, silos are not typically dealt with through the strategic planning process itself. Transformational change involves far more than basic "strategy." To ensure an effective transformational plan, all of the elements of an organization must be aligned, as depicted in Fig. 1.1.

For example, if a strategy calls for more nursing staff—possibly even playing new roles in community health initiatives—but resources and organizational structures are not adjusted to provide for these initiatives, implementation will fail. Or, if people across the organization do not understand and support culturally the organization's evolving mission and vision, any resulting plan will face significant barriers.

Of course, in a strategic planning process, an organization cannot specify and respecify in detail all of its organizational elements. However, at a minimum the process can and must identify and address major misalignments.

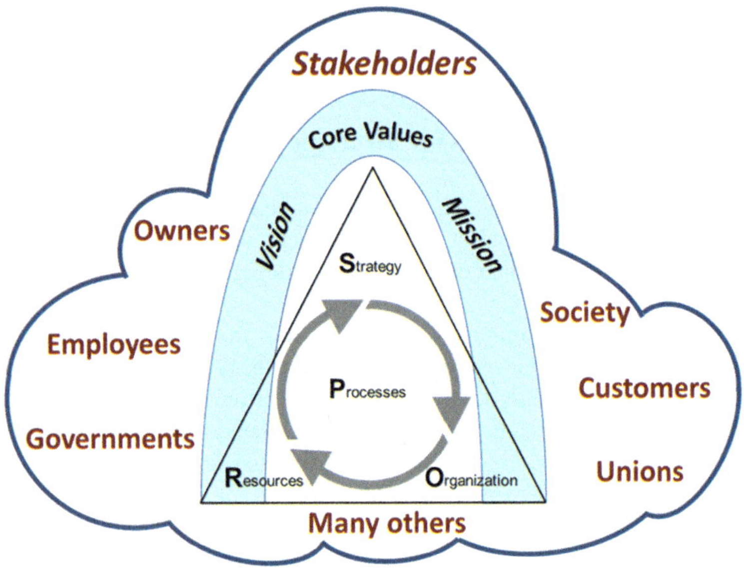

Fig. 1.1 Elements of the high-performance model

Chapter 4—Tools for Transformational Strategic Planning

Myriad approaches to strategic planning exist. Leaders must assemble an appropriate set of tools for use in an environment of uncertainty to achieve transformation. Such an approach must meet three attributes:

- **Visionary thinking**—The approach must permit nontraditional, creative thinking throughout the planning process. Such perspectives are needed to break out of the status quo, and to see more than incremental, short-term requirements.
- **Methodical**—While the approach must be open to new directions, it must also include tried-and-true planning techniques to ensure the approach is practical. The approach must also be tailored to the rate and magnitude of external change.
- **Measureable**—Finally, the plan must be quantifiable. Implementation is difficult or impossible without clear metrics—otherwise, leaders will not be able to define and demonstrate success.

This chapter explores different tools that satisfy these attributes. For example, scenario planning can be used to identify visionary options in times of uncertainty. The tool allows planners to portray a series of plausible alternative futures, methodically. Each scenario tells a story of how various forces might interact under certain conditions. Scenarios open up new ways of thinking about the future and provide a platform for strategic dialogue—new questions, new conversations—as the basis for strategic action.

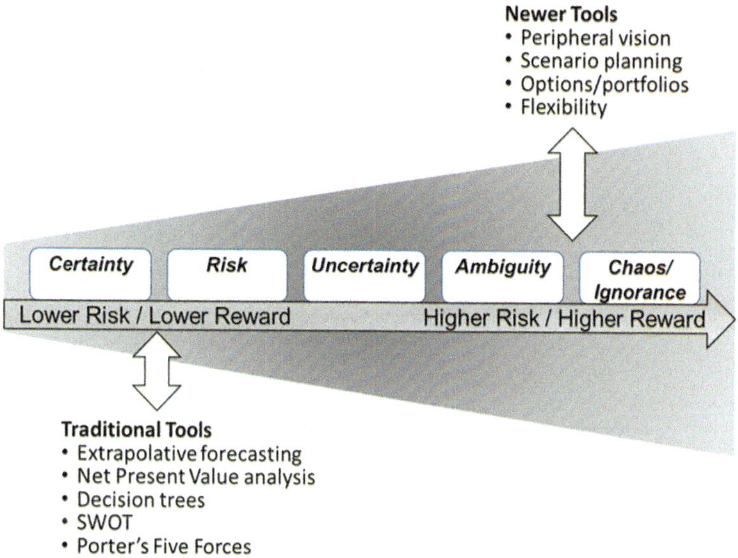

Fig. 1.2 Evolving trends and focus of strategic planning tools. (This framework, developed by Decision Strategies International, Inc., was established by P.J.H. Schoemaker)

The chapter also discusses other strategic planning frameworks—SWOT (Strengths, Weaknesses, Opportunities, Threats), Porter's Five Forces, etc. The point is, the tools must be relevant for the situation or environment facing an organization. Too often leadership teams pull out the simplest approaches, or the tools that were successfully used in the past, not realizing that in times of true uncertainty—as typifies the future of healthcare—the "past is not prologue." Five Forces and SWOT are best suited for more certain and moderately risky situations. As outlined in Fig. 1.2, given the high level of uncertainty and need for transformation in healthcare today, scenario planning is a more relevant tool to address the ambiguity and challenges healthcare leaders face.

Since visionary thinking is so critical to the kinds of transformation needed in healthcare organizations today, the chapter concludes with a more detailed guide to scenario planning, walking the reader through a step-by-step process to develop relevant scenarios—their own "alternatives" for the future. Using the futures developed, the reader can "stress test" existing strategies to develop new strategic options that reduce risk and increase growth opportunities. The goal of scenario planning is to enable healthcare leaders to develop strategies that both improve core operations *and* explore experimental or innovative opportunities. The ability to do both—focus on required, short-term, incremental changes while also seeking transformational opportunities—literally "painting with two paint brushes"[3]—is critical in times of uncertainty and change.

[3] The analogy from Professor Joe Ryan, Wharton, as often mentioned in his lectures.

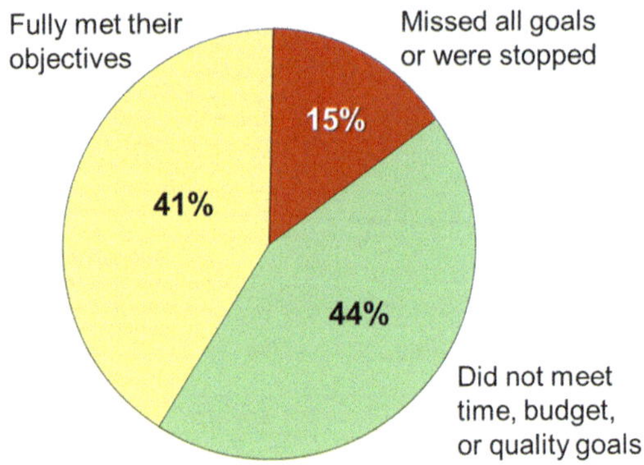

Fig. 1.3 Project success rates

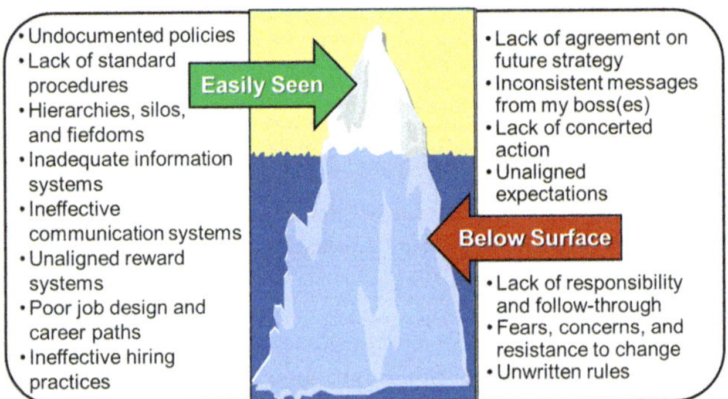

Fig. 1.4 Barriers to change

Chapter 5—Driving Successful Implementation

Leaders face the brutal reality that the vast majority of change initiatives fail to achieve their full objectives. About 15 % fail outright and another 41 % are "challenged" in some significant way. Only 44 % fully succeed (Jørgensen et al. 2008) (see Fig. 1.3).

This chapter explores the reasons behind implementation failure and proposes a series of positive actions that can be taken to optimize the likelihood of success. A leader must understand, evaluate, and mitigate the barriers to change summarized in Fig. 1.4.

This chapter describes additional actions, including:

- Establish a three-step process: agree clear priorities, ensure adequate resources to carry out the priorities, and hold individuals/teams responsible for results
- Create an effective governance infrastructure

- Implement a multifaceted communications program
- "Chunk" implementation and achieve a stream of quick wins
- Get beyond compliance to ensure widespread enrollment

Parts II, III, and IV—Case Examples of Strategic Transformation

Parts II, III, and IV provide case examples of strategic projects, primarily as developed and implemented by executives in Brown's Executive Masters in Healthcare Leadership Program. Each of their chapters includes a description of the case, tools/frameworks utilized, lessons learned, and key questions healthcare leaders should ask themselves in undertaking comparable transformational change.

Part II—Case Examples of Institutional Change: Hospitals, Treatment Centers, and Provider Groups

Chapter 6—The Pursuit of the Integrated Multidisciplinary Service Line

Brigham and Women's Hospital; Boston, Massachusetts

Mr. James Andrews, Administrative Director of Brigham and Women's Heart and Vascular Center, summarizes the integration of six cardiovascular specialty areas to create a more efficient, patient-focused cardiovascular service line.

Chapter 7—Creating Ever Better Ways to Provide Cost-Effective Care for Our Community: The Coastal Medical Journey

Coastal Medical, Rhode Island

Coastal Medical, a large, physician-led, primary care practice, underwent a major organizational and cultural change to meet the future demands of the Affordable Care Act.

Chapter 8—Transforming the Facility Master Planning Process: How to Manage Risk in Times of Uncertainty

2dplanning, Massachusetts

This case describes architect David Deininger's integrated healthcare master planning process used with his hospital/provider clients. The process provides a 360-degree, high-level view of their context and a flexible framework/vision for development that embraces future uncertainty.

Part III—Population Health Change

Chapter 9—Buprenorphine Integrated Care Delivery Project: Genesis of the Howard University Urban Health Initiative

Howard University's Urban Health Initiative, Washington, DC

This case describes a community-based medical practice focused on high-risk patients receiving buprenorphine therapy for chronic opiate addiction. Innovative approaches—comprehensive healthcare services via care-coordinating patient navigation, telehealth services, and a common Electronic Health Record (EHR) platform—are highlighted, resulting in improved clinical outcomes, enhanced health behaviors, and improved family-health dynamics.

Chapter 10—Transforming Cancer Survivorship Care

Lifespan Healthcare Systems, Rhode Island

In 2012, Lifespan Healthcare System launched the Women's Medicine Collaborative to address the gender-specific healthcare concerns of women. The aim was to develop an evidence-based, integrative cancer survivorship program to serve the needs of female cancer survivors and their families. This case examines the progress made, as well as the remaining development issues, as the program seeks to fulfill multiple stakeholder needs for improving gender-specific survivorship care.

Part IV—Market Transformation

Chapter 11—Importance of a Vision: Licensure of Medical Dosimetrists

Massachusetts General Hospital, Boston, Massachusetts

Medical dosimetrists, part of the clinical care team, strive to administer therapeutic radiation safely and effectively. To date, the profession lacks formal requirements for clinical practice with no route to licensure in Massachusetts. This case describes Brian Napolitano's efforts to achieve licensure status for improved patient care and growth of the profession.

Chapter 12—Transforming Health Information Management: AHIMA and Scenario Planning

Kloss Strategic Advisors, Chicago

Highlighting the tool of scenario planning, this case outlines how a major association assessed the changing requirements of their members, evolving the role of the association to aid members in transition. Written by the past-Chief Executive Officer (CEO) of the American Health Information Management Association

(AHIMA), the case highlights the difficulties, trade-offs, and different stakeholder perspectives that arise in times of major change and uncertainty.

Chapter 13—Transformation of Brand Planning to Embrace Future Uncertainties: A Pharmaceutical Company's Voyage

Decision Strategies International, Philadelphia

The North American affiliate of a major, international pharmaceutical firm faced major change from increased market uncertainty with the Affordable Care Act to increasing competition. The case examines how the marketing department utilized the tool of scenario planning to help the senior leadership move from short-term tactics to a discussion of future challenges and alternatives. Out of these discussions came future guidelines that enabled the brand teams to realize new growth opportunities.

Part V—Concluding Remarks

Chapter 14—Conclusion

The final chapter summarizes the major points made in the book and provides a checklist to drive transformative change. Strategy requires trade-offs and focus. The challenge is to develop critical short-term priorities that keep one's operations functioning, while laying the groundwork for broader, longer-term transformational change. It demands greater efficiency while at the same time experimenting … trying new endeavors. To ensure focus and the necessary resource commitments, in driving transformational change healthcare leaders should ask themselves what will they:

- **Eliminate**: What activities are healthcare leaders doing that are of *minimal or little value* in driving sustainable competitive impact?
- **Ease**: What activities could leaders *minimize*, thus providing more energy to focus on more critical endeavors to minimize risk and increase opportunities?
- **Elevate**: Where do healthcare leaders need to *raise the bar* to drive strategic change?
- **Explore**: What new capabilities do healthcare leaders need to acquire in order to drive strategic transformation in their organizations?

References

Christensen CM, Bohmer R, Kenagy J. Will disruptive innovations cure healthcare. Harvard Business Review 2000 Sep–Oct.

CMS (Centers for Medicare & Medicaid Services). Value modifier results. Department of Health & Human Services, Washington, DC; 2015. http://www.cms.gov/Medicare/Medicare-Fee-for-

Service-Payment/PhysicianFeedbackProgram/Downloads/2015-Value-Modifier-Results.pdf. Accessed 20 July 2015.

Daniel JM Jr, Kupper BP. Ambulatory strategies in a changing reimbursement environment. In: Session 44 AB, American College of Healthcare Executives Congress on Healthcare Leadership, Chicago; 2015. 16–19 March 2015.

Halfon N et al. Applying a 3.0 transformation framework to guide large-scale health system reform. Health Affairs. 2014;33(11):2003–11. doi:10.1377/hlthaff.2014.0485.

Jørgensen HH, Owen L, Neus A. Making change work. New York: IBM Global Services; 2008. http://www-07.ibm.com/au/pdf/making_change_work.pdf. Accessed 12 June 2015.

Marušić A. Commentary: multiple definitions, common goal. Ann Ist Super Sanità. 2013;49(1):2–3.

Rachman A. Indonesia health-care program struggles. Wall Street J 2015 Oct 8.

Roland D. Virtual doctor created for diabetes. Wall Street J 2015 Dec 11: B4.

Ulwick AW, Christensen CM, Grossman JH. A prescription for health care cost reform. Strategy Innovation 2003;1 No. 1, March–April.

Part I

Strategic Issues and Frameworks

Setting the Stage: Today's Healthcare Challenges

2

Jim Austin, Judith Bentkover, and Laurence Chait

Abstract

This chapter summarizes the key issues facing all healthcare leaders—how to improve quality, expand access, and manage (ideally lower) costs. Every major healthcare system struggles to balance these, especially restraining costs as technology increases, populations age, and governments seek to expand healthcare access. The theme of this book is that these challenges present healthcare leaders with the need to manage simultaneously for the short-term, while also investigating longer-term, transformational change. In this way, leaders can learn to embrace future uncertainty, not flee from it.

Challenging Leaders for Generations

The delivery and payment of healthcare services entered the modern age when Germany enacted compulsory sickness insurance in 1893, soon to be followed by Austria, Hungary, Norway, Britain, Russia, and the Netherlands. Other European countries, including Sweden, Denmark, France, and Switzerland, subsidized the

J. Austin (✉) • J. Bentkover • L. Chait
Executive Master of Healthcare Leadership, Brown University, Providence, RI, USA
e-mail: james_austin@brown.edu; judith_bentkover@brown.edu; Lpchait-ca@chait.net

J. Austin et al. (eds.), *Leading Strategic Change in an Era of Healthcare Transformation*, Management for Professionals,
DOI 10.1007/978-3-319-30776-3_2

mutual benefit societies that workers formed to protect income against wage loss due to illness and infirmity rather than payment for medical expenses, which came later (Palmer 1999). Early healthcare programs were originally conceived as a means of maintaining both incomes and political allegiances of the working classes; only a select few programs became regarded as "universal" for their country's residents, such as Britain and Sweden.

Through World War I, healthcare insurance efforts in the United States were voluntary, utilizing private means to cover the costs associated with chronic or acute care. No legislative or public programs existed. Although Theodore Roosevelt supported a healthcare program, believing that no country could be strong with people who are sick and poor, he was unable to gain sufficient Congressional support for a federal healthcare policy.

In the early 1900s, the American Association of Labor Legislation (AALL), seeing the gains of working-brethren in Europe, began supporting healthcare insurance coverage for their members. In 1915, they created a legislative bill to cover expenses for physicians, hospitals, nurses, maternity, and worker death benefits; funds paid by workers, employers, and the state would support dependents.

As was to typify US healthcare policy initiatives over the ensuing nearly 100 years, multiple constituencies had a hard time agreeing on a common agenda. The American Medical Association (AMA) initially stood behind the AALL healthcare coverage legislation. However, due to disagreements within the AMA on specifics of physician payment, the AMA soon withdrew its support.

Similar discord within the labor movement occurred when the American Federation of Labor denounced compulsory health insurance, concerned that a government-based health insurance system would weaken union-power. The commercial insurance industry, whose primary revenues were based on coverage for funeral and other death benefits, also opposed this bill due to challenges to the bill's death-benefits schemes. As a result, nothing came of these early efforts.

With the advent of World War I, political ideology precluded financing compulsory social services that in any way appeared similar to German "sickness funds." In the 1930s, the focus changed from financing healthcare to providing healthcare services. At this time, medical costs for workers were regarded as a serious problem. Rising healthcare costs provided the stimulus for several public and private efforts to attempt to transform the US healthcare system.

Fast forward to the early 1960s when healthcare transformation again dominated Congressional and public debate. Through several political compromises, Medicare and Medicaid were born in 1965, offering public health insurance for those over age 65 and low-income populations. States slowing began to roll out implementation of Medicaid throughout the late 1960s and early 1970s.

> The problems we face today are a direct consequence of actions that we failed to take yesterday. Since Teddy Roosevelt first called for reform nearly a century ago, we have talked and we have tinkered. We have tried and fallen short, we've stalled for time, and again we have failed to act because of Washington politics or industry lobbying (Obama 2009)

Today, the US healthcare system is one of the most technologically advanced in the world. But while the United States is perceived as a global healthcare leader and spends much more on healthcare than other countries, its outcomes and rates of mortality are at best comparable to those of the developing world. As with most other major economies, the United States continues to grapple with how citizens can access high-quality healthcare at a reasonable cost.

Why Is Healthcare So Perplexing to Local and Global Leaders?

Innovation and transformative change in healthcare differ in many ways from innovation in other industries. In most industries, access to innovation is readily accepted, and the economic forces of supply and demand govern the rate of change. For example, smartphones revolutionized communication and multiple related industries. In India, roughly 75 % of the population accesses a mobile telephone. In Kenya, payment and banking services are more ubiquitous on mobile platforms than in many developed markets. As a result, government payment and support transfers to remote areas is dramatically increasing, while reducing transfer inefficiencies and graft in both countries.

Innovations in healthcare, on the other hand, are ripe with tension about whether access to these innovations is a basic human right or a privilege for those who can afford them. The tension between healthcare as a universal right and healthcare as a commodity or "privilege" that should be paid for individually is at the root of much of today's complexities in many healthcare systems. This tension drives how healthcare is consumed, paid for, experimented with, and delivered. In addition, normal market conditions of supply and demand that lead to greater efficiency and higher quality seem sadly lacking in healthcare (Porter and Teisberg 2006). As one writer dryly commented, if other industries operated like healthcare:

- Banking: Automated Teller Machine (ATM) transactions would take days or months because records would be unavailable or misplaced.
- Home Building: carpenters, electricians, and plumbers would work from different blueprints, with little coordination.
- Shopping: prices would not be posted and the price would vary widely within the same store, depending on the source of payment.
- Automobile Manufacturing: warranties for cars would not exist. Factories would not monitor output and would not have the data or incentive to improve production line performance or product quality.
- Airline Travel: each pilot would be free to design his or her own preflight safety check, or not to perform one at all. On average, one jumbo jet would crash each day and result in no changes to the system (Braithwaite 2014).

Today, the United States is not alone in its struggles with improving access, lowering costs, and improving quality. Around the world, countries face challenges to care for aging populations, manage more prevalent chronic diseases, and improve

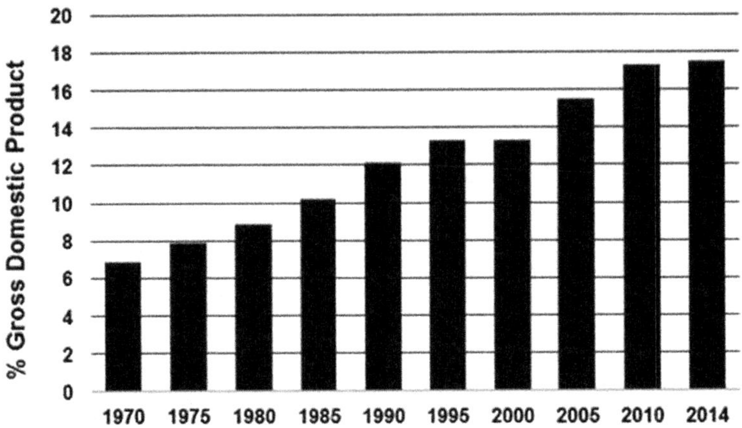

Fig. 2.1 Average percent of gross domestic product spent on healthcare, US, 1970–2014

access to basic medical advances. The "iron triangle" of healthcare—access, quality, and cost—where one can improve two out of the three—but rarely all three simultaneously—seems to bedevil every healthcare system.

The persistence of these issues and the snail-like or nonexistent pace of change led to this book. At the heart of today's issues, lie four questions:

- **WHY** change?
- **WHAT** to change?
- **HOW** to change?
- **WHEN** to change?

We will examine each of these questions in more detail throughout the rest of this book. In summary:

Why Change?

The answer is simple: the current situation is untenable.

Technology advances are ever more expensive, and big data systems collect more data but do not necessarily communicate the right information at the right time to the right party. At least in the United States, players scramble to forge alliances deemed as essential to survive in an ever more chaotic healthcare economy. Providers deliver care in a variety of settings; payers pay for care with a variety of plans. Patients and providers are both confused. Manufacturers of healthcare products face increasing challenges regarding how to recoup their costs of research and development. Politically polarized, local, regional, and federal constituencies are unable to forge consensus on the best way forward. Overall, these are uncertain times, with problems that increasingly defy incremental solutions.

Trend lines show healthcare spending moving higher and at an increasing rate, as shown in Fig. 2.1 (CMS 2015). What was troubling a few decades ago has become increasingly unsustainable. The impact of rising healthcare costs causes problems throughout the United States and global economies (Economist 2015). Simply put, resources devoted to healthcare preclude availability of resources to improve infrastructure, educate the population, or spend in other ways. For example, in Massachusetts, according to past State Treasurer Timothy P. Cahill:

> The universal [health] insurance coverage we adopted in 2006 was projected to cost taxpayers $88 million a year. However, since this program was adopted in 2006, our healthcare costs have in total exceeded $4 billion. The cost of Massachusetts' plan has blown a hole in the Commonwealth's budget (Bandow 2011).

The same holds true in private industry: the US auto industry faces a competitive disadvantage because of its comparatively large expenditures for healthcare benefits compared to other foreign automobile companies. Rising healthcare costs and their displacement effects underlie the calls for reform. As shown in Fig. 2.1, US healthcare costs have risen dramatically over the past 40 years.

Both governments and healthcare organizations have begun to make efforts to shift or at least reduce the healthcare cost "upward creep." For example, the United States has begun to experiment with healthcare financial incentives that pay for outcomes—such as "risk-based, capitated arrangements" that pay a per-member-per-month rate to providers—rather than pay for inputs, as typified by the historic fee-for-service arrangements permeating the US healthcare system. In the United Kingdom, the National Institute for Health and Care Excellence (NICE) establishes the treatments and drugs the National Health Service (NHS) will support and fund. Approaches like this emerge through a fundamental shift from paying for volume to paying for value and for outcomes, as well as trying to connect compensation for services provided and outcomes realized. Data and information on costs and consumption are slowly becoming much more transparent and generally available—to providers, regulators, and consumers.

The question is: will incremental changes be sufficient or do organizations and healthcare leaders need to embrace transformational change if healthcare systems around the world are to improve access, increase quality, and manage (ideally lower, at least in the United States) costs? This book argues for transformational change.

What to Change?

Three specific areas stand out.

Transforming healthcare organizations. Reflecting on the last 100 years, we see dramatic shifts in medical innovations to improve health, but organizations often adopt those innovations at a slow, evolutionary pace. New procedures can take decades—or medical generations—to become standards of practice.[1] New drugs, on average, take over a decade to go from initial identification to market launch, at over a $1 billion in R&D costs. While research in fields such as genetics and nanotechnology holds the promise of groundbreaking results, realizing those results more rapidly will take far more funding, time, and collaboration.

Yet, even given the barriers, change is possible—change that can set the path for further innovations. While change is hard, the case example in Chapter 9—Buprenorphine Integrated Care Delivery Project—is indicative of how creative teams use new tools, such as telemedicine, to drive more cost-effective, accessible care. Changes such as these can be leveraged and used by healthcare leaders as demonstration projects to help transform healthcare.

Transforming healthcare delivery. The strong influence of human factors and "decision traps" complicates achieving change in healthcare delivery (Kahneman 2011). One prime example of this influence is "evidence-based medicine." On the surface, having strong evidence for a procedure or treatment plan makes sense. But in reality, providers and patients are often slow in following new evidence, especially data that challenges existing orthodoxies (Gawande 2013). On average, following established protocols will yield the best results—but how can a clinician be sure it will be best for a specific patient in a specific situation?

Also, changing healthcare delivery systems can run counter to the natural tendency to "stick with what got us here." Finding solutions that both support short-term, operational requirements, while allowing for longer-term, more transformational change should bridge the gap between past and future requirements.

Finally, consumers armed with information (though not all of it quality information) influence delivery—or over-delivery—of care. Willing or compliant practitioners driven by past payment systems, too, influence care delivery.[2] In the United States, this situation generates large numbers of often-unnecessary tests, procedures, and prescriptions. Change is occurring: for example, changes to medical-service compensation models. But much more change is needed in delivery and payment models.

The case studies in Chapters 6-13 highlight real-world examples of significant change aimed at counteracting these trends. Chapter 9, for example, summarizes how a major teaching hospital collaborating with a community-based medical practice was able to provide comprehensive healthcare services to a disadvantaged population, thereby facilitating improved clinical outcomes, reduced chronic disease burden, enhanced health-seeking behavior, and improved family and community health dynamics.

Transforming healthcare financing. Healthcare payment systems are equally challenging. In most healthcare systems, the national or federal government can

---

[1] See the amusing, yet challenging article by Dr. Atul Gawande (2012).

[2] Fee-for-service, in the United States, for example, see the section: *Transforming healthcare financing*, below.

radically change healthcare through regulations and payment systems; achieving the necessary political support for such changes is daunting. In the United States, for example, while politicians continue to battle about the merits of the Affordable Care Act (ACA), new options for payment models are being tested, such as Accountable Care Organizations (ACO), Patient-centered Medical Homes, and Accountable Communities of Health (ACHs). ACOs are entities including hospitals, physicians, and other healthcare professionals responsible for delivering coordinated patient care for a defined population, not just individual patients. Rather than being paid for each service intervention, providers are typically rewarded based on group outcomes, including reduced hospital visits, increased quality, and management of chronic diseases. The Patient-centered Medical Home is a care delivery model in which the primary-care physician is responsible for coordinating treatment to ensure patients receive the care they need when and where they need it. Accountable Communities of Health build on these ideas by developing shared community health goals and bringing together public and private entities to achieve identified health metrics.[3] But these are nascent models, indicative of the range of experiments underway rather than the optimal solution(s).

How to Change?

Given the challenges faced by healthcare systems, and the lack of a clear way forward, it is no surprise that the future is highly uncertain. For any organization—within or outside of healthcare—the problem is how to balance the need for short-term improvements to keep current operations functioning … while simultaneously launching transformative initiatives that can substantially improve the likelihood of long-term success. It is, as one often hears, akin to creating the airplane of the future while flying the prop-plane of the past.

Different organizational challenges require different magnitudes of improvement, which, in turn, result in different types of change. At the low end of the change scale is *incremental change,* which results in small, ongoing improvements in current processes, resources, and organizational elements (Kaplan and Haas 2014). A higher magnitude of improvement, often referred to as *radical redesign,* looks beyond narrow or siloed processes and redesigns the way work is done across an organization. At the top of the scale is *transformation*. In this mode of improvement, discontinuous change occurs, often by taking totally new directions or introducing disruptive technologies into existing business models. (Uber, and its impact on the taxi industry, is a good example.)

[3] In Washington state, for example, ACHs will (1) establish collaborative decision-making on a regional basis to improve health and health systems, focusing on social determinants of health, clinical-community linkages, and whole person care; (2) bring together all sectors that contribute to health to develop shared priorities and strategies for population health, including improved delivery systems, coordinated initiatives, and value based payment models; and (3) drive physical and behavioral healthcare integration by making financing and delivery system adjustments, starting with Medicaid (Washington State 2015).

Magnitude of Improvement	Type of Change	Example
Small and local	Incremental	More efficient intake system in an ER or physician's office
Large and cross-organizational	Radical redesign	New, more efficient and effective care model that improves patients' outcomes from intake to discharge and beyond
Major and disruptive	Transformation	New reimbursement model throughout a delivery or healthcare system

Fig. 2.2 Level of organizational change and corresponding magnitude of improvement

Figure 2.2 distinguishes between levels of change and magnitudes of organizational improvement in healthcare.

Around the world today, countries struggle to care for aging populations and pay for new drugs, technologies. Healthcare consumers want improved access, greater quality, and lower costs, but the necessary trade-offs and the pathways forward are far from clear. And while other nations, such as Norway and Sweden, are much further along than the United States in their use of electronic medical record (EMR) systems, most countries struggle with data accessibility across all healthcare components that could inform treatment protocols, day-to-day administrative decisions, and longer-term transformational efforts.

Hospitals scramble to forge alliances deemed essential for surviving in an ever more chaotic healthcare economy. Pharmaceutical companies are combining in unprecedented numbers, at often staggering costs. Patients and providers are both confused about healthcare insurance options. Overall, these are uncertain times, with problems that increasingly defy incremental solutions.

In the midst of these tumultuous times, healthcare leaders grapple with future challenges and opportunities. The old adage, "If you are a hammer, everything looks like a nail" is too often typical of the strategic initiatives pursued by various healthcare players.

The level of strategic change required today is transformative. But note that incremental change and radical redesign are still required—it is just that those two modes of change, while necessary, are not sufficient. Transformation of organizations is needed to reach a tipping point that will result in broad, industry-wide transformation. Here is the rub: organizations know well how to change incrementally, and many can manage radical redesign. But precious few know how to be successful in transformation. Enabling organizations to achieve transformation is the challenge—and promise of the rest of this volume … while balancing the needs for the short-term, the need to "keep the doors open and business running."

When to Change?

Again, the answer is simple: Change *now!*

If you want to improve your organization's chances for long-term sustainability, start transforming now. It all begins with a well-designed strategic planning process and successful execution. We know it's possible—as the included case studies outline:

- Chapter 7: A large, primary-care practice underwent a major, transformational organizational and cultural change to meet the future demands of changing healthcare systems and the Affordable Care Act.
- Chapter 8: An architect created a new, integrated healthcare master planning process that aligns strategy, finance, and operations for hospitals and providers as they design and develop new facilities to meet the needs of healthcare into the future.
- Chapter 6: A major hospital redesigned its organizational and financial structures to improve its service line offering, yielding efficiencies, higher quality standards, and improved patient satisfaction.

They changed; now you can too! Chapters 3-5 discuss the building blocks needed, from an appropriate approach to transformative strategic planning to the keys for successful execution. Chapters 6-13 summarize examples where different groups within the healthcare ecosystem used these tools and frameworks to drive significant change.

Now, it's your turn: Transform!

Questions Healthcare Leaders and Teams Should Ask

As healthcare leader and author Quint Studer explains, "At one time the healthcare industry operated in a state of episodic change. Today, we've moved to a state of continuous change" (Studer 2013).

Chapter 2 offers a glimpse into why we believe healthcare leaders need to embrace transformational change, balancing short-term requirements (incremental change) with longer-term needs, to be successful in the future. To start on this journey, healthcare leaders should ask themselves and their teams four questions:

1. Why change?
   - What are critical challenges you see in the future?
   - Can you handle these with your current operations, actions, or do you need to assess radical or transformational opportunities?
2. What to change?
   - What are the critical areas in your organization that need to evolve in the future?
   - What current activities will you continue, and what new efforts, capabilities might you look to evolve in the future?

3. How to change?
   - Will you look to make short-term incremental changes … medium-term, more radical changes … or longer-term transformational changes and why?
   - How will you know if changes are successful … what are your goals in undertaking?
4. When to change?
   - Is there a "burning" platform—we have to change now!—or can you take a more gradual approach? Is this true for all your organization's activities?
   - What might be "triggers"—internally or externally—to shift the urgency of change?

References

Bandow D. Romney health plan a bust for Massachusetts. Real Politics. 2011 Sep 22. http://www.realclearpolitics.com/articles/2011/09/22/romney_health_plan_a_bust_for_massachusetts_111436.html#ixzz3qS4AN2gz. Accessed 9 Sep 2015.

Braithwaite WR. HIPAA on ICD-10. In: WEDI 2014 winter forum, Coral Gables, 8 Jan 2014 slide #11; 2014.

CMS (Centers for Medicare & Medicaid Services). NHE fact sheet. Department of Health & Human Services, Washington, DC. 2015. http://www.cms.gov/Research-Statistics-Data-and-Systems/Statistics-Trends-and-Reports/NationalHealthExpendData/NHE-Fact-Sheet.html. Accessed 10 July 2015.

Gawande A. Big med: restaurant chains have managed to combine quality control, cost control, and innovation. Can health care? The New Yorker 2012 Aug 13.

Gawande A. Sharing slow ideas. The New Yorker 2013 July 29.

Kahneman D. Thinking fast and slow. New York: Farrar, Straus and Giroux; 2011.

Kaplan RS, Haas DA. How not to cut health care costs. Harvard Business Review 2014 Nov.

Obama B. Remarks by the president at the opening of the White House forum on health reform. 2009. https://www.whitehouse.gov/the-press-office/remarks-president-opening-white-house--forum-health-reform. Accessed 30 Dec 2015.

Palmer KS. A brief history: universal health care efforts in the US. San Francisco: Physicians for a National Health Program; 1999. http://www.pnhp.org/facts/a-brief-history-universal-health-care-efforts-in-the-us. Accessed 15 June 2015.

Porter M, Teisberg EO. Redefining health care. Boston: Harvard Business School Press; 2006.

Studer Q. A culture of high performance: achieving higher quality at a lower cost. Florida: Fire Starter Publishing; 2013.

The Economist. The pause before fast-forward. The Economist 2015 Oct 10: 76.

Washington State Healthcare Authority. Accountable communities of health. 2015. www.hca.wa.gov/hw/Pages/communities_of_health.aspx. Accessed 15 Aug 2015.

Building Blocks for Strategic Planning

3

Jim Austin, Judith Bentkover, and Laurence Chait

Abstract

The aim of strategy—sustainable competitive impact—sounds simple. But it is not. This chapter lays the groundwork for strategic thinking, from developing a different mindset to ensuring a focus on creating and maintaining a high-performance organization. Outlining a holistic, flexible approach to strategic planning, the chapter provides the basic processes that will allow organizations to embrace uncertainty, balancing short-term incremental changes with longer-term transformational initiatives.

Introduction

Strategy is about three words: sustainable competitive impact. Whether in a for-profit or nonprofit environment, each of these three words is important. First, while short-term tactical necessities may exist to deal with immediate external challenges, the primary aim of strategic planning is to make choices that will produce longer-term sustainability. Second, all entities face competition. In the for-profit world, competition may be for market share or "share of wallet." Nonprofits compete for

J. Austin (✉) • J. Bentkover • L. Chait
Executive Master of Healthcare Leadership, Brown University, Providence, RI, USA
e-mail: james_austin@brown.edu; judith_bentkover@brown.edu; Lpchait-ca@chait.net

J. Austin et al. (eds.), *Leading Strategic Change in an Era of Healthcare Transformation*, Management for Professionals,
DOI 10.1007/978-3-319-30776-3_3

2000		2013	
1. Microsoft	(US)	1. Apple	(US)
2. General Electric	(US)	2. Exxon Mobil	(US)
3. NTT DoCoMo	(Japan)	3. Microsoft	(US)
4. Cisco	(US)	4. Google	(US)
5. Walmart	(US)	5. Berkshire Hathaway	(US)
6. Intel	(US)	6. General Electric	(US)
7. Nippon T&T	(Japan)	7. Johnson & Johnson	(US)
8. Exxon Mobil	(US)	8. Walmart	(US)
9. Lucent	(US)	9. Hoffmann-La Roche	(Swiss)
10. Deutsche Telekom	(Germany)	10. Chevron	(US)

Fig. 3.1 Top ten global entities, 2003–2013 (based on data from New York Times and Financial Global Times)

talent and stakeholder support. Finally, think of impact as leverage: does the entity "produce" or yield more output from given inputs than competing alternatives for these resources, whether financial, managerial, or social? David Dranove further explores this relationship as he writes, "A firm in a competitive market can earn a profit only if it creates more value than its rivals." And value "is the difference between the benefits enjoyed by a firm's customers and its cost of production" (Dranove and Marciano 2005).

This definition of strategy holds true in a stable environment, when a plan may result only in incremental change, as well as in an environment of rapid change and uncertainty, when there may be a greater necessity for organizational transformation. In either situation, achieving sustainable competitive impact over time to "stay at the top" is challenging (see Fig. 3.1).

Of those publically traded entities that had the highest global market capitalization at Year End 2000, there were only four "repeats" at Year End 2013: Exxon Mobil, Microsoft, General Electric, and Walmart. If one looks at a country level, the story is much the same. Why? Certainly macroeconomic factors could impact an entire industry, such as the recent drop in oil prices affecting all the major oil producers. At the enterprise level, many possible explanations exist: from hubris to poor leadership, from an internal focus goaded by short-term incentives to lack of vision and risk-taking, and from too narrow definitions of the business model to poor scanning of disruptive technologies.

When a past successful business or product begins to wane, it is really hard to transition (in time) to a new, alternative product, service, or business that is typically less profitable, requires different capabilities, and may even be of lower "quality."[1] Leaders of the business or product tend to try to "run

[1] See Christensen (2007) for a discussion of how disruptive technologies typically enter a market at a cheaper price point and lower quality than the established brands, leading the entrenched interests to proclaim: our customers won't want such products … until they do.

harder"—doubling-down on the "known" instead of making fundamental, transformational changes. Examples of such strategic challenges can be found in Kodak's inability to transition to digital (a technology they developed in the late 1970s); or Cisco System's current challenges in shifting from its legacy internet hardware products to a cloud oriented, service model, or Blackberry's rapid demise with the introduction of the iPhone.

As Richard Rumelt (2001) argues, part of the problem is most strategic planning efforts yield "bad" strategies. Such plans too often simply articulate generic goals (e.g., "improve our costs," "increase our market share," "grow into new markets," "be the world-wide leader in… ") that are not truly differentiable. Developers of the plan do not really engage in the hard work of looking into the ever-changing future to make choices that optimize current and longer-term opportunities. Worse, most strategies do not explicitly link to budgets, resource allocations, and specific actions for execution.

In addition, as strategy scholar Dr. Rita McGrath (2012) argues, entities that consistently outperform their competitive set simultaneously are "champions of stability" and "rapid adaptors." In their core, these companies promote from within, retain talent, maintain long-term customer relationships, and have management that does not make radical strategic shifts, maintaining a laser-like focus on culture and shared values. At the same time, these entities experiment: they make small bets seeking business diversification, they actively acquire new ideas as well as opportunities, they seek processes that build flexibility, and they incorporate innovation across the organization. This framework—building a portfolio of initiatives that balances current, short-term requirements with longer-term, more transformational efforts—is one of the key themes of this book. This framework is simply the best way to deal with rapidly changing, uncertain times that typifies healthcare environments around the globe.

Updated Perspective on Strategic Planning

Chapter 2 (*Setting the Stage: Today's Healthcare Challenges*) outlined the historical, political, and economic forces that led to today's challenging situation in healthcare. While the United States is most glaring in its relatively high costs, low quality (in comparison to other countries), and poor access—all major economies struggle to afford high-quality medical care for their populations. And as argued in Chapter 2, while incremental changes may help in the short-term, more fundamental—transformational—changes are required for long-term sustainability of our healthcare system. Unfortunately, no "silver bullet" exists that will solve all our issues. Rather, the future is truly complex, with multiple potential paths forward. Across most major economies, the future of healthcare is, by definition, uncertain (Courtney et al. 1997). Times of rapid change and uncertainty call out for innovative ways to think about "strategic planning" and "value creation" that produce a new set of questions:

- Where are we today?
- How did we get here?
- What is needed for sustainable competitive impact?

Evolution of Strategic Planning. Strategic planning's etymological roots are found in military planning. In fact, the word "strategy" is derived from the ancient Greek "*strategia*," which means "generalship." Planning for wars and battles involved the positioning and movement of troops. In the halcyon days of old, the generals and their senior staff devised the plans—their *strategy*; the troops followed orders.

More recently, business strategy came to refer to "competitive strategy" as moving chess-pieces on a board. Beginning in the 1950s, strategic planning became the battle for competitive position. Enterprises were "at war" with each other, and only those with the most effective competitive strategies would survive. The options were relatively simple. For example, an organization could buy another company or sell a division. An organization could compete on price or quality or features (Porter 1980). Or it could enter or exit a market. Senior management determined competitive strategy; as in the military at the time, the staff implemented management's decisions. Once a competitive strategy was set, a manufacturing strategy, marketing strategy followed, as did a human resources strategy, financial strategy, and so on.

Strategic Planning Issues. This model of planning worked in a world of relatively slow-moving competitors, trade barriers, domestic market dominance, and less-than-fluid capital movements. But even then, it did lead to various issues. First, misalignments arose between the views and plans of senior management and the realities that existed further down in the organization. And second, sequential, siloed planning often resulted in little congruence among the various plans. However, since the environment was relatively stable and certain, the difficulties encountered could be corrected and their possible risks managed.

Over time, with greater data access and the rise of strategy consultants such as Arthur D. Little, McKinsey, Boston Consulting Group (BCG), and Bain, corporate strategic planning became a complex, time- and resource-consuming activity. Because of that, and given the relative stability and slow pace of change in many business environments, large-scale planning efforts were undertaken every 5–10 years.[2]

Today, if a healthcare organization seeks transformation, the "top-down," resource-intensive, more static strategic planning models of decades past simply do not apply. Market conditions change too rapidly. In the past, governments moved slowly. With increased costs, access challenges, and quality-control issues, the healthcare environment is hardly stable. The pace of change seems to constantly increase, resulting in ever-higher degrees of uncertainty, especially the further out institutions attempt to plan.

In addition, given the pace of change and uncertainties in their environments, organizations cannot tolerate misalignments. The time allowed to take corrective

[2] For a history of strategic business planning, see McKinsey (2000).

action is significantly shorter. Five-to-ten-year planning cycles are simply inappropriate. Look back and see how quickly things evolved: the World Wide Web had its fledgling start in 1990, and the iPhone, with all its capabilities, was only released in 2007!

Furthermore, a strategic planning process that only involves senior management working largely in isolation from the rest of the organization causes problems. Information access and relevant knowledge that exists at lower organizational levels—fueled by technology advances and globalization of businesses—argue for much broader staff involvement. Senior management can no longer sufficiently stay in touch with markets, suppliers, and the operational realities faced by staff members to strategize on their own.

Planning and Implementation. Obviously, transformation depends upon successful execution. Yet senior managers working in isolation, with the planning function separated from operations, result in many of the execution failures that bedevil plan implementation. These major factors contribute to the low success record of many major change projects.

Chapter 5 will explore in more depth the issues with implementation and change management. But a large part of implementation success is inexorably tied to the strategic planning activity itself. Seeds for successful implementation are often sown in the planning process and how leaders undertake the planning process.

For example, in our own experience, implementation is most successful when the people responsible for that implementation are involved in the initial planning process. As Gary Hamel, founder of Strategos, writes, "The objective is not to get people to support change but to give them responsibility for engendering change, some control over their destiny" (Hamel 1996). Individuals involved in the planning process—people who are heard and own a part of the plan—are much more likely to support implementation. The bottom line: the people who will be responsible for implementation must be involved in planning.

The Strategic Journey. Research by McKinsey & Company suggests a new way to conceptualize strategic planning. The research holds that in today's uncertain, rapidly changing environment, planning is much less of an event than it is a journey (Bradley et al. 2012). In their model, strategic planning must be an ongoing process to deal with the changes and uncertainties in the environment. They suggest that senior managers frequently come together to identify critical issues, assess them, and agree on how to respond. The time suggested for such activities is significant. McKinsey argues that senior teams should devote roughly 25 % of their time on a continuing basis to strategic planning activities or discussions. McKinsey equated this strategic commitment as equivalent to the time senior management devotes to operating issues.

And McKinsey is not alone. Boston Consulting Group also speaks to the need to change our approach to strategy:

> Strategy, under relatively stable conditions, has historically relied on concepts of scale, efficiency, and first-order capabilities. But in a world of increased turbulence and unpredictability, leadership is less durable, industry boundaries are blurring, and forecasting has

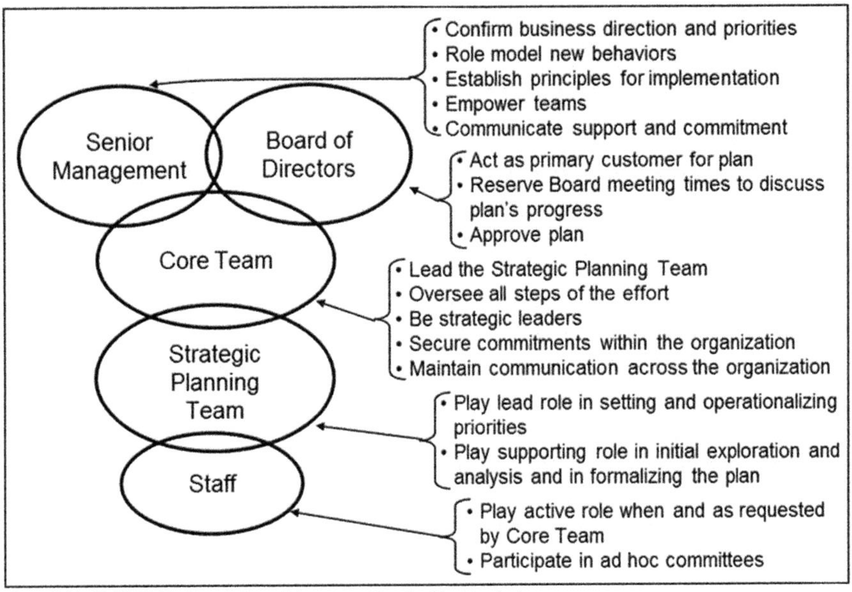

Fig. 3.2 Potential team responsibilities for strategic planning

> become much harder. We must therefore supplement traditional bases of competitive advantage with dynamic, adaptive capabilities and strategies (BCG 2015).

For transformational change, updating your perspective on strategic planning to reflect and embody today's realities is critical to success.

Building Blocks for Good Strategy

In our experience, four building blocks are essential for strategic planning efforts in today's complex, uncertain environment:

- Updated perspective on strategic planning
- Broad workforce involvement
- Unconstrained, open mindset
- Holistic approach to strategic thinking

Broad Workforce Involvement

As indicated previously, strategic planning for transformation requires broad workforce involvement. In our own strategic planning work, the model portrayed in Fig. 3.2 is typically utilized to delineate responsibilities in the planning process.

The sizes and numbers of ovals, as well as the names within them, change from situation to situation and organization to organization. However, two core concepts are always present:

- Strategic planning must always involve multiple groups, with different perspectives. The purpose of these groups is to spread the planning responsibility down and across the organization. This supports the mandate that those who implement must also plan. In addition, those further down the organizational ladder understand many aspects of the enterprise that senior leaders do not. Being close to markets and customers, they see valuable opportunities (as well as challenges), from which the executive suite is simply too removed. And finally, they are the leaders of tomorrow—the people who will be leading the organization as it lives through the consequences of current strategic planning and change initiatives.
- The groups (ovals) always overlap. These overlaps indicate shared memberships that enable much more effective communication. The absence of these overlaps can result in a siloed planning process with very poor communication across and down the organization.

In staffing the teams, planners must select the best team members to support the goal of achieving and sustaining high performance. Team attributes should include:

- Individuals receptive to the concept of creating a new future for the organization
- Open thinkers, willing to share their insights and ideas—rather than people who are likely to rubberstamp the senior team's perspective
- All team members must be trusted by their sponsors and the organization at large as such trust can be a major factor in the ultimate acceptance of the planning team's deliverables[3]
- One or two members might be outsiders—patients, suppliers, or others who represent the organization's key external stakeholders—to provide a perspective on future opportunities/challenges that employees or organizational insiders all too often lack
- One or two members should be selected due to their experience and skills to lead implementation efforts; ideally, the individual who will manage the implementation should come from the "core" strategic planning team (see Fig. 3.2)
- Team members should be individuals who will likely be impacted by the plan and its implementation
- Some members should be people with tenure who know the organization well, while others should be more recent hires bringing fresh ideas from outside the organization
- Most important, they should be the people with the *least* available time to spend in the planning effort—the *busiest* people in most organizations are usually the most valuable

[3] For how to establish and maintain trust, see Covey (2005).

When building the primary planning team, referred to above as the "Strategic Planning Team," it is important to include a mix of viewpoints. Given challenges inherent in any transformational or major change effort, some members should be known as innovators and future thinkers—the kind of people who will bring fresh ideas into discussions. Some members should represent owners/doers—people in supervisory or middle management positions who are integral to the work of the organization. And other members should represent those whose resources will be needed to ensure successful change.

Improvements to the patient experience undertaken at Augusta Health illustrate this strategic change process. August Health, in Fishersville, Virginia, is a 255-bed community hospital ranked by *Healthgrades* as one of the top 50 hospitals in the United States. According to Mary N. Mannix, Chief Executive Officer (CEO):

> Our biggest critical success factor is that <the patient experience> isn't just a top-down process; it cuts across all employee lines … It's not just leaders who have a voice; it's our frontline staff as well, because that's where our mission is fulfilled every day (Poore 2015).

According to Mannix, all stakeholders within and outside the hospital engaged with leadership to create "The Augusta Way":

> One of the biggest and earliest surprises during this cultural transformation was the high levels of employee engagement. The Augusta Way isn't about chasing a number or improving patient satisfaction scores, although that is clearly a desirable outcome. Our entire organization came together to decide how we will treat our patients and their families and how we will treat each other (Poore 2015).

Unconstrained, Open Mindset

Strategy, by its nature, is a creative act. Strategic planning is the one moment for most organizations to challenge the past, assess different opportunities and threats, and chart a course into the ever-evolving future. Unfortunately, as this book argues, most strategic planning efforts do little more than make incremental changes to past results.

Before we discuss our approach to strategic thinking, recognize that strategic planning is only as good as the *decision-making processes* that lead to strategic choices. One difficulty in times of uncertainty is how *individuals* make choices, how individuals process information—what they are willing to consider. Healthcare leaders must help their teams overcome the all-too-human tendencies to be "predictably irrational" (Ariely 2009). Daniel Kahneman, noted for his work on judgment and decision-making, articulated the leader's role this way:

> Executives can't do much about their own biases … But given the proper tools, they can recognize and neutralize those of their teams (Kahneman et al. 2011).

Good decisions involve three distinct steps:

1. Outline the issue(s)
2. Gather information
3. Make a decision[4]

Unfortunately, as behavioral psychologists explain, individuals are "hard-wired" to fall into the following "decision-traps" at each of these decision steps:

- Frame Blindness
- Overconfidence
- Groupthink

Healthcare leaders and their teams must consciously work at overcoming these decision-traps. How?

According to Kahneman et al. (2011), our brains process information in two distinct ways: intuitively and reflexively. Processing information intuitively "produces a constant representation of the world around us and allows us to do things like walk, avoid obstacles, and contemplate something else all at the same time." Processing information reflexively "is slow, effortful, and deliberate. This mode is at work when we complete a tax form or learn to drive."

While both operate simultaneously, the first determines the context or the situation for bringing to bear—if necessary—the analytic components of decision-making. Most of the time, decisions are made intuitively, quickly, and subconsciously. The challenge is when those "quick calls" lead to decision-errors. While Kahneman is not very sanguine about the ability of individuals to correct their own decision-errors, "There is reason for hope, however, when we move from the individual to the collective, from the decision maker to the decision-making process, and from the executive to the organization." In this vein, we explore the following three "decision-traps."

Frame Blindness: Today, data permeates the world. Possibly based on cave-dwellers' primordial necessity to decide quickly whether or not that movement in the bush is a man-eating lion or only the wind, humans "frame" problems rapidly, intuitively, and almost effortlessly. Rarely are assumptions made explicit, or adequate time spent assessing: *what is the real problem?* Senior leaders, especially those with strong personalities, want to "get to a solution."

To begin a transformational strategic planning effort, request that each participant list his/her assumptions about the effort. More specifically, ask each participant to outline:

- Why was our institution/group successful in the past?
- What do we need to do in the future to maintain/increase our success?
- Looking forward, what could derail, or impact those assumptions?
- Why are we undertaking this strategic planning effort?

[4] For further detail on these steps, see Russo and Schoemaker (2002).

For example, if several members of the strategic planning team assume the Affordable Care Act will minimally impact operations, while several other team members assume just the opposite, participants will struggle to find common ground due to their subconscious assumptions. Only in calling out those assumptions and in establishing awareness of one's "frame" can teams begin to search more creatively for solutions.

Overconfidence: As Paul Schoemaker (2002), founding partner of Decision Strategies International, writes, "We are too sure of our single view about the future, and we fail to consider alternative views sufficiently." Leaders use their experience to assess future opportunities or challenges. Unfortunately, it is hard to change beliefs; disconfirming evidence, or challenges to existing orthodoxy, are all too often pushed aside as "not relevant." As a result, individuals are notoriously bad at assessing risks of a given situation *objectively*. For example:

- 84 % of Frenchmen estimate that they are above-average lovers.
- 93 % of US student drivers think they are "above-average" drivers.
- 68 % of University of Nebraska professors rated themselves in the top 25 % for teaching ability.
- Entrepreneurs starting new businesses say their chances for success are 90 %—when statistics show on average a 50 % failure rate (Dobelli 2013; Thaler and Sunstein 2008).

As a strategy team begins to examine the strategic implications of health reform and gather relevant data, discuss the following questions:

- Where are we most vulnerable in relying on a single, common view of the future?
- Who can provide us with a fresh perspective on the data or reports we will be examining to help us broaden our strategic planning efforts and avoid "tunnel vision"?
- What can we do to leverage perspectives inside and outside of our institution or group to help avoid overconfidence?

Groupthink: This is one of the most difficult, insidious problems teams face when developing strategies for the future. Quite simply, groupthink is rooted in the all-too-human desire to be part of a group, to belong, to feel "connected." At a subconscious level, most individuals want to be part of the "A-Team." And that results in feeling emotionally conflicted when arguing against the assumptions, conclusions, and operating procedures of the group. Individuals quickly figure out what is and is not acceptable in their team … what does the boss, or most senior person "want to hear" … and what is "out of bounds?"[5]

To assess transformational change, groups must be willing to challenge existing orthodoxy. But how? Kleiner Perkins Caulfield and Byers (KPCB)—arguably one of the most successful venture capital firms ever—employs what they call the "Balance Sheet" to bring forth different points of view. Whenever the partners at

[5] For example, the experiments of Dr. Solomon Asch in the 1950s on groupthink.

KPCB face a major strategic decision—to buy a company, sell a company, or change the management of an acquired firm—all the partners must fill in what they label "their balance sheet": what are the "pluses" and "minuses" of this idea, action *from each individual partner's point of view.* Then, *before* discussion begins, each partner reads from his or her "balance sheet." Two things happen: first, everyone must prepare; and second, partners report they have changed their points of view "by being forced to listen to the views of others first" (Lovallo and Sibony 2010). The key is to *delay* discussion. The minute discussion begins, individuals stop listening as they (subconsciously) prepare to explain their own ideas and justify their own points of view. Leaders find it really hard to elicit different perspectives in any meeting—and even harder for groups to listen to ideas presented with a totally open perspective. But, as David Cote, CEO of Honeywell, states:

> Your job as a leader is to be right at the *end* of the meeting, not at the beginning of the meeting. It's your job to flush out all the facts, all the opinions, and at the end make a good decision, because you'll get measured on whether you made a good decision, and not whether it was your idea from the beginning (Bryant 2013).

Approaching the strategic planning process with an unconstrained mindset is critical to identifying and being open to transformational possibilities. Without such a mindset, the resulting plan will be doomed … doomed to repeat actions from the past, incrementally moving the healthcare organization forward, lacking the creativity and insight to layer on transformational changes critical for future success in the ever-challenging, evolving future of healthcare.

Holistic Approach to Strategic Thinking

As indicated above, early approaches to strategic planning—based on a stable, more certain view of the world—are insufficient to deal with the challenges and uncertainties facing healthcare leaders today and into the foreseeable future.

The need for transformation in healthcare—in an environment of significant change and uncertainty—demands a new strategic planning framework and process. The high-performance model (HPM) fills this void. First conceived in the 1990s at Arthur D. Little, Inc., (Nayak et al. 1992) and further developed by the authors, the HPM focuses on four questions that healthcare leaders should ask themselves:

- Why does my organization exist?
- How does my organization create sustainable value?
- How should my organization strategically position itself for the longer-term?
- How will we achieve our goals and measure our progress to achieving those goals?

The model is best explained from the "outside in." An organization's strategies and operations exist in a complex ecosystem. The external environment—the economy, regulatory environment, global issues, competitors, and suppliers—surround and impact every organization.

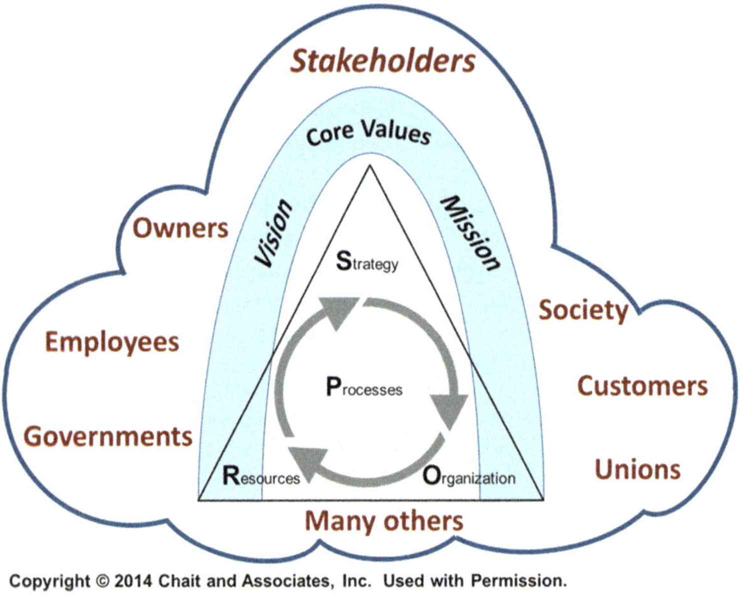

Fig. 3.3 Elements of the high performance model

Fundamentally, an organization exists to create value for its stakeholders. This model applies to both for-profits with requirements for financial returns to investors and nonprofit stakeholders seeking to further their mission. However, the power and impact of different stakeholders changes over time. Based on an organization's strategic assessment of short-term and longer-term changes in the external environment, as well as different stakeholder requirements in those evolving futures, the organization sets its future direction consistent with its mission, vision, and core values.

In the center of the model are the organization's strategies and operations. As outlined below, this triangle is really four connected triangles through which the organization plans and executes its plans.

Most organizational planning and operational models treat elements such as strategies, processes, and implementations as discrete, addressing them sequentially. Traditionally, the calendar year was divided into quarters with a strategic planning period (typically Q1), a budgeting cycle, building off the agreed strategy (often Q2) and then functional group roll-outs with implementation metrics measured the rest of the year. But, in times of rapid change, with great future uncertainties, continuous and accelerated improvement *requires* that all business processes—from strategic planning to budgeting and operational management—are functioning on *parallel* tracks and continuously feeding new information to the other processes.

At its core, high performance is achieved when all of the elements of an organization, shown in Fig. 3.3, are aligned and moving toward a common, shared, aspirational vision. Sustaining high performance requires ensuring continuity of that alignment even as situations change.

Value Creation: Evolving Definitions of "Stakeholders"

Over the decades, the focus of value creation dramatically changed. In the 1960s, the target was the shareholder, and the goal was to maximize earnings or long-term return on investment (ROI). In the 1980s, that singular focus on shareholders was extended to include two additional stakeholders: customers and employees.

More recently, the focus of value creation expanded even further. Strategic planning today certainly includes customers, employees, and owners as stakeholders—but also incorporates any entity or individual that the organization serves or that can make demands on it. In healthcare, stakeholders can be quite extensive, ranging from unions, hospitals, patients, clinicians, researchers, service staff, insurers, governments, regulators, to community organizers.

Today, another stakeholder is often added to the mix: society (Porter and Kramer 2011). More and more organizations articulate and measure their broad "social impact," not just their financial results. To some, this social role simply fulfills a "Public Relations" effort added to the environmental and other regulatory requirements organizations face; other organizations take this social role quite seriously with goals, objectives, costs, and actions that they undertake and ask their stakeholders to support. For example, Novo Nordisk subscribes to a "triple bottom line" of financial, social, and environmental responsibility[6]; Whole Foods has a core value of sustainability.[7]

To achieve high performance in healthcare, the issues and concerns of multiple stakeholders must be taken into account. Organizations address the complexity of their environments through this effort. Organizations must understand their stakeholders' often-competing needs and demands and weigh them against each other—as it is simply not possible to satisfy the full requirements and demands of all stakeholders simultaneously. Needs of nursing staffs in a hospital are different from those of patients and administrators—to say nothing of regulators and the community. Needs of pharmaceutical patients differ significantly from those of a pharmaceutical company's stockholders. Understanding and prioritizing stakeholder needs is the foundational step to developing unique value positions for sustainable competitive impact.

[6] For details on Novo Nordisk's triple bottom line, see Novo Nordisk (2015).

[7] For details on Whole Foods' core value of sustainability, see Whole Foods (2015).

Aspirational Vision	A clear, compelling statement of the future the organization wants to create, one that will act as a magnet, pulling people toward that future
Mission	The purpose of the organization—why it exists, what it does, and what it does not do
Core Values	The principles and beliefs that determine how people in the organization will behave

Fig. 3.4 Mission, vision, and core values

Mission, Vision, Aspirations, and Core Values

As the Cheshire Cat so correctly told Alice, "If you don't know where you're going, any road will get you there" (Carroll 1865). A high-performing organization knows—with considerable precision—where the organization is heading. That direction is aspirational—and yet practical—and is unique to the institution. That "true North" direction helps answer the question: Why do we exist?

Internally, the HPM begins with a vision, mission, and core values (see Fig. 3.4). Organizations must get these elements right as they form the foundation for the organization and its strategic plan. They set the aspirational rationale for the organization's existence, as well as the practical "boundaries" for action, internally and externally. Ideally, they should serve as a magnet towards which the organization and everyone in it are drawn—and the embodiment of the organization that everyone on the outside can see and appreciate.

How is this different than culture? Ideally, the vision, mission, and core values reflect and grow from an organization's culture. Unfortunately, there can be a fundamental difference between the "expressed" culture and the "embedded" culture.[8] Expressed culture is what an organization says, what it wants employees and external stakeholders to believe. Unfortunately, the embedded culture is how employees and others actually behave. Enron in its values statement claimed: "As a partner in the communities in which we operate, Enron believes it has a responsibility to conduct itself according to certain basic principles" (Kunen 2002). How employees actually behaved at Enron was dramatically different. While challenging, leaders must be honest about any potential gaps between what leaders say and do. More importantly, leaders must ask themselves: is our culture, today, the right culture to realize our future aspirations? And if not, what do we need to change?

Aspirational Vision. The Alzheimer's Association provides an example of an exemplary vision statement from a healthcare organization: "A world without Alzheimer's disease®." The statement is simple, aspirational, comprehensible, powerful, and unique. Their vision is magnetic, drawing people toward it. As author and business consultant Jim Collins writes, "Enduring companies have clear plans for how they will advance into an uncertain future. But they are equally clear about how they will remain steadfast, about the values and purposes they will always stand for" (Collins and Porras 1996).

[8] From private conversation with Dr. Mario Moussa, Wharton School.

Powerful visions balance *what* the institution stands for and *how* it will advance into an uncertain future. One approach to defining such a vision is to begin with the question: *If we did not exist, what would the world lose?*

Who should be involved in developing an institution's vision? Two extremes exist. At one end, senior managers meet in the executive suite, develop a vision statement, and then share it throughout the organization. At the other end of the spectrum, people in the organization are brought together in groups to share their own aspirations, relate them to the future of the organization, and from that work, derive an aspirational vision in which they are all enrolled.

While both methods can yield a "shared vision," the resource requirements and time necessary for communication are often quite different. In the HPM, a shared vision developed by multiple layers of an organization creates a strong alignment of the staff toward a common purpose—a fundamental requirement for high performance. When people are involved in creating a vision, they feel a sense of ownership, ideally an emotional commitment. While an organization may take more time to create the vision by engaging different levels of an organization, much less time may be required to gain its acceptance. And with broad employee engagement comes a much lower probability that the embedded and expressed cultures will be at odds over the new vision.

Mission. A mission defines what an organization does, whom it serves, and (at a high level) how it creates value. A clear mission statement sets boundaries; it can help keep an organization focused and prevent it from wandering and expanding its scope in unproductive ways.

Examples of healthcare mission statements appear in Fig. 3.5.

Core Values. Core values succinctly give people—employees, stakeholders, and the public at large—a clear view of what is important to an organization. Many organizations' value statements do not really meet this standard. Instead, the organization may use generic words that can be applied to all organizations, words like integrity, sustainability, and creativity. As James Kunen (2002), a leading corporate communications expert, writes:

> Then again, maybe adherence to ethical conduct really should go without saying. Every company's statement ends up rehashing the same things, anyway: We will maintain the highest ethical standards, treat our employees with respect, encourage teamwork, make quality products, and respect the environment … As opposed to what? We will maintain fair-to-middling ethical standards? Treat our employees like old shoes, foment backstabbing, make shoddy products and lay waste to the environment?

Core values must be something more than that. The *Harvard Business Review* provides an excellent definition:

> Core values are the deeply ingrained principles that guide all of a company's actions; they serve as its cultural cornerstones … They are the source of a company's distinctiveness and must be maintained at all costs (Lencioni 2002).

Examples of core values of healthcare organizations appear in Fig. 3.6.

The Mayo Clinic was established in the early 1900s in Rochester Minnesota. Today, the Mayo Clinic serves over one million people a year from over 150

Organization	Mission
Large, regional, integrated healthcare provider	We are committed to serving the community. We are dedicated to enhancing patient care, teaching, and research, and to taking a leadership role as an integrated healthcare system. We recognize that increasing value and continuously improving quality are essential to maintaining excellence.
Worldwide leader in medical care, research, and education	To inspire hope and contribute to health and well-being by providing the best care to every patient through integrated clinical practice, education. and research.
Academic medical center	We are dedicated to helping people achieve and maintain healthy lives and restoring wellness/health to maximum attainable levels
Major-city hospital for children	Provide the highest quality care, be the leading source of research and discovery, educate the next generation of leaders in child health, and enhance the health and well-being of children and families in our local community.

Fig. 3.5 Examples of mission statements of healthcare organizations

countries. Mayo is a large organization, operating three campuses, a 70-hospital/clinic health system, and several medical colleges.

A large part of the Clinic's success can be ascribed to its simple, yet powerful core value: "The needs of the patient come first." That value statement was first expressed by Dr. William Mayo over 100 years ago, and today is part of Mayo's embedded culture. As former CEO Dr. Glenn S. Forbes said:

> If you've just communicated a value but you haven't driven it into the operations, into the policy, into the decision making, into the allocation of resources, and ultimately into the culture of the organization, then it's just words (Berry and Seltman 2008).

The Mayo Clinic relies on the "patient first" value as a qualifier in hiring new practitioners. "Patient first" is also a key criterion in winnowing out staff from the organization. In these ways, the culture "self-corrects," demonstrating the power and longevity of the Mayo values.[9]

[9] For more information on the Mayo Clinic and the impact of its core value, see Berry and Seltman (2008).

Organization	Core Value
Pharmaceutical company	Preserve and improve human life
Rehabilitation services firm	Help people with mental impairments realize their full potential
Medical device manufacturer	Help all people lead healthy lives

Fig. 3.6 Examples of core value statements of healthcare organizations

Strategy

Moving even further into the HPM comes strategy. An organization's strategy presents the primary, high-level actions it will follow—actions designed to achieve its vision and mission and satisfy its stakeholders. Strategy establishes the road map for the future: key priorities, choices, and trade-offs necessary for future sustainability. The tools for developing strategy will be covered in Chapter 4. Before discussing them, what are the key processes that good strategy should be concerned with, but all too often is not?

Processes, Resources, and Organization

The HPM elements of processes, resources, and organization (PRO) are all too often not covered during strategic planning. Most often, these elements are relegated to the realm of implementation. During implementation, leaders design and redesign processes, bring to life resource plans, and establish supportive organizational elements.

However, not considering processes, resource plans, and organization during the planning process can be a potential cause of failure when the plan moves to implementation. For example, a plan that implicitly assumes new processes may fail in implementation if the planning does not recognize and address the need for new capabilities, such as financial management capabilities in moving from a fee-for-service to a risk-based, capitated world. Similarly, a plan that involves physically moving groups of people around is likely to run into rough sledding if it does not consider the physical resources available to the organization. And finally, a plan that assumes a new, transparent management style will not prove successful unless it recognizes the need to address several cultural issues.

This is not to argue that the PRO should be fully designed during the planning phase; rather, the implications of the strategy on PRO must be recognized and taken into account in the plan.

At Rush University Medical Center (RUMC), Chicago, leadership established a separate "Office of Transformation" during Rush's strategic planning efforts to change major care delivery infrastructure. According to Peter Butler, President RUMC, "It has never been more challenging to prioritize the work that needs to be done when you are not sure how fast and in what ways the market will change. As a result, you need to be nimble and patient but nevertheless decisive." The Office of Transformation was created "...to make sure that we could think freely about the future and not drag along some of the past processes and behaviors" (Hegwer 2015).

Therefore, when developing a strategic plan, be sure to ask the following questions:

- Are the current resource and organizational processes aligned with the strategies?
- What new processes and/or additional resources will be required to support the strategic plan?
- What resources will be required, for how long, to move from the institution's current state to what the strategy envisions for the future?

Finally, new strategies may imply the elimination of some current processes and resources. It is important to recognize such impacts during the strategic planning process and develop tactics to effect such changes. Elimination of processes and resources will be disruptive and emotionally draining for all involved. If not addressed proactively, these disruptions can significantly hamper or derail implementation efforts.[10] These themes will be more fully explored in Chapter 5, Driving Successful Implementation.

Processes. Processes are the vehicles through which organizations achieve their strategies. Everything that is accomplished in an organization is done through a process.

In every organization, low-level processes exist as sets of steps to accomplish a task; such processes are normally called "procedures." At the highest level, an organization is constituted of six-to-ten "core" processes—broad collections of subprocesses that cut across an organization. It is through these core processes that virtually all of an organization's primary work is done. Generically, such processes are typically marketing, service, finance, and information technology. In a hospital setting, core processes often include admitting, billing, pharmacy, and patient care.

Often, what people call "core processes" are really subprocesses or physical departments (that can include many lower-level processes of their own). But core processes include much more. For transformation, such misunderstandings of what constitutes a core process can be a significant barrier to change.

For example, imagine a generic hospital "patient process." The process would begin when the patient's first entered the institution—whether through a medical-staff admission, referral, or Emergency Room (ER) visit. It would cover admitting, diagnosis, transport, all aspects of treatment, discharge planning—and possibly post-hospital activities, such as rehab and home care. By assessing the core patient process holistically, not department-by-department, an institution may be able to improve access, lower overall costs, and raise care standards.

[10] For an excellent discussion of how to handle eliminating resources, personnel, see Mishra et al. (2009).

But such a perspective would be a radical departure from the current reality for most hospitals. It could only flow from a different vision leading to potentially transformative strategic planning efforts.

Resources and Organization. If processes are the vehicles through which organizations achieve their strategies, then the resource and organization elements provide the fuel to power those processes.

In a healthcare setting, resources includes buildings, diagnostic equipment, computers, information technology, and the people who employ all of these resources. Analogous resources exist in pharmaceuticals, insurance, and all other industries.

The "organization" element of the HPM represents the "soft side" of the enterprise. It includes roles and responsibilities, policies and procedures, structure, climate and morale, and management systems. Most important, it includes the organization's culture—the behaviors that are embedded into how people do their work and relate to others.

Strategic plans often impact the in-place organization elements of the HPM. They can require changes to training and reward systems, the organization chart, and expected behaviors. When these changes will be significant, they should be carefully analyzed, as they may indicate the need for changes in the emerging plan, itself—either to add action plans to address them, or to reconfigure components of the strategies, themselves.

PRO Alignment. Processes, resources, and organization (PRO) must work hand-in-hand to achieve an organization's objectives and sustain high performance. Strategic leaders need to ask: What could happen if our institution gets two of these elements right, but fails with the third? If honest, the answer is that the plan will likely fail.

Research supports what should be obvious—that organizational performance increases or decreases depending on the alignment of PRO (Maira and Scott-Morgan 1997; Womack et al. 1990). The closer the alignment of these three elements, the higher the performance of the organization and the better its results.

As stated earlier, while the elements of process, resources, and organization are not the focus of strategic planning, their alignment with each is critical to achieve and sustain high performance.

HPM Alignment. Just as processes, resources, and organization must be aligned with each other, so too must they be aligned with strategy, mission, vision, and stakeholder needs—with all of the elements of the HPM. In fact, the goal in planning for high performance is to ensure that each of the elements of the HPM is aligned with the others. Misalignments—especially in times of change and uncertainty—will render strategic plans very difficult to implement successfully. And if the plans call for transformation, significant misalignments will make implementation impossible. Tests of alignment across the HPM are important steps in the development of a strategic plan for high performance—and critical steps if that plan calls for transformation.

Strategy Creation

Chapter 4 will focus on the tools or specific models for strategy creation. As will be discussed, in times of complexity and uncertainty, leaders need strategic tools—such as scenario planning—that can help examine strategic initiatives against different future environments, assess options, and then build a balanced portfolio of incremental (short-term) actions, as well as transformational (longer-term) moves. In this way, the organization can prepare itself for sustainable competitive impact no matter how the healthcare system evolves.

Questions Healthcare Leaders and Teams Should Ask

This chapter begins outlining our approach to Strategic Planning for times of uncertainty. All healthcare systems around the world face fundamental cost, access, and quality issues. While country systems may vary by degree of challenge and the willingness of political entities to embrace systemic change, the future is likely to be very different from the past. This chapter outlines a holistic, flexible approach that allows organizations to embrace uncertainty, balancing short-term, incremental changes with longer-term, transformational initiatives. The key questions healthcare leaders and their teams should discuss as they begin the Strategic Planning journey are summarized below.

Setup

- Why are we undertaking a strategic planning process?
- How far out will the plan look: 3 years, 5 years, or longer?
- What is our view of the external environment: fairly stable (and so the plan can focus on more incremental changes), or more uncertain, complex (requiring a blend of incremental and more transformative initiatives)?
- Who will be involved in the strategic planning effort:
  - Only senior management?
  - A "blend" of senior management and other organizational groups?
  - A number of working teams engaging various levels of the organization and external stakeholders?

Unconstrained, Open Mindset

- Framing/Assumptions
  - Why were we successful in the past?
  - What do we need to do to be successful in the future?
  - What could disrupt these assumptions?
- Overconfidence

  - Where are we most vulnerable in relying on a single, common view of the future?
  - Who can provide us with a fresh perspective on the data or reports we will be examining to help broaden our strategic planning perspectives?
  - What can we do to leverage perspectives inside and outside of our institution or group to help avoid confirmation bias?
- Groupthink
  - How do we challenge "prevailing wisdom"?
  - How do we surface all the points of view in the room?
  - How do we reach a decision? Who has decision-rights?

External Environment

- Who are our primary, secondary, and tertiary stakeholders that the Strategic Plan should be built around?
- What are their expectations today … in the future?
- Are the external stakeholder requirements primarily financial … or are there broader, more social imperatives?
- How will we gather their perspectives and input for the Strategy?

Vision/Mission/Values

- Vision
  - If we did not exist, what would the world lose?
  - What are our aspirational goals … that might never be achieved?
  - What is unique about this organization and our role going forward?
- Mission
  - What is our core purpose?
  - Who will we serve … why?
  - How will we qualitatively measure our impact?
- Core Values
  - What are our enduring, core values we would follow even if it meant taking a financial loss?
  - What actions, behaviors will we not tolerate?

Throughout your strategic planning processes, seek a blend of short-term, critical operational priorities with a few experiments for greater future flexibility, embracing future uncertainty. And engage a broad array of viewpoints. As Teri Fontenot, President and CEO of Women's Hospital, Baton Rouge, LA, argues, "The key is looking at your particular market and scope of services and figuring out how you can experiment. We included people in every decision that we could allow them to make, and this helped to earn their trust and engagement" (Hegwer 2015).

References

Ariely D. Predictably irrational. New York: Harper-Collins; 2009.
BCG. Choosing the right approach to strategy. BCG perspectives. Boston: Boston Consulting Group; 2015.
Berry LL, Seltman KD. Management lessons from mayo clinic. New York: McGraw Hill; 2008. p. 20.
Bradley C, Bryan L, Smit, S, Managing the strategy journey. McKinsey Quarterly 2012 July.
Bryant A. Decisiveness is a two-edged sword. New York Times 2013 Nov 3: B2.
Carroll L. Alice in Wonderland. London: Macmillan and Co.; 1865.
Christensen C. The innovator's dilemma. New York: Harper Business; 2007.
Collins J, Porras JI. Building your company's vision. Harvard Business Review 1996 Sep–Oct.
Courtney HG, Kirkland J, Viguerie P. Strategy under uncertainty. Harvard Business Review 1997 Nov–Dec.
Covey SMR. The speed of trust: the one thing that changes everything. New York: The Free Press; 2005.
Dobelli R. The art of thinking clearly. New York: Harper; 2013.
Dranove D, Marciano S. Kellogg on strategy. New York: Wiley; 2005. p. 30.
Hamel G. Strategy as revolution. Harvard Business Review 1996 July–Aug.
Hegwer LR. Leading change from the c-suite: 3 leaders share their strategies. Healthc Exec. 2015;30(6):12.
Kahneman D, Lovallo D, Sibony O. Before you make that big decision. Harvard Business Review 2011 June.
Kunen JS. Enron's vision (and values) thing. New York Times 2002 Jan 19.
Lencioni P. Make your values mean something. Harvard Business Review 2002 July.
Lovallo D, Sibony O. The case for behavioral strategy. McKinsey Quarterly 2010 March.
Maira A, Scott-Morgan P. The accelerating organization. New York: McGraw Hill; 1997. p. 125.
McGrath R. How the growth outliers do it. Harvard Business Review 2012 Jan–Feb.
McKinsey. Thinking strategically. McKinsey Quarterly 2000 June.
Mishra AK, Mishra KE, Spreitzer GM. Downsizing the company without downsizing morale. MIT Sloan Manage Rev. 2009;50(3):39. Spring.
Nayak PR, Drazen E, Kastner G. The high performance business: accelerating performance improvement. ADL Prism. 1992;1997(1):5–29.
Novo Nordisk. Triple bottom line. 2015. http://www.novonordisk.com/sustainability/Focus/Our-Sustainability-Approach/Triple-Bottom-Line0.html. Accessed 15 Sep 2015.
Poore JM. When culture and strategy collide. Healthc Exec. 2015;30(4):52.
Porter M. Competitive strategy: techniques for analyzing industries and competitors. New York: The Free Press; 1980.
Porter M, Kramer M. Creating shared capital. Harvard Business Review 2011 Jan–Feb.
Rumelt R. Good strategy, bad strategy. New York: Crown Press; 2001.
Russo JE, Schoemaker PJH. Winning decisions: getting it right the first time. New York: Doubleday; 2002.
Schoemaker PJH. Profiting from uncertainty. New York: Simon & Schuster; 2002. p. 225.
Thaler RH, Sunstein CR. Nudge. New Haven: Yale University Press; 2008.
Whole Foods. Our core values. 2015. https://www.wholefoodsmarket.com/mission-values/core-values. Accessed 24 Dec 2015.
Womack J, Jones DT, Roos D. The machine that changed the world. New York: Free Press; 1990.

Tools for Transformational Strategic Planning

4

Jim Austin, Judith Bentkover, and Laurence Chait

Abstract

How should healthcare leaders begin a strategic planning effort given future uncertainties? This chapter provides a summary of key strategic planning tools from SWOT (strengths, weaknesses, opportunities, and threats) to scenario planning. While the aim of strategy—sustainable competitive impact—is the same no matter which tools are utilized, this chapter argues that more dynamic tools, such as Hambrick's Strategy Diamond and scenario planning, are best suited for healthcare's increasingly uncertain future. Robust strategy efforts should yield a portfolio of strategic initiatives—short, medium, and longer-term—that can "bend" with future uncertainties while lowering the risk of being truly unable to respond as the future unfolds.

Introduction

Genentech, one of the world's foremost biotechnology companies, had a problem. Its cancer drug, Avastin, was used "off-label" by many ophthalmologists as a lower-cost option to Genentech's more-expensive drug, Lucentis. While not cleared by the Food and Drug Administration (FDA) for treatment of macular degeneration in

J. Austin (✉) • J. Bentkover • L. Chait
Executive Master of Healthcare Leadership, Brown University, Providence, RI, USA
e-mail: james_austin@brown.edu; judith_bentkover@brown.edu; Lpchait-ca@chait.net

J. Austin et al. (eds.), *Leading Strategic Change in an Era of Healthcare Transformation*, Management for Professionals,
DOI 10.1007/978-3-319-30776-3_4

2007, Avastin had the same mechanisms of action as Lucentis—and at 2.5 % of the per-dose cost of Lucentis. Genentech's response was to restrict the usage of Avastin by "halting sales of Avastin to compounding pharmacies that have been dividing Avastin into the smaller quantities needed for treating the eye." This led to a public relations nightmare (Haddrill 2014). In a quarterly earnings teleconference with analysts, a Genentech executive said that Lucentis was used to treat 55 % of new patients and 50 % of all patients. Ophthalmologists say Avastin accounted for most of the remaining patients—nearly half the market (Pollack 2007). How could this happen? Did Genentech not think through alternatives … or were they blindsided by rapidly evolving market conditions, possibly the very conditions they helped set in motion?

As discussed in Chapter 3, organizations find it hard "to stay at the top." Steve Lohr (2007), in exploring some of the business challenges facing Microsoft, writes:

> One of the evolutionary laws of business is that success breeds failure; the tactics and habits of earlier triumphs so often leave companies—even the biggest, most profitable and most admired companies—unable to adapt.

Difficulties of adapting to changing environments pervade all types of corporations. Consider the case of rural hospitals in the United States, institutions originally begun to serve populations facing many healthcare challenges including high rates of heart disease, diabetes, tobacco use, and other chronic health conditions. These hospitals face two significant challenges. First, the healthcare delivery system in rural areas frequently confronts health professional shortages, and most importantly, a lack of primary care physicians (Bodenheimer and Pham 2010). Second, their payer mix weighs heavily toward government payers. Due to the rural poverty rates, higher incidences of chronic disease, and generally older populations, Medicare and Medicaid comprise the majority of healthcare funding, and generally reimburse below the actual costs of care (Steinberg 2015).

The Affordable Care Act (ACA) extracted Medicare cuts from all providers, under the premise that a provider's uninsured population would be reduced by Medicaid expansion and by the purchase of new insurance products from health exchanges.

In some rural areas, such as some Southern states, minimum increases in health insurance coverage occurs. States that rejected health reform, declined to operate an exchange, and refused to expand Medicaid also experience deterioration of the financial health of their rural healthcare infrastructure. Operating margins of rural healthcare providers may be one of the failures bred by state implementation of the ACA, whose primary goal was to improve access to healthcare.

Globally, every major economy struggles with rising healthcare costs. Are healthcare leaders, irrespective of national boundaries and expectations, able to adapt to the demands of a growing population with a greater proportion of that population aging, manage more chronic conditions, and utilize more healthcare services?

Failures of strategy are often failures to anticipate a reality different than what organizations are prepared or willing to see. So as the healthcare environment changes, how can healthcare leaders plan for the future? The challenge is to utilize the *appropriate* strategic planning tools for an entity's environment and time frame. Such tools must meet three attributes:

- **Visionary thinking**. The approach must ensure that the planning process allows for nontraditional, creative ideas. Such thinking helps to break from the status quo and realize opportunities in times of uncertainty and rapid change.
- **Methodical**. While the approach must be open to new directions, it must also emphasize practical application. And all the parts of a strategy—from vision to options to priorities and execution—must fit together, mutually reinforcing each other.
- **Measureable**. Finally, the approach must ensure that the plan can be tracked and adjusted based on variations in key plan assumptions, such as those concerning the external environment, internal capabilities, and competitor actions. Successful implementation is difficult or impossible without clear metrics that tie back to planning and resource allocation updates.

This chapter explores different tools that satisfy one or more of these attributes, principally SWOT (strengths, weaknesses, opportunities, and threats), Five Forces, Hambrick's "Diamond," and scenario planning. In summary:

- **SWOT** examines the internal Strengths and Weaknesses of an entity, as well as the external Opportunities and Threats facing an organization. The framework seeks to leverage positive factors and mitigate negative ones. The primary question SWOT seeks to answers is where to focus given internal capabilities and the external, competitive environment?
- **Porter's Five Forces** considers different competitive aspects within an industry, specifically threat of new entrants, degree of competitive rivalry, supplier power, buyer power, and threat of substitution. Application of the Five Forces seeks to determine the relative power or control within an industry in order to answer the question: how can we gain greater power and leverage given our position and industry structure?
- **Hambrick's Strategy Diamond** provides leaders with key components to an integrated, overarching strategy (Hambrick and Frederickson 2001). Hambrick argues that most strategies are little more than "catch-all terms," lacking necessary specificity, alignment, and purposeful design. This framework asks: how will we achieve our strategic objectives in an integrated fashion that is also unique and sustainable?
- **Scenario planning** can be used to identify visionary options in times of uncertainty. The tool allows planners to portray a series of plausible alternative futures, methodically. Each scenario tells a story of how various forces might interact under certain conditions. Planners design scenarios to open up new ways of thinking about the future and provide a platform for strategic dialogue—new

Strengths	Weaknesses
• Strong sales & marketing infrastructure • Ability to drive cost elimination • Industry-leading early stage R&D pipeline • Robust balance sheet	• Mature portfolio with increasing exposure to generic competition • Lack of blockbuster product launches • Failure of R&D pipeline to deliver initial commercial expectation
Opportunities	**Threats**
• Movement into high growth foreign market • Potential to increase sales growth in emerging markets • Strong cash position facilitates potential M&A	• Impact of generic erosion to sales • Development setbacks impacting late stage R&D pipeline

Fig. 4.1 Sample SWOT analysis for pharmaceutical company

questions, new conversations—as the basis for strategic action. Scenario planning seeks to answer: how can we survive—ideally prosper—no matter what the future brings?

The strategic planning tools chosen by an organization must be relevant for its situation or environment. SWOT and Five Forces are best suited for more stable, moderately challenging situations. One of the themes of this book is that Hambrick's Strategy Diamond and scenario planning are more relevant tools for the uncertain, highly challenging environments facing most healthcare entities.

Key Strategic Planning Tools

SWOT

The easiest, most approachable planning tool for any organization is a SWOT analysis, examining the Strengths, Weaknesses, Opportunities, and Threats facing the organization in the future. The first two areas—Strengths and Weaknesses—typically explore the internal operations or capabilities of the organization. On the other hand, Opportunities and Threats examine the external environment. Figure 4.1 shows an example of a SWOT analysis for a pharmaceutical company.

The intent of a SWOT is to focus management on the critical internal and external issues facing the organization. Through structured discussion, analyses, and follow-up, leaders can orient their organization to maximize strengths, while seeking to shore-up or offset challenges. For example, in Fig. 4.1, management of this

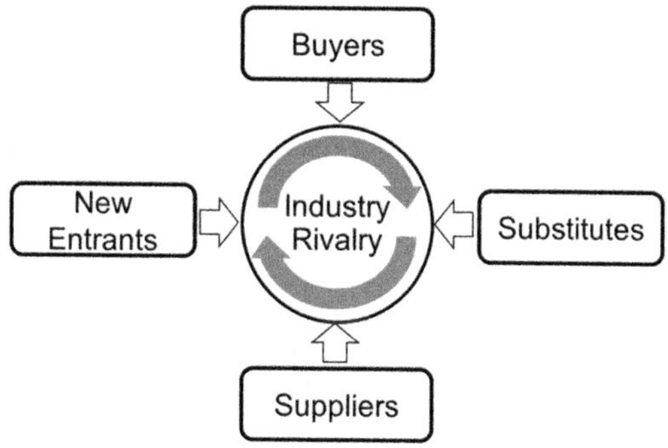

Fig. 4.2 Porter's Five Forces (Porter 1980)

particular pharmaceutical company faced a declining (internal) R&D pipeline. To offset this, they developed a series of external partnerships with promising, smaller bio-tech labs, as well as explored generic manufacturing of company brands that were soon to come off-patent.

While a quick "diagnostic," SWOTs often are insufficiently dynamic for complex situations and suffer from overly simplistic portrayals of evolving environments. They are often used in the context of shorter planning periods, or for more mature market assessments.

Porter's Five Forces

Michael Porter (1980) developed the Five Forces framework in his seminal work, "Competitive Strategy." He sought to add greater rigor to existing strategic analyses by focusing on specific industry structures, competition, and potential for profitability within different industries. For Porter, power over one's environment is key: the greater the influence an entity exhibits over the forces that characterize specific industries, the greater the profit-generation potential. Figure 4.2 summarizes Porter's Five Forces.

Some analysts add a "sixth force"—government—which may be very relevant for healthcare leaders in their application of this planning tool.

After outlining the components for each force, those conducting the strategic planning exercise must assess how to gain greater power or control over these forces going forward. Some typical ways entities seek to shift relationships, gain more power, and improve their future returns include:

- Leverage power over buyers (e.g., build customer loyalty)
- Offset supplier power (e.g., locate alternative supply sources)
- Avoid excessive rivalry (e.g., attack weak or emerging entities)
- Raise barriers to entry (e.g., make preemptive investments or seek regulatory barriers to new entrants)
- Reduce the threat of substitution (e.g., incorporate their benefits)
- Reduce governmental power (e.g., invest in lobbying and coalition building)

Several challenges exist in using the Five Forces tool in healthcare planning, such as:

- What is the definition of an "industry"? And what is the "competitive set"? Within healthcare, multiple overlapping industries and ever-emerging competitors muddy the "industry-definition" waters. For example, are hospitals competing against other hospitals? Or are they also competing with specialty outpatient clinics or even retail pharmacies, such as CVS and Walgreens with their urgent care centers?
- What is the goal or vision for healthcare entities? Is their aim primarily to drive profits, or broader social goals such as improving population health or taking care of the neediest?
- Over what time period are leaders planning? The further into the future one looks, the less likely the existing "rules" pertain. For example, by 2025, could US healthcare expenditures consume 25 % of Gross Domestic Product (GDP)? If so, what could be the regulatory, public sector actions to curtail such cost growth? The ACA changed the "rules of the game" in the United States in ways that were only imagined before the Obama presidency.

Innovation Analysis

An alternate strategic framework for groups seeking to develop new, creative growth opportunities in healthcare is Dr. Regina Herzlinger's (2006) work on barriers to healthcare innovation. She starts by asking the provocative question: Why do most healthcare transformation efforts fail? Specifically, she points to two major initiatives: integrating hospital groups vertically to provide "one-stop-shop" for patients and combining physician practices horizontally for economies of scale. Both were financial disasters, the former losing more $112,000 per owned physician, while most physician-practice management firms are bankrupt.

As Dr. Herzlinger argues, the challenges facing healthcare leaders require more than incremental updates and extensions to products, processes, and services. Based on her studies of innovation in healthcare, Dr. Herzlinger concludes that most innovations fail due to the six forces summarized in Fig. 4.3.

For success, Dr. Herzlinger argues that healthcare innovation must create viable business models that explicitly manage her "Six Factors" in Fig. 4.3. She further refines this framework by applying it to the three broad categories of innovation that promise to make our healthcare systems "both better and cheaper":

- Consumer-Focused Ventures, which involve the patient in the processes of healthcare delivery
- Technology-Based Ventures, from integrating disparate data to gene therapy
- Integrator Ventures, which realize economies of scale through vertical and/or horizontal integration efforts (Herzlinger 2014)

Forces	Analysis Required	Action Needed
Players	Understand the expectations and relative power of stakeholders involved in or impacted by the innovation	Develop a plan to ensure stakeholders' continuing support or neutrality
Funding	Analyze financial aspects of the innovation in light of healthcare's unique investment and payment models	Determine how to navigate investment and payment models successfully
Policy	Determine which of the myriad laws and regulations that touch every aspects of healthcare can impact the innovation	Develop plans to address the laws and regulations
Technology	Understand the constant and rapid changes in healthcare technology related to the innovation	Determine how to (1) best leverage appropriate technologies and (2) ensure that an innovation will not arrive too soon—before infrastructure elements are ready, or too late—after a market opportunity has passed
Customers	Analyze the potential impacts on innovation from increasingly empowered consumers	Plan how to neutralize or leverage consumers to advance the innovation
Accountability	Determine the direct and often public demonstration stakeholders may require of how an innovation is pursued and/or what specific results are achieved	Develop action plans to satisfy those stakeholders requirements

Fig. 4.3 Herzlinger's six forces impacting healthcare innovation Herzlinger (2006)

If innovation is required for a transformation—in products, processes, or services—analyzing one's current context by Herzlinger's six forces can help determine how to overcome barriers and leverage potential growth opportunities.[1]

[1] Note: there is an extensive literature on Innovation, which we will not be covering here as we prefer to focus on how best to balance short-term with longer-term requirements that concern most operating entities. However, if the reader seeks innovation-specific perspectives, see Christensen (1997), Kim and Mauborgne (2005), and Terwiesch and Ulrich (2009).

Do healthcare leaders allow themselves the creative room to "step outside" of today's current realities to find those innovative future opportunities? As discussed below, scenario planning can help open up such critical strategic discussions. In addition, as Hambrick's Strategy Diamond highlights, what of segments and differentiation, critical elements to any strategy discussion?

Hambrick's Strategy Diamond

Hambrick argues comprehensive, value-adding strategies need to answer two fundamental questions: Where to play? and How to win?

- Where to Play?
  - What business will we be in?
  - What are our key customer segments, geographies, today and in the future?
  - What products, services, and technologies will we focus on?
- How to win?
  - Within those segments, geographies … why will customers (patients) choose us?
  - Where will we match the competition and where do we need to excel?

The Strategy Diamond puts segmentation and differentiation at the center of strategy development.

Where to Play? While healthcare players may say "we serve all patients," the most successful healthcare leaders segment their markets, for two reasons: (1) The size and scale of segments are different and (2) the needs of segments differ greatly.[2]

These segments should reflect the vision and business definition of the entity, as outlined in Chapter 3's discussion of the high-performing model. Entities can segment based on traditional criteria, such as demographics, location, economic status, and payment source (private, Medicare, Medicaid, etc.). However, the most effective strategic segmentation efforts seek creative, more unique delineations. For example, one pharmaceutical company segmented its potential subspecialty provider market as outlined in Fig. 4.4.

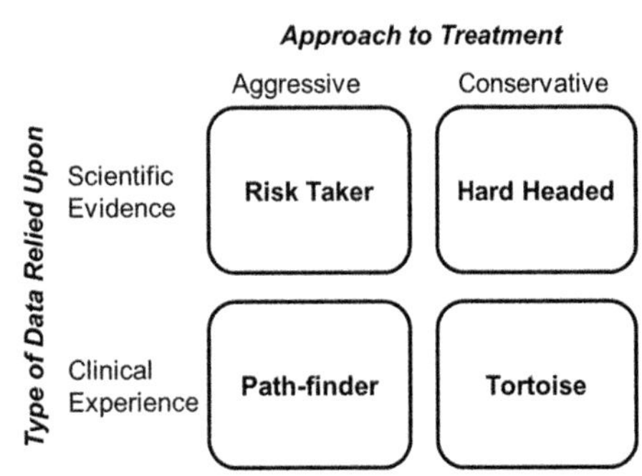

Fig. 4.4 Segments of physicians (from private conversation with professor Jagmohan S. Raju, Wharton School, University of Pennsylvania)

[2] For further discussion of segmentation, see Dranove and Marciano (2005).

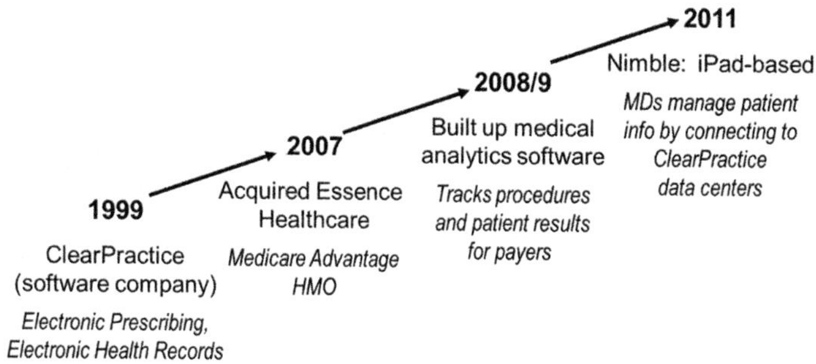

Fig. 4.5 Essence Healthcare "Adjacency" moves

Focusing on the most attractive segments, growth options typically include: (a) stay with core or current market segments, services and/or (b) grow into adjacencies, or related arenas. According to Chris Zook (2010), entities that grow from a strong core into directly related activities are three times as likely to be successful as those that jump into totally new or unrelated efforts.[3] Figure 4.5 illustrates an example of a healthcare enterprise's growth efforts over several years.

Note how Essence evolved: the organization did not suddenly leap from a software company to managing patients on the iPad. Rather, Essence made a series of small steps, consolidating each stage and then moving on given their capabilities (or gaps in capabilities) and assessment of opportunities in the context of their vision—to create a "unique health plan that would work side by side with doctors to guarantee every person on Medicare had access to great healthcare" (Essence Healthcare 2015).

How to Win? What is the unique value or differentiation any entity brings to its segments? One way of thinking about these "value differentiators" is to ask:

- What are *basic* requirements, like "cleanliness in a hospital?" These do not "win," but rather are the "ante" to be able to play.
- What are the *normal performance* value drivers? These are the traditional competitive differentiators, such as quality, access, reputation, range of services, etc.
- What are the *"wow" or unique* differentiators? For example, the Mayo Clinic's reputation is so strong that the normal performance value drivers are irrelevant.[4]

A dynamic aspect to these relationships also exists. Over time, "wow" factors become "normal performance," while the performance become "basic."[5] So entities need to replenish "how to win," continually refreshing their capabilities and support for key segments.

[3] These "new-new" efforts are often called "Blue Ocean," or uncontested space initiatives; see Kim and Mauborgne (2005).

[4] This model of value differentiators builds from the Kano Model, developed in the 1980s; see Kano et al. (1984).

[5] An example would be Anti-Lock Brakes (ABS), pioneered by Ford and BMW in the 1980s ("wow" then), and now found on all makes and models (basic).

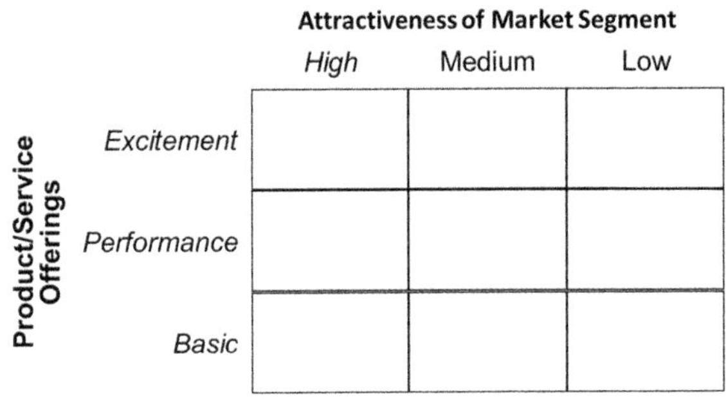

Fig. 4.6 Combining "where to play" with "how to win" *Source*: *Professor Jagmohan S. Raju, Wharton*

One approach to combine these two strategic components—Where to Play? And, How to Win?—is shown in Fig. 4.6.

Which to focus on—segments or offerings—and how to balance? According to McKinsey, "…a company's choice of *where to compete*[6] is almost four times more important than outperforming *within* its market"[7] (Viguerie et al. 2008). For large entities, the McKinsey data argue that 46 % of growth differences are due to "portfolio momentum," or organic growth; 33 % are from M&A (Mergers and Acquisitions); and only 21 % result from share gains. Back to this book's argument that to survive in the rapidly evolving, uncertain healthcare arena requires a *blend* of short-and longer-term initiatives, McKinsey states:

- Finding new "where to play" segments or geographies can take "5 or more years"
- M&A gains are short- to medium-term
- Share gains—How to Win—can be both from short-term, tactical actions and longer-term, transformational efforts (reinventing the business)
- "Exceptional" performance requires doing well in *each* of these three areas (Viguerie et al. 2008)

From there, entities should further assess and answer three additional questions:

1. First, how will we realize our strategies? Will we realize our strategies through organic growth, partnerships, joint ventures, etc.? A good example of one vehicle to realize one's strategy is the path Takeda Pharmaceutical took to enter the United States. In 1977, they formed a joint venture with Abbott—creating TAP Pharmaceutical—to gain US market exposure and knowledge. The 30-year arrangement was dissolved in 2008; since then, Takeda expanded its portfolio of products, selling directly into the United States as Takeda Pharmaceuticals U.S.A., Inc.
2. Second, what will be the speed and sequence of our strategic moves? What resources are available and what is required short-term, as well as long-term? What is the urgency behind different moves? Is there a "first-mover" advantage or is it better to wait until the market becomes more established? Are there

[6] i.e., Where to Play.

[7] i.e., How to Win.

"threshold" requirements that until achieved can prevent other parts of the strategy from being realized?
3. Finally, through all these choices, how will we earn money—and profit? This last query refers back to the David Dranove quote at the beginning of Chapter 3: sustainable competitive impact is realized when a firm "creates more value than its rivals" (Dranove and Marciano 2005). Recent media reports about the pricing policies of pharmaceutical companies like Valeant Pharmaceuticals International highlight the need for long-term value creation—either greater benefits relative to costs or a better cost position relative to competitive offerings—not simply short-term price differentials based on channel or availability loopholes.[8]

Only in wrestling with and seeking answers uniquely relevant for each institution can strategies then lead to institutional alignment, requisite organizational structures, operating processes, and execution priorities for future success.

While the Strategy Diamond is a powerful framework for healthcare institutions grappling with setting a course into the future, several issues may arise:

- Creatively looking beyond short-term responses to changing environments is hard to do
- How should strategic teams identify gaps or missing elements in current operations and capabilities for longer-term impact?

Scenario planning builds on the Strategy Diamond, but explicitly seeks to deal with the above two issues.

Scenario Planning

As argued before, with greater complexity and increasing rates of change, incremental strategies may be necessary in the short-term, but not sufficient for long-term success (Courtney et al. 1997). The past is not prologue in today's global healthcare marketplace, replete with rapidly expanding technologies, exploding online sources of patient information, and ever-more-rapidly evolving alliances among healthcare providers. For healthcare and life sciences companies, provider groups, healthcare consultants, payers, and patients—all the major players in the global healthcare marketplace—incremental strategies and "waiting to see what will happen" are the *wrong* approaches to deal with this complexity. Leaders need different tools, different "mental models"[9] to produce transformational strategies for success in the rapidly evolving, uncertain world of healthcare in the twenty-first century.

One such tool is scenario planning. Scenarios portray a series of plausible alternative futures. Each scenario tells a story of how various forces might interact under certain conditions. Scenarios are designed to open up new ways of thinking about

[8] For more on Valeant, see McCoy (2015).

[9] The flexible mindset, aware of "decision traps," was discussed in Chapter 3.

the future and provide a platform for strategic dialogue—new questions, new conversations—as the basis for strategic action. Scenarios are *not* predications or forecasts; rather, they combine existing trends and key uncertainties[10] into a few "future worlds" within the realm of possibility.

Scenarios benefit organizations by stimulating leaders to think together and prepare for change systematically. Scenario planning trains teams to recognize change without overlooking or denying it (Schoemaker and van der Heijden 1992). A survey of 77 large companies by René Rohrbeck, of Aarhus University, and Jan Oliver Schwarz, of Germany's EBS Business School, found that scenario planning generates strategic foresight and an enhanced capacity to perceive, interpret, and respond to change (Rohrbeck and Schwarz 2013). According to the annual Bain & Company survey of top management "tools" (Rigby and Bilodeau 2015), scenario planning applications increase in times of greater external complexity and uncertainty, as typifies the healthcare sector today and for the foreseeable future.

Figure 4.7 summarizes our approach to scenario planning and its key steps to drive transformational strategies in healthcare.[11]

As portrayed in Fig. 4.7, scenarios create a range of potential futures (A, B, C, and D) from the interaction of multiple forces (technology shifts, political changes, etc.) that "bracket" future possibilities. Different than traditional strategic planning, scenario planning:

- Starts the strategic discussion "in the future" to develop a reasonable range of alternative futures.
- Across those futures, asks the question, "How will a particular strategic initiative fare?" And not just in the best case, but also in "challenging" future states.
- Finally, focuses on developing a portfolio of initiatives that meets both short-term requirements and longer-term opportunities and challenges.

The purpose of outlining these potential futures is *not* to predict the future; rather, it is to foster strategic discussions around questions such as:

- Can our organization survive and prosper in different futures?
- What new investments and capabilities will our organization need to be successful no matter how the healthcare system evolves?
- What should we, as healthcare leaders, watch to identify early on where the healthcare industry might be heading so we can be optimally prepared to respond?

[10] In scenario planning terms, a "trend" is a force whose timing and impact all can agree on (e.g., demographic trends); an "uncertainty" is a future force that could evolve in a multiplicity of ways, with varying degrees of impact (e.g., technology breakthroughs or major disease cures).

[11] Many approaches exist to develop future scenarios, e.g., Ringland (1998). The approach outlined here is based on Schoemaker (1995).

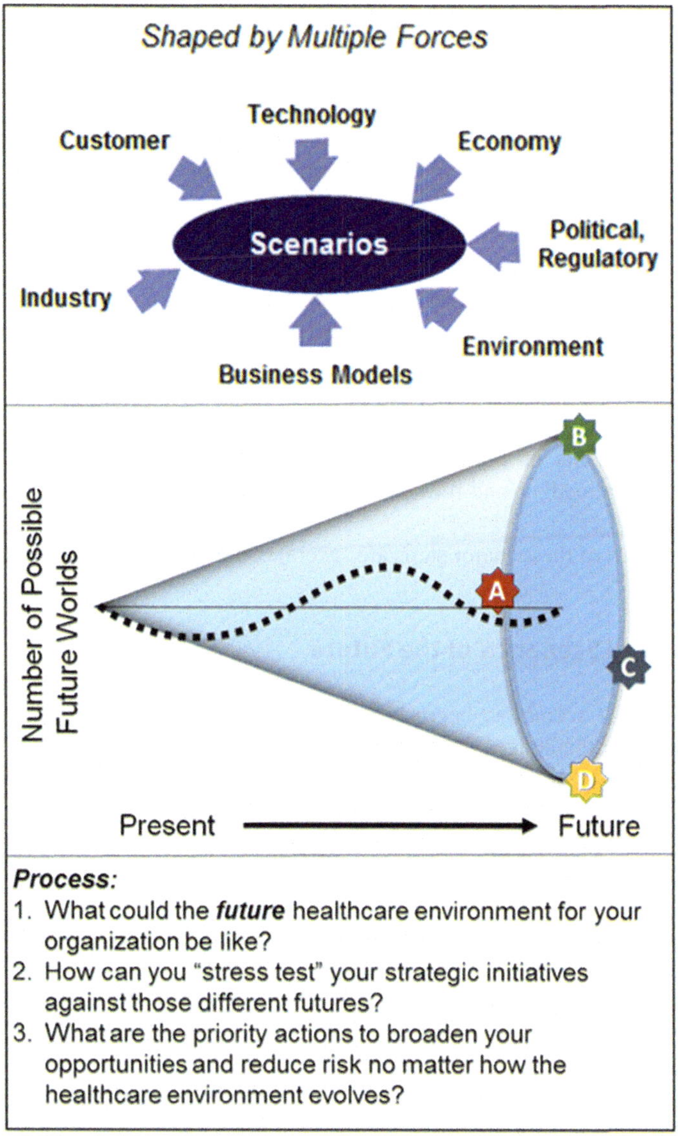

Fig. 4.7 Scenarios and developing strategic priorities

In times of uncertainty and complexity, leaders need different tools and a different mindset. Scenario planning starts from the future and works back and in that process ideally reveals more creative opportunities for future success.

This approach remains very relevant for healthcare institutions. In the face of major change—such as the shift from fee-for-service, component-specific payment systems to value-based, risk-adjusted payment schemes—leaders all too often default to short-term requirements. Unfortunately, incremental cost-saving strategies in today's world will be inadequate to prosper in an era of population health.[12] Worrying about "smarter" ways to reduce capital spending or utilize nurse techs will not help hospitals shift from fee-for-service to totally new payment regimes, or satisfy population health requirements.

Rather than projecting from past experience and data, the fundamentally different approach of scenario planning is to start in several, possible futures and *work back to today*. When executives can position themselves outside of today, they become remarkably creative. The key is to come back to choices for today, in the light of a range of potential futures, thereby overcoming the very real human response to change and uncertainty: becoming "anchored in the past."[13]

Building scenarios requires three distinct steps:

- Create scenarios of the future
- Use the scenarios to "stress test" current strategic initiatives
- Build a portfolio of strategic initiatives—short, medium, and longer-term—to meet *both* immediate and future challenges

Within each of these major steps are several components, as outlined below.

Step 1: Build Scenarios of the Future

To build robust scenarios, begin by asking the question, "What are the critical uncertainties or challenges we face in the foreseeable future?" Start by listing the STEEP factors—*S*ocial, *T*echnological, *E*nvironment, *E*conomic, and *P*olitical—that could dramatically change the organization's operating or external environment. For example, the following indicative list of high-impact uncertainties might be a starting point for a major tertiary-care center:

- Reimbursement levels and payment arrangements for in-patient and outpatient services?
- Patient volumes? By specialty?
- Competition? Both current and new?
- Affiliations?
- Changes in eligibility requirements for Medicare? Medicaid?
- Payment cycles from Medicaid? Medicare?
- Level and type of philanthropy?
- Political support for current delivery models?
- Environmental requirements?
- Regulatory requirements?

[12] This incremental, short-term view of what needs to change is reflected in Kaplan and Haas (2014).

[13] A good example of potential healthcare scenarios of the future and their implications can be found in Institute (2012).

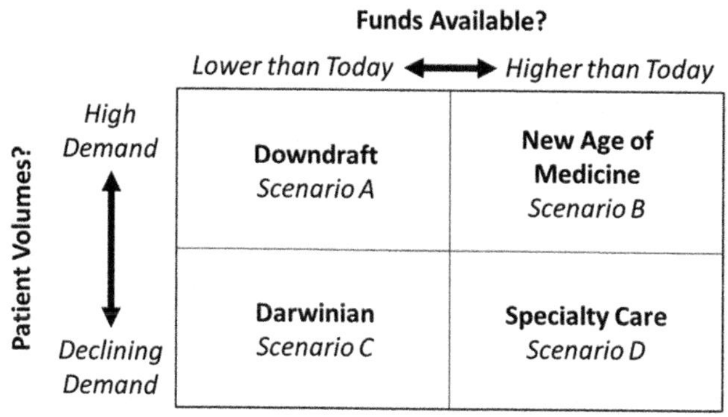

Fig. 4.8 Example of future scenarios for major tertiary-care center (scenario "names" or "titles" are typically indicative of the "world" they are summarizing and created as a playful reminder of that future environment. In the Scenarios of the Future for Major Tertiary Care Center (this figure), the different titles indicate: *Downdraft,* difficult conditions that can lead to a crash; *New Age of Medicine,* implies a future that is resource rich, supported by patient demand; *Darwinian,* a "dog-eat-dog" world of diminishing resources and declining patient volumes; *Specialty Care,* a potential future where patient demands are generally declining but resources are available for more targeted, specialty efforts such as orphan drugs)

- State of the economy?
- Overall healthcare spending and implications?
- Funding availability for and support of teaching initiatives?
- Supply of physicians, nurses, technicians, and other healthcare providers?
- Access to capital?
- New technologies? New treatment paradigms?
- Integration (horizontal, vertical) opportunities and challenges?[14]

Once you generate the list of uncertainties, pick the two most interesting, most dynamic uncertainties that will form or "bound" a 2×2 Scenario Matrix. This is the "messy part" of scenario planning. No algorithm exists that will determine which two uncertainties are best. Beware of uncertainties that move together—e.g., "future number of jobs" matched against "state of the economy." Both of these uncertainties directly influence each other and so respond to other forces in the same direction. Ideally, seek two, major uncertainties that could evolve in different directions, or only indirectly influence each other, and are likely to significantly impact the organization's future. For example, from the list above, a major, tertiary-care hospital system might chose "Patient Volumes" and "Fund Availability." These two uncertainties then form the *X*-axis and *Y*-axis of the two-by-two matrix shown in Fig. 4.8.[15]

[14] These critical uncertainties can also be generated by surveys asking respondents both to rank a supplied list of possible future uncertainties (developed through interviews) for their degree of uncertainty *and* impact.

[15] Personal information from authors.

The next task is to add a brief description for each of the four scenarios. To do this, go back to the other uncertainties: how would each play out to create the worlds identified? For example, in Scenario (A) of Fig. 4.8 (entitled "Downdraft"), the following are possible events that might "explain" how the healthcare environment evolved from today to that possible future:

- A troubled economy translates into a 25 % reduction in dollars available for hospitals, including funding formerly found in philanthropic networks.
- With expanded healthcare coverage from the ACA, patient volumes at hospitals increased by more than 40 % over the past, but hospitals see reimbursement at lower rates.
- Increasingly ineffective antibiotics and vaccines make it nearly impossible to treat several recurring infections, including those associated with H1N1 influenza.
- Healthcare reform, along with the implementation of a "zero-growth" clause for Medicare, puts adult providers in survival mode.
- Broadened eligibility for Medicaid and other programs results in declining net reimbursements under healthcare reform.
- A spiraling federal deficit leads to cuts to the US Centers for Medicare and Medicaid Services (CMS), federal match programs, and funding for the expansion of electronic medical records (EMRs).

Are any of these possible? Certainly—but that is not the point. The idea is to develop plausible futures to test assumptions about what it will take to succeed, and to determine the critical areas for healthcare transformation. Try to tell a story, a flow of events that could lead from today into each of the four, different futures. Do not worry about exactitude. Rather, aim to challenge how one might shift from today into different, yet plausible futures. The uncertainties are the critical variables that could move us from one world to another. Try not to predict the likelihood of one future over another. Rather, the aim is to seek a reasonable range of possible futures that will challenge the strategic planning team to critique their strategy and major initiatives, as outlined in Step 2, below.

One further point: how far into the future should healthcare leaders look when building scenarios? And how broad should their scope be? Envisioning too far out risks that everything could change. On the other hand, too close in—unless there is a major upheaval—and not much is likely to change. For example, will the ACA change dramatically in the next 12–24 months? It's possible, but not very likely, and thus is too "close in" for good, strategic discussions on future opportunities and challenges in the US healthcare system. On the other hand, could the United States face a very different healthcare system by 2050? If healthcare costs continue to rise faster than the growth of GDP—which is their historical path—and unless there is a significant change in the structure of our US system, healthcare will "crowd out" investments in multiple other sectors from the military to education. 2050 may literally be "too far out" as so many variables could change; only in the broadest sense will most organizations or groups need to plan for futures so far away.

Strategic Options	Scenario A	Scenario B	Scenario C	Scenario D
Maximize Profit: "Stay the Course"	—	0	++	+
Maximize Revenue: "Go Big"	++	++	— —	—
Improve Operational Cash Flow	+	+	— —	—

How attractive is each strategic effort across the scenarios?
(+) = more attractive (0) = same as today (-) = less attractive

Fig. 4.9 Stress test example

Second, what about scope? For example, should the scenarios be at a national, regional, or individual state level? It depends on the entity's environment. If the group engaged in the scenario planning exercise is a multistate healthcare institution, a regional or even national perspective is best, as the environment in which this team will succeed or fail is likely to be influenced by forces at the national level. On the other hand, a subspecialty group of physicians will probably be most influenced by local or state issues and should stay at that level in developing its scenarios of the future.

Several other issues can arise with scenario planning. First, how many possible futures are there? *MILLIONS*! But the aim is not to be exactly right … rather, to approximate alternative futures to spur discussion, different perspectives, and ideas on how to win in different futures. Second, what should leaders be prepared for, if the future begins to evolve in very different ways from what is imagined today? And finally, how do future scenario discussions tie back to current budget realities and today's short-term requirements? The remainder of this Chapter and Chapter 5 will seek to answer these critical questions.

Step 2: "Stress Test" Current Strategic Initiatives

With the scenarios, run a simple test: how well will current strategic initiatives fare in each of the different futures? For example, in a world of incremental change, constant challenges to the ACA, and modestly rising healthcare costs (basically the world of 2015 projected into the future with only incremental changes from today), cost control and EMR expansion will be very important. While there may be some growth in Accountable Care Organizations (ACOs), for example, widespread acceptance of these new models of care is likely to be isolated to a few, demonstration projects funded by CMS. On the other hand, is it possible that by 2020, fueled by spikes in healthcare costs and studies "proving" the link between wellness campaigns and declining rates of obesity, there could be much more emphasis on population health ? In such a future, focusing on incremental cost controls will be grossly insufficient for hospitals or healthcare provider groups to survive, much less prosper.

- Figure 4.9 illustrates a simple way to evaluate an institution's major initiatives against different scenarios. Typically, this is only a qualitative assessment:
- If the initiative does well in the future, it receives a (+).
- If it does as well in the future as it does in the current environment, it is graded with a (0) or neutral rating
- If it does worse, or does not contribute to the healthcare institution in the future—as with short-term cost controls in a world of population health and outcomes-based reimbursement schemes—it receives a (−).

One can color-code the various estimated impact outcomes to reveal strengths—where an initiative can have impact across multiple futures—and potential issues—when an initiative might only work in one or two possible futures.

Of course, it is not wrong to pursue an initiative that seems best suited for a limited number of futures. In the same way that one might invest a large portion of one's retirement income in growth stocks for the greater potential gain, just beware of the greater variability or risk with such a strategy. Leaders cannot foretell the future, but only outline a reasonable range of potential futures (Step 1, above). Across those futures, how well will an institution's different strategic initiatives fare? And how can leaders build the optimal portfolio to reduce risk, while increasing expected return or potential for future success?

Referring back to the earlier discussion about Hambrick's Strategy Diamond, that framework and scenario planning build on each other. While tempting to stay at the macro-level, trade-offs and "stress test" discussions are most informative at the segment level, asking in the context of different scenarios: where to play and how to win? For example, strategic options for a particular subspecialty (such as anesthesiology) will be very different in a fee-for-service environment as compared to a capitated, fixed-fee world emphasizing patient outcomes. In the former, the subspecialist simply charges for their time; in the latter, they have to establish relative value and possibly branch into related activities, such as perioperative home care, for future professional sustainability.

Step 3: Build a Portfolio for the Future

Given future uncertainty—which only increases the further out healthcare leaders look—what does it mean to employ an "options" mentality? Different than traditional strategy formulation with slower moving external environments and less medium-to-longer term uncertainty, what could be the demands of the healthcare marketplace five years from now? Ten years from now? According to a study by the Robert Wood Johnson Foundation, US healthcare futures could be described as either:

- Absorbing more than 20 % of Gross National Product (GNP) *or* facing sharply reduced spending levels (less than 15 % of GNP) and
- Be constituted of patients seeking incrementally "better health" *or* more aggressively "a culture of health" defined by population health and wellness campaigns (Institute 2012).

These variables then constitute radically different futures for healthcare leaders and their organizations. What strategic initiatives make the most sense given these uncertainties?

In a rapidly changing, uncertain environment, the best strategy is to create a flexible portfolio of initiatives that can pivot, as needed, to meet emerging future opportunities and challenges. Specifically, from Steps 1 and 2, above, strategic planning teams should identify three types of initiatives: Core initiatives, New initiatives, and Wow initiatives.

Core Initiatives. What are key short-term, immediate activities, or priorities that keep current operations performing ever more efficiently? For example, what are essential quality and operational investments critical to meet immediate budgetary and payer/patient requirements? In our experience, these Core strategic initiatives represent 70–80 % of what existing institutions should focus on.[16] The primary strategic aim for Core initiatives is to increase efficiencies in current operations … not transformational change. The reason is simple: unless the institution or group can realize additional returns in the near-term while continuing current operations, there will be few if any resources to invest in the longer-term.

New Initiatives. What are medium-term, medium-risk priorities that over time can replenish the Core? For example, might forming an ACO or a new relationship with several payers be part of the strategy? These might be "radical redesign" or transformational initiatives articulated in Chapter 2, depending on the capabilities of the institution, and the lifecycle of the initiative. Again, in our experience, groups target 10–20 % of their resources, capabilities for initiatives in this area.

Wow Initiatives. What are a few experiments or transformational opportunities that can be pursued? What are a few, wild ideas that are really only at the prefeasibility stage, but could open up major new future possibilities? While such initiatives can be very attractive, beware of focusing more than 5–10 % of resources and management time on the ideas in this group. Unfortunately, most of these ideas will *not* be realized, and that is to be expected. Potential transformational initiatives might be new social media platforms for reaching out to younger patients, or in-patient institutions partnering to develop Accountable Communities of Health prototypes.[17] While financial metrics, such as Net Present Value or Break-Even analyses should be used to prioritize initiatives in the Core and New categories, they should *not* be used to prioritize the Wow ideas. They are simply too new, too unformed, and typically too far out into the future to stand such comparisons. As Dr. Roch Parayre recommends, "Use ROI (return on investment) to prioritize your core or new ideas … but to use ROI for the experimental investments is really short-hand for **R**educe **O**ur **I**nnovation."[18]

---

[16] Percentage allocations are at best indicative based on the state of the industry sub-sector, and the lifecycle of the firm or entity. For example, with a start-up, there may be little "core;" a more mature business, in a fairly stable environment, may have relatively fewer "wow" initiatives.

[17] For example, see Chapter 2 discussion of Washington State ACH efforts.

[18] Personal comment from Dr. Roch Parayre, Professor, Wharton School University of Pennsylvania and Senior Partner, Decision Strategies International, Inc.

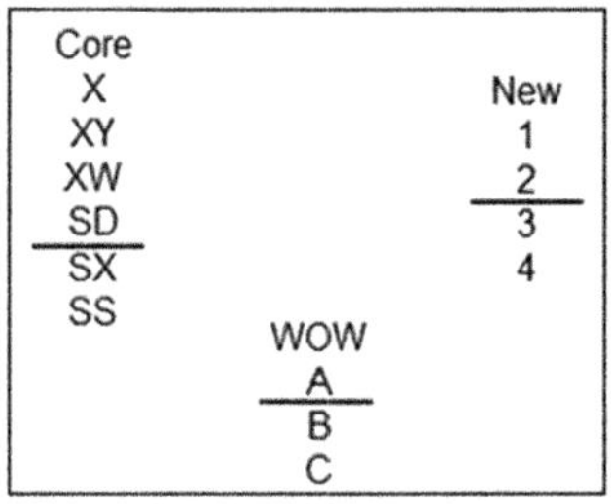

Fig. 4.10 Ranking of strategic initiatives

The portfolio percentages (70/20/10) are suggestions, allowing for both optimizing current operations and transforming into new areas. But they certainly can (and should) vary by situation, competitive pressures, external pressures, etc. A high percentage of core initiatives might be seen as counter to our central argument for transformation. But in reality, if you are a hospital or a pharmaceutical company, you still need to do the basic things a hospital or pharmaceutical company does—you can't simply stop doing all of that to focus on new and wow initiatives. Transformation does involve doing new things, but more important, it means adopting a new mindset about how both new—and old—things are done. If you are able to maintain the current environment with fewer resources, you will be able to devote more to new and wow initiatives—and speed your journey toward transformation.

Organizations that effectively manage transformational or more risky efforts are both unafraid to change direction and employ clear metrics to determine "go/no go" decisions. No one likes to fail. But by their nature, transformational efforts have a higher risk of failure and must be managed extremely closely to ensure success.[19] The key is to cast these initiatives as "learning experiments," proving hypotheses, but not yet establishing a business. And those entities that do this well, use clear metrics to make decisions for stopping or continuing programs. They use set decision-criteria to counter the emotional issues inherent in "sunk costs" (e.g., "Just let's try for another six months given all we put into it...") or emotional appeals ("But think of all the lives we will save if we can get it to work..."). For example, Google employs the following four criteria to decide whether or not to continue funding a radically new idea (in their terms, a "moonshot"):

- Popularity with customers
- Ease of attracting Google employees to work on the effort
- Solves a "big enough" problem
- Achieves internal performance targets or objectives and key results (Goel 2009)

In summary, scenario planning (and all robust strategic planning efforts) should end with a ranked set of strategic initiatives that might look like Fig. 4.10.

[19] Dr. George Day, Senior Professor of Marketing at Wharton, estimated across industries nearly 90% of new innovation efforts—new markets and new technologies, classic "Blue Ocean" efforts—fail. From personal communication.

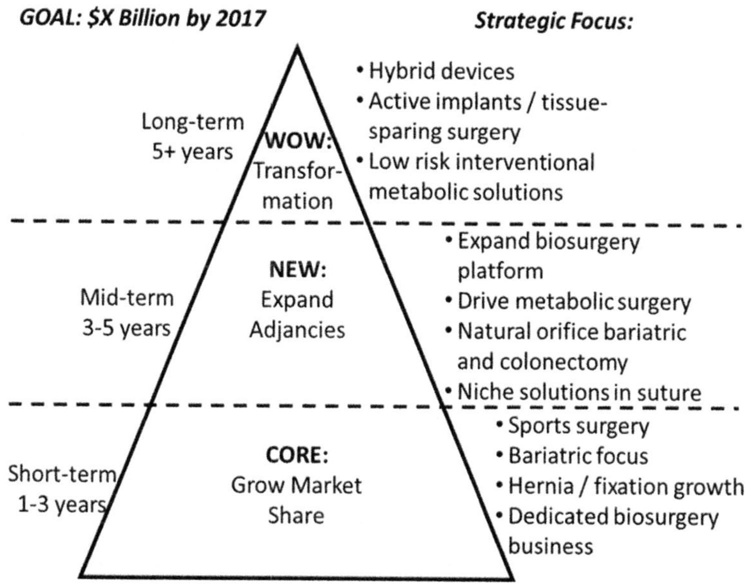

Fig. 4.11 Strategy focus of a medical device company (author's personal knowledge)

Note: there are *not* 50 items listed! Teams run into problems when they try to accomplish too many things. As Jim Collins (2009) writes, one of the signs of organizational decline is "undisciplined pursuit of more." Strategy and transformation is all about doing a few things really, really well … not trying to do everything. As Laura Ramos Hegwer (2015) recently wrote in her article on "Leading Change from the C-Suite":

> Many healthcare executives aim to transform how their organizations think about delivering care. However, the most successful leaders recognize that what they choose *not* to do is just as important as what they actually do during times of change.

Based on resources and capabilities, the management team "draws a line" as to what is included or not in the current strategic plan moving forward (see Fig. 4.10). Those projects "below the line" are held in abeyance, to be activated if an "above the line" project fails, or there are additional resources available. Conversely, if resources become strained, management can "raise the line," putting certain projects on-hold until the budget or operating pressures abate. The example in Fig. 4.11 shows how a major medical device company categorized its key initiatives.

Projects are aggregated by category and then prioritized within each category. If all major initiatives were grouped into one, catch-all budget and cuts had be made, inevitably, the further out, more experimental, transformative efforts would not survive. If savings must be made, first decide how they should be allocated *across* the different groups, and only then reprioritize *within* each group.

The listing of major strategic initiatives is also the key to execution. In our experience, most plans are not realized because they fail in their execution, as will be further explored in Chapter 5. By listing the major strategic initiatives, the critical linkages between strategy and execution are clearly defined with understandable priorities that all organization members can identify and help manage. Of course, below the high-level summary example in Fig. 4.11 are portfolios for each business unit or operating group. But these lower-level portfolios should *all* be based upon the overall set of institutional or group-wide priorities.

Summary

Ahh, for the good old days! While tempting to long nostalgically for the past, how best to deal with the range of future healthcare uncertainties, such as:

- Will organizations face more significant resource constraints as cost-pressures rebound with greater patient volumes from the implementation of the ACA?
- What will be the federal vs. state roles in the future of establishing quality metrics and payment reforms, in the United States or in other countries?
- Will CMS take a more direct role in establishing national pricing bands in the United States for major pharmaceuticals?
- What will be the public's reaction to population health?

The challenge healthcare leaders face is how to balance the short-term necessities of keeping current operations functioning *while* laying the groundwork for future transformational change. To do this:

- Use the tool of scenario planning to challenge current orthodoxies and identify potential future threats, opportunities
- Develop a portfolio of strategic initiatives that can "bend" with future uncertainties while lowering the risk of being truly unable to respond as the future unfolds
- Drive execution with a few, clearly defined areas of focus, as will be further explored in Chapter 5.

Questions Healthcare Leaders and Teams Should Ask

Chapter 4 outlines typical tools that leaders employ in their strategic planning efforts. The challenge for healthcare leaders is to apply the right tool for their unique situation. While Porter's Five Forces and SWOT analyses are powerful frameworks that can help teams assess strategic leverage, challenges, and opportunities, they are best suited for more stable, mature markets that do not typify healthcare in general. For longer-term, more transformational efforts in times of uncertainty, Hambrick's Strategy Diamond and scenario planning are much more robust, powerful frameworks to challenge current orthodoxies. The following are some of the key questions healthcare leaders and their teams should discuss as they wrestle with different tools to aid in their strategic planning efforts:

Future Uncertainties. What are the STEEP factors—*S*ocial, *T*echnological, *E*nvironment, *E*conomic, and *P*olitical—that could dramatically change our operating or external environment?

- Of all those uncertainties, which are the most critical ones … the ones with the greatest likelihood of occurring *and* impacting our organization?
- From these uncertainties, what future scenarios can we construct that are both possible and challenging?

Stress Test. Given those scenarios, how well will our current strategic initiatives fare?

- Are we unconsciously banking on one or two scenarios of the future to be successful?
- Where are our largest gaps or blind spots if the future is very different from our current environment?
- What will it take to be successful not just in today's world, but in a range of possible futures?
- Who are our key customer or patient segments today and in the future?
- How might the definition of "how to win" in different segments change with alternative future scenarios?

Portfolio of Strategic Initiatives. What are our mission-critical strategic choices in the short-medium-and-longer-term?

- Core: What are the short-term, relatively low-risk investments, and strategic initiatives that we must undertake to keep the current organization functioning, meeting our immediate stakeholder targets? And how can we be more efficient with these efforts to free up resources for investing in more transformative initiatives (New and Wow)?
- New/Transformational: What projects are medium-term, medium-risk that over time will replenish, ideally expand, our current operations?
- Wow/Transformational: What are those longer-term, higher-risk—but much greater potential impact—strategic initiatives for future growth and flexibility? How will we manage these … and what are the clear "stop/go" metrics to ensure we do not either short-change or needlessly prolong these experiments?

References

Bodenheimer T, Pham HH (2010) Primary care: current problems and proposed solutions. Health Affairs 29(5):799–805

Christensen C (1997) The innovator's dilemma. Harper Business, BostonCollins J. How the mighty fall: and why some companies never give in. New York: HarperCollins Publishers; 2009.

Collins J (2009) How the mighty fall: and why some companies never give in. New York: HarperCollins Publishers.
Courtney HG, Kirkland J, Viguerie SP. Strategy under uncertainty. Harvard Business Review 1997 Nov–Dec.
Dranove D, Marciano S (2005) Kellogg on strategy. Wiley, New York, p 30, 38–9
Essence Healthcare About us. 2015. www.essencehealthcare.com/member/about-us.aspx. Accessed 30 Dec 2015.
Goel V. How Google decides to pull the plug. New York Times 2009 Feb 14.
Haddrill M. Lucentis vs. Avastin: a macular degeneration treatment controversy. 2014. http://www.allaboutvision.com/conditions/lucentis-vs-avastin.htm. Accessed 10 June 2015.
Hambrick DC, Frederickson JW (2001) Are you sure you have a strategy? Acad Manage Exec 15(4):51–62
Hegwer LR (2015) Leading change from the c-suite: 3 leaders share their strategies. Healthc Exec 30(6):12
Herzlinger RE. Why innovation in healthcare is so hard. Harvard Business Review 2006 May.
Herzlinger RE. Innovating in healthcare—framework. Harvard Business Review 2014 March.
Institute for Alternative Futures. Health and health care in 2032: report from the RWJF futures symposium, 20–21 June 2012, Alexandria, VA; 2012.
Kano N, Seraku N, Takahashi F, Tsuji S (1984) Attractive quality and must-be quality. J Jpn Soc Qual Control 14(2):39–48
Kaplan RS, Haas DA. How not to cut healthcare costs. Harvard Business Review 2014 Nov.
Kim WC, Mauborgne R (2005) Blue ocean strategy. Harvard Business Press, Boston
Lohr S. Preaching from the Ballmer pulpit. New York Times 2007 Jan 28.
McCoy K. Valeant shares plunge amid questions, investigation. USA Today 2015 Nov 5.
Pollack A. Maker seeks to restrict cancer drug used on eye. New York Times 2007 Oct 11.
Porter M (1980) Competitive strategy: techniques for analyzing industries and competitors. The Free Press, New York
Rigby D, Bilodeau B. Management tools & trends 2015. Bain & Company; 2015. http://www.bain.com/Images/BAIN_BRIEF_Management_Tools_2015.pdf. Accessed 24 July 2015.
Ringland G (1998) Scenario planning: managing for the future. Wiley, New York
Rohrbeck R, Schwarz JO (2013) The value contribution of strategic foresight: insights from an empirical study on large European companies. Technol Forecast Soc Change 80(8):1593–1606
Schoemaker PJH (1995) Scenario planning: a tool for strategic thinking. MIT Sloan Manage Rev 36:25–40
Schoemaker PJH, van der Heijden CAJM, Integrating scenarios into strategic planning at Royal Dutch/Shell. Strategy Leadership 1992 May–June.
Steinberg C. Underpayment by Medicare and Medicaid fact sheet. American Hospital Association; 2015. http://www.aha.org/research/policy/finfactsheets.shtml. Accessed 20 Apr 2015.
Terwiesch C, Ulrich KT (2009) Innovation tournaments. Harvard Business Press, Boston
Viguerie P, Smit S, Baghai M (2008) The granularity of growth. Wiley, New York, p 41, 53, 68–9
Zook C (2010) Profit from the core. Harvard Business Press, Boston

Driving Successful Implementation

5

Jim Austin, Judith Bentkover, and Laurence Chait

Abstract

Strategies are only as good as their execution. Unfortunately, most major change initiatives fail to realize their objectives. This chapter outlines the major barriers to change, and what healthcare leaders can do to improve the likelihood for driving transformational change. There are many parts to execution: from prioritization to team structure, metrics to commitment, and expressed values to embedded culture. All require special focus. Throughout, it is the balance between short-term, tactical goals and longer term, transformational efforts that healthcare leaders need to embrace.

Introduction

To achieve sustainable competitive impact in healthcare, especially given future complexity and uncertainty, strategies should balance short-term operating requirements with longer term, transformational initiatives, as outlined in Chapter 4. However, this is a necessary—yet not sufficient—condition for success. High performance and transformation require effective *execution* of strategic plans and, for

J. Austin (✉) • J. Bentkover • L. Chait
Executive Master of Healthcare Leadership, Brown University, Providence, RI, USA
e-mail: james_austin@brown.edu; judith_bentkover@brown.edu; Lpchait-ca@chait.net

J. Austin et al. (eds.), *Leading Strategic Change in an Era of Healthcare Transformation*, Management for Professionals,
DOI 10.1007/978-3-319-30776-3_5

many organizations, *change management*. Unfortunately, major change efforts have a dismal track record. In multiple studies, highlighting the experiences of hundreds of companies initiating large-scale changes, the overwhelming results are poor. For example:

- John Kotter's seminal research in the field of change management half a century ago revealed that only 30 % of change programs succeed (Aiken and Keller 2009).
- A 2008 global IBM study of major change initiatives found that only 41 % fully met their objectives, while 44 % missed their budget, time, or quality goals, and 15 % were seen as total failures (Jørgensen et al. 2008).
- In 2013, a report that aggregated over 6,000 senior executive surveys revealed that 70 % of change efforts fail to achieve their target impact (Kitching and Shaibal 2013).

As the Harvard Business Review's editor articulated so well in discussing why so many transformation efforts fail:

> … no business survives over the long term if it can't reinvent itself. But human nature being what it is, fundamental change is often resisted mightily by the people it most affects: those in the trenches of the business. Thus, leading change is both absolutely essential and incredibly difficult (Kotter 2007).

Transformation implies—and requires—change. But healthcare organizations—given their operational complexities and entrenched behaviors and hierarchies—are especially difficult to change. What can be done?

This chapter presents a series of positive actions that should be taken to improve the odds for implementation success:

- Start implementation *during* planning
- Establish governance infrastructure
- Articulate value propositions that emotionally connect at an individual level
- Agree on unambiguous priorities, and the process to update
- Establish program principles, especially clear scoreboards/metrics of success
- Maintain active, ongoing oversight with leadership team commitment

Start Implementation During Planning

Too often organizations wait until strategic planning is complete before beginning implementation. While distinct sequencing sounds logical, the seeds of implementation success or failure are sown early in the strategic planning process.

As discussed in Chapter 3, decisions made regarding the composition of the teams involved in strategic planning directly impacts implementation success. To the extent that the strategy teams include people who will be affected by the implementation—not just the senior team—these individuals will be better able to share their ideas, represent their cohorts, and support the strategy early on.

Engaging key implementation leaders in the strategy development teams ensures a natural leadership progression from planning through implementation. On the other hand, waiting to choose implementation managers until strategic planning is complete leads to two problems. First, a delayed start to implementation is often created by the time required to identify, vet, and choose candidates—and the time it takes to free the selected individual from his/her current responsibilities. Second, if the chosen individual was not part of the strategic planning process, his/her learning curve will be extended as that individual studies, discusses, and ultimately internalizes the execution requirements of the strategic plan.

How leaders identify and set priorities in the strategic planning process will also impact implementation success. For major change, ask the strategy team arguing for such an investment to complete a "premortem": If our plan failed, what went wrong (McGrath and MacMillan 1995)? Identify critical assumptions and then ask the following: Can we realistically overcome them, or are we overconfident? What are the historical rates of success with projects like this in our own organization? What are the experiences *outside* of the organization against which we can benchmark?

For example, electronic medical record (EMR) implementation in most healthcare organizations has been typically much more difficult and costly than originally envisioned. One major tertiary care center in the northeast, before beginning implementation of a system-wide EMR, asked the following: What assumptions are behind this project? In benchmarking other tertiary-care center experience with similar efforts, they quickly learned that the staff training time assumed for the new system's rollout was woefully inadequate. By dramatically increasing the training time and resources supporting the project, its implementation—while still difficult—was completed on schedule.

Finally, in some cases, high-value, core projects can be launched during the strategic planning effort itself. As these projects move forward, more transformational—New and Wow projects—often emerge. Healthcare leaders quickly learn the execution limits to what they can accomplish. In the EMR case outlined above, the institution realized that this project alone would take more than 50 % of allocated resources for future investments, leading to re-prioritization of other efforts, as well as a more conservative rollout plan for the EMR.

Establish Governance Infrastructure

As discussed in Chapter 3, for effective, transformational strategic planning, multiple, overlapping groups provide one key to success. This structural model applies to implementation, as well. A generic structure for implementation can be seen in Fig. 5.1.

The concept of overlapping groups shown in this graphic is particularly important. Overlapping groups ensures cross-group interactions, thereby avoiding the miscommunications that often occur when multiple groups work on the same program in a fragmented fashion. Given their scope, in transformational efforts,

Fig. 5.1 Implementation governance infrastructure

cross-group interactions are especially important. The specific groups, and their execution roles, can be described as follows:

- **Senior management**—Starting at the top of this chart, direct, continuing senior-management involvement is critical. Senior managers must "speak with one voice" regarding priorities and implementation timetables. For example, in an healthcare insurance company, the heads of agency, actuarial, and customer service must be consistent in what they say and do relative to the plan and in its resource requirements. Different messages from different leaders cause confusion in the ranks, which can lead to two equally undesirable results: conflicting actions or worse, passivity and no action.

During implementation phases, senior managers must over-communicate key messages. Frequent repetition helps embed priorities into the psyche and culture of the organization. As John Kotter (2007) writes, in driving change, senior leaders consistently underestimate the need for communication—not just the *what*, but the *why*. These simple, consistent messages should be about the importance of major strategic initiatives tied to the organization's vision, mission, and values—the building blocks underpinning execution.

Where new behaviors are necessary or desired tied to culture-change efforts, senior managers must be role models of those behaviors. If senior managers try to drive a message that "we are all equal in these times of change," but senior leaders still keep their preferred parking spaces, the embedded culture (i.e., what we do, not what we say) will quickly realize that the stated new behaviors are not really that important. If the plan calls for greater collaboration, then the chief executive officer (CEO) must involve all relevant parties in internal deliberations—be they doctors, nurses, administrative staff, or unions. "Setting a good example" is just as relevant in implementation as it is in other situations. Should others in the organization fail to exhibit the new behaviors, senior managers must ensure that corrective actions are taken.

In successful change efforts, senior managers create the overall context, establishing and approving—and then ensuring adherence to—a set of principles for implementation. Such principles define the "playing field" and provide a high-level guidance for how the work of the implementation will be carried out.

In addition to setting principles, speaking as one, and serving as role models, senior managers must empower teams across the organization to conduct the frontline work of implementation. People on these teams must truly believe that they have the right and obligation to enact whatever charters they are given. For example, if an EMR implementation plan is "critical," but the next week senior leaders put new priorities out to the organization, the message will be clear: "We have no priorities, it's just flavor of the week."

Senior managers must agree in full with the plan and make their expectations clear—and then take a step back to let the implementation teams do their work. These managers should step forward only to answer questions and provide general guidance and support (and, of course, to mitigate disasters). An all-too-common occurrence is the senior manager who steps in late in the game and says, "That's not what I had in mind." When people in an organization repeatedly get this message, they lose their commitment to their work and to management. Management's responsibility is to think through—up front—what needs to be done, and why it is critical. Then management must clearly and consistently provide help if and when needed. In the military, every leader is responsible to leave a better command/team than the one they were first given. This means articulating expectations and the rationale for actions, but then giving their reports and staff the latitude to deliver, learn, and grow.

The role of senior management in the implementation of strategic plans is always critical. And the ante increases when major change and organizational transformation are involved. Success requires that senior managers do all of the things discussed above, remaining fully and vocally committed to the plan's priorities.

Finally, divisional leaders may be the business unit general manager, or the president of a community hospital owned by a third-party corporation. This level may or may not be relevant for different organizations based on size and organizational structure. If such a layer exists between the most senior leadership and the execution teams, these individuals must play the same roles as the executive team: "walk the talk."

- **Implementation manager** —Leaders must select a strong implementation manager (IM) to execute the strategic plan. Ideally, the IM will be a widely known and well-respected, emerging leader, someone with a track record of positive accomplishments that support the institution's core values. This individual must be relieved from all or a majority of his/her day-to-day duties—and ensured a return to a position of responsibility at some defined point in the future, or when the work of several key transformational efforts is complete. The IM leads the core team and guides and coaches the implementation teams. His/her role is to keep all of the implementation teams on track, liaise between the execution efforts and senior management, and ensure simple, consistent communication throughout the organization.

- **Core team** —The core team supports the implementation manager. The core team is comprised of representatives from the leadership team, each of the implementation teams, and any organizational functions (e.g., human resources, information technology, and finance) that are not already represented but may be impacted by and/or have key inputs into the various projects. The core team oversees all of the moving parts of the implementation effort. The core team supports all of the implementation teams, integrating and synthesizing their efforts. The team also ensures needed commitments from within and outside of the implementation effort, and oversees the communications effort (discussed below).
- **Implementation teams**—The implementation teams manage one or more threads of the overall effort. Where feasible, the teams should be cross-organizational, representing different segments and subcultures of the overall enterprise. When these teams are empowered, and led by a strong individual reporting directly to the IM, they will make change happen. Finally, whether naturally or through training and coaching, they must be highly collaborative and constantly ask the following: What do we need to accomplish, by when, for the good of the organization?

A positive by-product of such efforts can be the delegation of responsibilities that provide long-term staff-development opportunities. Of course the rub is for staff to manage ongoing operations *plus* the additional requirements of any change initiative(s). In addition, some functions—such as nurses and physicians—are historically protective of their relative positions and responsibilities. While they may seem to agree on change initiatives within a meeting, back on the floor, traditional roles and responsibilities quickly resurface. In our experience, such barriers to change should be expected and mitigation options included in the implementation plan. Thus, it is even more important for leadership to consistently over-communicate the "what and the why" for the change, celebrate its success, and be ready for inevitable challenges.

Articulate Value Propositions That Emotionally Connect at an Individual Level

A value proposition clearly and succinctly communicates the benefits of a strategic effort. If the value proposition hasn't been developed as part of the planning process, an early step in implementation must be to ensure that a clearly articulated value proposition exists for each of the major initiatives, as well as the overall execution effort. For successful implementation, this value proposition must be understood, accepted, and supported by all levels of the organization. Sometimes this approach is labeled "alignment." As an example, just after President Kennedy set the target of putting a man on the moon by the end of the decade, a reporter asked a NASA (US National Aeronautics and Space Administration) janitor, "What is your job?" Without hesitating the janitor replied: "To put a man on the moon."

In the healthcare field, Merck & Co.'s efforts to research, develop, and help distribute a cure for river blindness are symbolized to all employees by the statue in the lobby of their worldwide headquarters. The statue depicts an older African suffering from river blindness led by a young man with full sight (Ferrill 2013). River blindness, or onchocerciasis, primarily affects the poorest nations in Africa and Latin America. Merck knew early on that the company would never recoup its incurred research and development expenses, and yet pushed ahead, making real its stated vision: "To make a difference in the lives of people globally through our innovative medicines …" (Merck 2015).

Powerful value propositions must appeal to three levels:

- **Value to the Individual**—specific benefits "I" will get from the proposed changes
- **Value to the Team or Function**—value a change will bring to "our group;" how it will enable the team to achieve its priorities more productively and effectively
- **Value to the Enterprise**—value to the overall organization; this can be about its contribution to sustainable competitive impact, ideally linking to broader values and aspirational goals of the organization[1]

What should leaders do when certain projects run counter to these appeals? Not all projects undertaken in the execution phase will provide value in each of these areas. Change is often threatening and emotionally challenging. For example, a change in staffing responsibilities—nurses shifting from a focus on institutional patient care to population health initiatives—can cause *disruption* for an individual or a group. According to Vaneet Nayar (2010), CEO of HCL Technologies, in any major change initiative, there will be roughly 10 % of the population that will support you ("early adaptors"), 80 % that will "wait and see" ("fence sitters"), and 10 % that will never agree. The challenge is to convince the 80 % to support the change efforts.

It is these dynamics that make change so difficult; they are a key reason so few strategic initiatives succeed. In our experience, while not guaranteeing success, two steps must occur. First, the reason for the change must be clearly articulated. As discussed in the section above on the Role of Senior Managers, leaders must do more than simply push: "We need to do X." They must explain the "*why*." And part of that "why" must be clear and emotionally appealing to the broad majority ("What is in it for me?").

---

[1] See Chapter 3 and the discussion of Vision, Mission, and Values.

Second, leaders must articulate what they expect from different groups going forward. For example, if coders for ICD-10 (a set of standard codes for diseases) hear that a new, automated EMR may eliminate their roles and positions, they can hardly be expected to be wild supporters of the effort, no matter how often the CEO of the hospital explains its necessity. What coders want to hear is: "We will still need you and will pay for your training to take on newer, higher-level positions in …"

Throughout the organization, the aspirational vision developed as part of the strategic-planning process is a key determinant of the value propositions employees should hear and internalize during execution. These value propositions—*such as each of us will share in the rewards and opportunities of the proposed changes*—should become part of the shared vision that pulls the organization toward the desired changes. It should focus on the benefits that will accrue from the strategy and its implementation. And it should be explicitly aligned with the organization's vision, mission, and core values that were articulated in the strategic planning process. Leaders face the challenge to connect emotionally, at the embedded-culture level, to lead staff through the change. Mere slogans are not enough. Success requires consistent, personal efforts to guide individuals through the change.[2]

One of the clearest signals that an execution priority really *is* a priority is to reduce team members' day-to-day commitments so they can *focus* on execution. As Sean Covey et al. (2012) explains so well:

> If you're currently trying to execute five, ten or even twenty important goals, the truth is that your team can't focus …[making] success almost impossible. This is especially problematic when there are too many goals at the highest levels of the organization, all of which eventually cascade into dozens and ultimately hundreds of goals as they work their way down throughout the organization, creating a web of complexity.

Establish Program Principles, Especially Clear Scorecards/ Metrics of Success

Every implementation can benefit from a set of guiding principles and metrics applied throughout the effort. The principles serve as underlying mandates for the conduct of the work. Principles vary depending on the organization and nature of the work, but often include guidelines such as:

- Regularly identify and mitigate barriers to change
- Establish proactive, two-way communications
- Ensure ongoing, adequate resourcing
- Seek program resilience
- Divide and conquer
- Establish scorecards/metrics for success
- Celebrate results

[2] For more on the emotional aspects to change, see Bridges (2004).

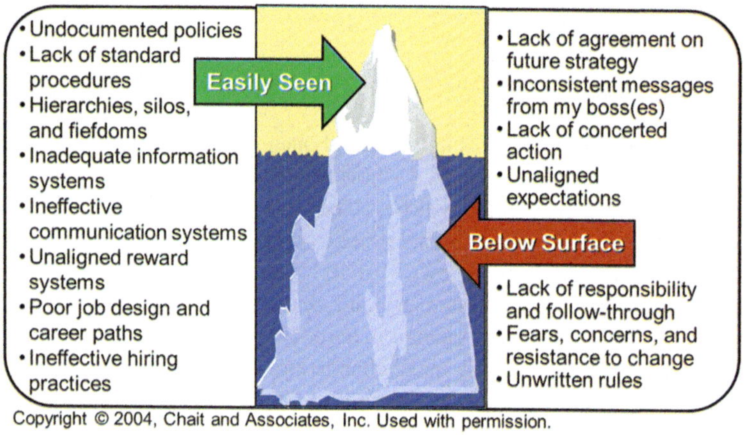

Fig. 5.2 Barriers to change

Regularly Identify and Mitigate Barriers to Change: Barriers to change exist in all organizations—though they are much more significant in some enterprises than in others. Of these barriers, some are easily seen (to those who take the time and effort to look!), while others are hidden beneath the surface, much like the part of an iceberg that cannot be easily observed, as portrayed in Fig. 5.2.

The implementation of a strategic plan can face multiple barriers. For example:

- Hierarchies and silos in a large teaching hospital can make it very difficult to get everyone moving in the same direction.
- Reward systems in an insurance company that encourage new memberships, when the plan is focused on retention, can make change very difficult.
- Employees' fears and lack of trust in any organization can provide a damper on change.

It may seem mundane and obvious to write that organizations must look for and eliminate barriers. Yet many implementation efforts end up in the "unsuccessful" category simply because potential barriers were missed, grew, and ultimately derailed progress.

The core and implementation teams are responsible to find and overcome these barriers. When they are identified early, they can be mitigated or eliminated long before they block progress and derail the implementation effort. When they are not recognized, or allowed to fester, they can certainly impede success. Ideally, the search for and mitigation of potential barriers will occur during the strategic planning effort. Still, ongoing, often more "embedded" barriers will surface during the implementation phase of any major change effort.

Thus "barrier busting" should be part of every agenda for core teams and working groups. And it's not that difficult, at least conceptually! Execution team members should periodically discuss:

- What *is really* getting in the way of progress?
- What *might* get in the way?
- What options can we devise to *neutralize or remove* the barriers?

But, embedded barriers, especially cultural ones, can make such discussions difficult. If most subspecialists are asked—how can nurses or techs take on part of your activities—the typical response will be, "They can't! And if you try, the hospital will be practicing bad medicine." This is not to pick on subspecialists. Rather, most of us, when confronted with our own "barriers," are very hesitant, at an emotional level, to discuss them, much less to try and change. Think how long most of our New Year's resolutions last … change is hard. However, if you avoid looking for and mitigating barriers, you only make change more difficult.

Establish Proactive, Two-Way Communications: Two-way communications mean that messages do not simply flow from the top down, but also from the bottom up. Further, such communications are more than simply messages sent and received; they involve active conversation between and among people all across and up-and-down an organization.

Implementation efforts need a clear principle that fosters effective *two-way* communications. While the core team, working groups, and management must all do some "telling," they must also listen. They need to hear what people think, understand their challenges and issues, and ask questions to clarify what they just heard.[3]

Part of the communications effort is education—what the new strategy is, why it is important, and how the changes included in the implementation effort will achieve desired goals. It also involves discussing the value proposition and key initiatives. The aim is to explain the "what and the why" of the change initiatives, reducing as much as possible incorrect, preconceived notions about the strategy, its rationale, likelihood of success, and impact on individuals in the organization.

In our experience, one reason many communication efforts fail is that they do not involve "active listening and discussion." They are all "push"—beginning with, "Let me tell you …." Successful communication efforts vary from situation to situation, but often include many or all of the following:

- **Walk the halls**—Senior managers, the implementation manager, and members of the core team should spend time physically walking the halls of the organization, looking for opportunities to discuss aspects of the implementation, identify issues, and take corrective action when necessary.
- **Various meetings**
  - All-hands/staff meetings—The implementation and its progress should be an agenda item for all staff meetings.
  - Lunch meetings—Whether organized or impromptu, those involved directly in the implementation should take the opportunity to provide information and get feedback from their peers and subordinates over lunch.

[3] Remember Chapter 4, concerning Mindset issues, especially Groupthink, and the use of a "balance sheet" to surface different perspectives before discussion begins, forcing people to listen.

  - Core team meetings—The communications plan and any communications issues should be discussed at all meetings of the core team.
  - Local meetings—At all other formal or impromptu meetings—at peoples' desks, in conference rooms, or at the water cooler—at least some time should be spent on two-way communication regarding the implementation effort.
- **Buddy system**—Members of the core team are assigned to a "buddy" role with key senior and middle managers; the team members are given scripts to use in maintaining two-way communication regarding implementation progress and issues. This should be in addition to the common practice of assigning senior leaders as key strategic initiative sponsors.
- **"Ask Me" buttons**—Especially in large organizations, members of the core team should sport obvious "Ask Me" buttons to encourage people they meet throughout the day to ask questions—or make suggestions—regarding the implementation.
- **Newsletters and other internal communications vehicles**—For the duration of the implementation, all written communications vehicles should contain timely news items on the effort. During the merger of Raritan Bay Medical Center and Meridian Health, creating one of New Jersey's largest health networks, the Raritan CEO sent letters in both English and Spanish to all staff homes in an effort to "keep them updated on the merger and the rationale behind it" (Hegwer 2015).
- **Workshops**—To obtain ideas and feedback, workshops (implying task-oriented, collaborative sessions) should be held; the atmosphere of a "workshop" is much more conducive to active, two-way communication than that of a "meeting."

Such communication efforts should allow for two-way communication, enabling staff to ask their questions and submit their ideas. Of course, there must be a commitment to respond to these inquiries in a timely fashion … and stick to those commitments. At times, questions raised may not have an immediate answer. Senior leaders should respond truthfully, and when they don't know the answer, simply ask, "What do you suggest?"

Communication is an ongoing process that must continue in force for the duration of the major implementation phases. Often, a separate team is formed to manage/implement the communications effort and/or a specific person made responsible for the communications plan and its execution. However, its overall responsibility lies in the hands of the implementation manager; the senior team should be accountable for its direction, content, and impact.

Communications that are heard are based on trust. If staff is distrustful, no matter what is said, little will be heard. The keys to trust are:

- **Competency:** Do I believe you have the requisite capabilities, skills to accomplish what you say you can?
- **Reliability:** Do you "walk-the-talk"? If senior leaders say they will respond in 24 hours to any e-mail about ongoing change initiatives—is that commitment met?

- **Emotional Commitment:** Deep down, do you have my best interests at heart? Do I feel "good" being around you?[4]

In outlining these steps to execution effectiveness, remember throughout the need to retain trust.

Ensure Ongoing, Adequate Resourcing: For its duration, implementation of a strategic plan can be a major time- and resource-consuming process. The role of resources in the process/resource/organization triad of the high-performance model (HPM) is directly applicable to implementation efforts. Implementation efforts that are insufficiently resourced (time, people, dollars, etc.)—initially and going forward—are doomed to failure.

Thus, the budgeting aspects of implementation planning are critical, as is regular monitoring of plan and budget status. Any situation in which adequate resources are not available or may become constrained must be flagged and dealt with as quickly as possible.

Another potential resourcing barrier, especially in large organizations, is the demands of other projects and activities that may be competing for the same resources. For example, a move to a new EMR system in a hospital can be voracious in its consumption of resources. Such implementations are often so large that they delay or cancel other highly desirable projects. Implementations of these dimensions do not occur often, but when they do, their resource conflicts must be elevated to senior management for resolution. As the earlier example of a major tertiary-care hospital struggling to implement an institution-wide EMR highlighted, the executive team was forced to make some tough decisions, delaying other projects to retain the necessary focus on the EMR project.

However, day-to-day resource conflicts are virtually inevitable, and resolution of such conflicts is the responsibility of the implementation manager. He/she must either resolve them quickly or escalate them for resolution on a timely basis.

Seek Program Resilience: The details of the implementation plan should be intentionally left for the implementation team to fill in—given budgetary and timing constraints. As in the military, senior leadership must articulate the "what and the why"; it is up to the troops in the field to develop the "how." This is simply because those working on the floors, handling patient calls and visits, coding records, and so on are in the best position to understand how best to go about realizing any major change. The best performing execution plans begin with "minimum critical specifications," allowing those closest to the patient or issue at hand to determine how to achieve the specifications. Empowering these individuals will also serve to increase their ownership of the outcomes.

While an implementation effort needs to be carefully planned out, unforeseen circumstances always emerge. Thus, it is important that implementation efforts have built-in resilience—i.e., characteristics including pragmatism, and systemic thinking.

---

[4] For more on trust and its impact, see Covey (2006).

- **Pragmatism**—Dogmatic thinking and actions can provide undue constraints on implantation teams. There must always be the potential to search for practical solutions to emerging issues. Note the discussion about Mindset issues in Chapter 3, especially problems with Frame Bias, and Overconfidence.
- **Systemic thinking**—Every part of an implementation effort is related in some way to other components. Thus, it is possible that a small change made by one specification or effort can have a ripple effect—positive or negative—elsewhere in the implementation chain. A continuing effort is needed to review the consequences of what is being done by each team on other teams and the overall implementation effort. This is one of the key roles for the implementation manager, as well as the divisional leaders and/or senior management.

Divide and Conquer: Large, transformational projects can easily be pulled down by their own weight. To facilitate success, they should be divided—"chunked"—into bite-sized pieces that can be broken off and accomplished by smaller, nimble teams. Chunking can prevent working groups from being overwhelmed by the size and scope of their tasks—and they also enable the next principle discussed, "celebrate results."

Over the course of the implementation, these smaller pieces can become "short-term opportunities"—mini-projects that can yield an ongoing stream of benefits and can thus maintain support for the implementation should times become more troubled.

In addition, when dealing with uncertainty, it is best to take a "stage-gate" mentality to change initiatives. Agree on Phase I, but then review and reassess given progress to date, external issues, and how and when it makes sense to proceed to Phase II and beyond. The challenge, as discussed earlier, will be the tendency for teams to lose objectivity in assessing risks/rewards as they move forward, especially if there are high levels of individual commitment to the effort as originally defined. Again, the role of the implementation manager is critical to ask clarifying questions that challenge the team and their assumptions (Kahneman et al. 2011).

Establish Scorecards/Metrics for Success: Another key reason so few strategic initiatives succeed is the lack of clear metrics linking strategy to execution.[5] At the institutional level, as outlined at the end of Chapter 4, organizations must agree on key priorities that *both* keep the current operations going (ideally more efficiently) *and* layer on radical/transformational initiatives. With such a portfolio, healthcare institutions can deal more flexibly with future uncertainty while continuing to function as leaders today. Without such priorities, organizations will quickly fall prey to the "undisciplined pursuit of more"—as Jim Collins (2009) writes—that is an early indicator of incipient failure.

With these priorities, organizations must be able to measure their progress. Pioneered in the 1990s by Dr. Robert S. Kaplan and David P. Norton (1996), the Balanced Scorecard sought to expand the typical financial metrics for measuring implementation success to include categories such as employee engagement or

[5] According to the Center of Creative Leadership (2015), roughly 85 % of strategic initiatives fail.

learning, internal business processes, and customers. While certainly expanding the metrics that for-profit companies typically measured in their execution efforts, the implementation of the Balanced Scorecard can be an administrative nightmare, especially in trying to measure more "qualitative" factors such as "How do customers see us?" In moving from the priorities identified in building a portfolio of strategic initiatives—Core, New, and Wow—many organizations simplify the categories of the Balanced Scorecard. For example, Baxter Healthcare developed their scorecard categories as Employees, Stakeholders, and Financials.[6]

According to Sean Covey et al. (2012):

> The kind of scorecard that will drive the highest levels of engagement with your team will be one that is designed solely for (and often by) the players. This players' scorecard is quite different from the complex coach's scorecard that leaders love to create. It must be simple, so simple that members of the team *can determine instantly if they are winning or losing*. (*Italics added*)

Celebrate Results: When an implementation effort seems never-ending—with people "borrowed" from their normal work to serve on various teams, and deadlines missed—enthusiasm quickly wanes. People just wait for the effort to be over. Such situations create a *negative* momentum, further eroding support, effort, and progress.

On the other hand, when teams "feel" forward progress and positive change, they want to be part of the crusade. Positive momentum feeds on itself and propels implementation forward. The short-term opportunities described previously can help fuel this momentum. An ongoing stream of benefits can do much to maintain management's commitment and employees' involvement over the duration of the implementation effort.

As interim positive results occur, the results and the people who achieve them should be identified publically and the impacts celebrated. Such actions can become part of a continuing effort to tell the affirmative, observable story of any implementation effort, helping maintain the organizational interest and active support needed to ensure future success.

Maintain Active, Ongoing Oversight with Leadership Commitment

A major implementation has many moving parts. Many people are involved, numerable teams are at work, and a multitude of tasks must be accomplished. It is all too easy for a major effort of this scope to spin out of control.

Implementation and change, especially at the transformational level, include many "musts." Resources must be available when and where needed. Deliverables must be timely and budgets must be controlled. Individual efforts must all be

[6] Author's personal knowledge.

integrated into a consistent whole. Conflicts must be nipped in the bud and resolved. Communication—two-way communication—must happen regularly.

Execution efforts fail without clear focus, compelling scorecards/metrics, and emotional support throughout tied to the institution's vision, mission, and values. Everyone participating in the implementation can and must be involved in moving the effort forward. However, the primary responsibility to pilot the ship falls on the shoulders of the implementation manager, with accountability for success in the leadership team. And at the end of the day, it is the CEO and his/her team that will take the organization into and through transformational change.

It is necessary—but not sufficient—for senior leaders to approve an implementation plan. An analogy may help to clarify the level of support required. Imagine each of the senior leaders as having a small plate on which rest the primary programs he/she supports. The plate is crowded; for a new program to have a chance, another program must be edged off the plate. The implementation of the strategic plan must take its place on each senior leader's plate and remain there until its objectives are achieved. There must be focus and clear prioritization for the strategic planning initiatives to be executed.

Throughout, senior leaders must show an ongoing commitment to the strategic priorities and their implementation, in the short, medium, and long term. The implementation will cause disruptions that must be accepted, and involve costs that must be incurred, in order to achieve objectives. Sporadic statements of support and multiple changes in priorities will, in fact, lead to confusion, dissipation of resources, and ultimately failure. In short, senior management *must* stay the course.

But here is the rub: things change! That is the definition of uncertainty … we do not know what the future will bring. So how do teams both "stick to the plan" *and* flexibly respond to changing requirements, new information, and shifting environments? First, as outlined above, senior teams need to lead the charge in driving execution. They need to ensure that *all* groups are equally contributing to execution and are aligned to carry out the strategic initiatives. At the same time, senior executives need to review and be willing to shift resources when required. As a recent major study of the issues with execution revealed issues with alignment and flexibility:

- Alignment: Most executives believe that they and their teams are aligned to the strategy, but they do not trust or believe *that other functions* are equally aligned (see Fig. 5.3).
- Flexibility: Only 22 % of interviewed executives feel that their organization can kill projects that are not succeeding; even fewer feel that they can shift people to more successful efforts as required (see Fig. 5.4).

Senior leaders must ensure that the implementation is adequately resourced. As stated earlier, the effort requires the time, people, and dollars needed for its success, and it must be protected from competing with other organizational programs. It is senior management that ultimately controls the resources and purse strings; they own the resource allocation—the power to "feed or starve" the effort.

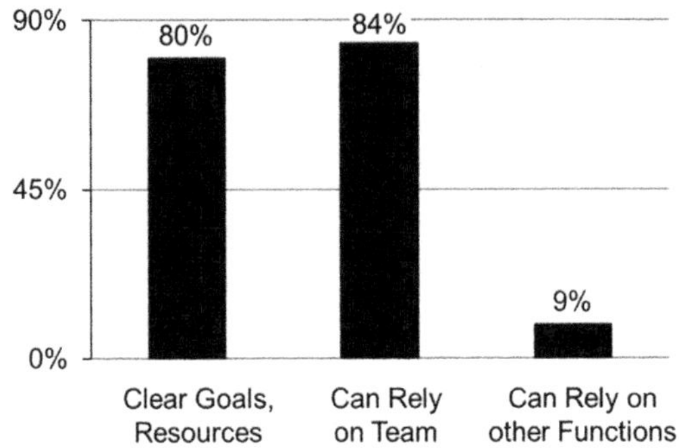

Fig. 5.3 Myth 1: Execution equals alignment (Sull et al. 2015)

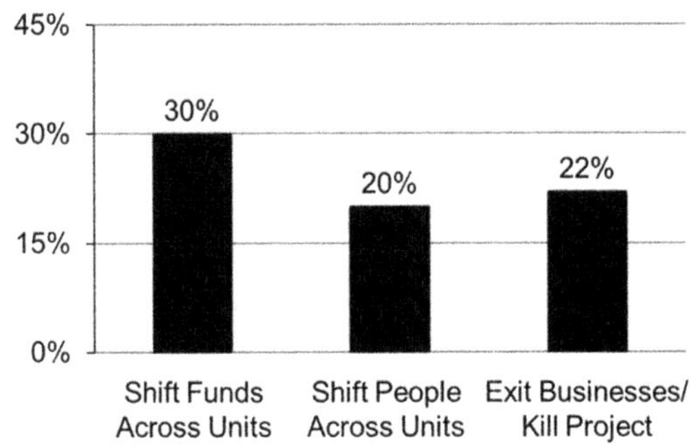

Fig. 5.4 Myth 2: Sticking to the plan (Sull et al. 2015)

But resources, while necessary, are not sufficient for success. As indicated above, the senior team must work to ensure that execution priorities are resourced and aligned not just within functions, but also across the entire organization. Second, the leadership team must be willing to *shift resources* as and when needed. In times of uncertainty, while the vision and goals should not change, the project priorities and the resources deployed need to shift as the fog of the future begins to dissipate (Day and Schoemaker 2005). Monitoring the environment and maintaining the ability to move as opportunities and threats arise is not just the key to execution, but to survival.

Finally, senior managers must do more than *guide and participate* in the implementation; they must be *active role models.* They themselves must do whatever the plan requires the people beneath them to do. Instead of "do what I say, not what I do," it must be "do what I say, which *is* what I do!"

Summary: Driving Successful Execution

Implementation is a risky undertaking. Implementing a plan for transformation, which implies change, increases the odds of failure. It takes an aspirational vision, a solid plan, committed management, engaged staff, and dedicated implementation infrastructure to ensure success.

Mario Moussa, in his research on driving change, argues that successful change initiatives (at the personal or professional level) are built on his STAR model:

- Get *S*pecific: Set realistic, step-by-step goals (*not* everything at once).
- *T*ake Small Steps: Break down actions into discrete actions that can be achieved. Once realized, go to the next set of steps—continually moving towards the overall goal.
- *A*lter the Environment: Develop reminders or change the workplace environment to make it easier to stay focused, on plan.
- Be a *R*ealistic Optimist: Anticipate roadblocks and be ready with a plan for overcoming (Moussa 2015).

The challenge is daunting, but Chapters 6-13 highlight a number of successful transformational efforts. Now it is your turn …

Questions Healthcare Leaders and Teams Should Ask

In 1737, Ben Franklin wrote: "Well done is better than well said."[7] While developing a strategy for healthcare's uncertain future is hard, the ongoing challenge lies in execution. At the end of the day, it is not what leaders say, but what they do, that will determine success or failure. As this chapter outlined, there are many parts to execution: from prioritization to team structure, metrics to commitment, and expressed values to embedded culture. Its very complexity is one reason so few strategic initiatives are successfully implemented. To help healthcare leaders and their teams navigate the perilous seas of execution, start by discussing the following:

- Start implementation *during* planning
  - What can be undertaken while strategic planning efforts are still under way?
  - Are there critical, short-term initiatives that must be tackled, no matter what the priorities for longer term, transformational efforts?
- Establish governance infrastructure
  - Is there a bias for action throughout the organization?
  - Are there clear roles and responsibilities established between the various execution teams and the senior leadership team?
  - Is there an implementation manager—responsible for all the execution efforts and reporting to the senior leadership team—in place?
- Articulate value propositions that emotionally connect at an individual level
  - What are the major strategic priorities to be executed against … and is it clear "why" they are essential to the organization?
  - Are other priorities and responsibilities—especially for execution team members—pulled back to enable focus on the *critical* initiatives going forward?

[7] Inscribed in the walkways of University of Pennsylvania, Philadelphia.

  - Are these priorities maintained, or are other priorities/initiatives/goals constantly being added … reducing clarity of focus?
  - How are all senior leaders, throughout the organization, helping all levels understand, accept, and move forward with major change initiatives?
  - What are the cultural implications of transformational efforts … and how are these being managed to overcome the emotional barriers to transitioning from today to tomorrow?
- Agree unambiguous priorities and the process for updating
  - What are the unambiguous strategic initiatives—short, medium, and longer term—that link the strategy to execution?
  - Does everyone understand the prioritization process for updating these initiatives given changing environments, capabilities, and project outcomes?
  - Are senior leaders utilizing the prioritization processes or circumventing to insert their favored projects?
- Establish program principles, especially clear scoreboards/metrics of success
  - What are the simple, team-driven metrics that enable team members to know: are we winning or losing?
  - How often are they updated?
  - What are the institution-wide metrics that enable all functions to align?
  - What is the process for slowing down, speeding up, or even killing projects based on outcomes and requirements? Are resources "moveable" based on need and results? And what are the criteria for making those shifts?
- Maintain ongoing oversight, especially senior leadership commitment
  - Are senior leaders "walking the talk"?
  - Does the senior team stick to overall agreed priorities, or does agreement break down outside of meetings?
  - Is the senior leadership team constantly seeking to balance short-term necessities with longer term transformational moves?
  - Is the senior team actively monitoring the environment and its periphery for signs of emerging threats or opportunities? Are they ready to respond? Are they "productively paranoid" or are they complacent, relatively secure in their position? (Collins 2011)
  - Are efforts being made to align all groups, across the organization, to the key strategic priorities and execution initiatives?
  - Are various action teams sharing information, supporting each other for the overall good of the organization … or hoarding talent and resources, protecting turf and function?

References

Aiken C, Keller S. The irrational side of change management. McKinsey Quarterly 2009 April.

Bridges W. Transitions: making sense of life's transitions. Boston: De Capo Press; 2004.

Center for Creative Leadership. Leading in times of transition. 2015. http://insights.ccl.org/multimedia/podcast/leading-in-times-of-transition-2/. Accessed 30 Dec 2015.

Collins J. How the mighty fall: and why some companies never give in. New York: HarperCollins Publishers; 2009.

Collins J. Great by choice. New York: HarperCollins; 2011.

Covey SMR et al. The 4 disciplines of execution: achieving your wildly important goals. New York: Free Press; 2012. p. 11.

Covey SMR. The speed of trust. New York: Free Press; 2006.

Day GS, Schoemaker PJH. Scanning the periphery. Harvard Business Review 2005 Nov.

Ferrill I. One in the eye for river blindness. Education in Chemistry. 2013. http://www.rsc.org/eic/2013/11/ivermectin-river-blindness. Accessed 18 July 2015.

Hegwer LR. Leading change from the c-suite: 3 leaders share their strategies. Healthc Exec. 2015;6(30):18.

Jørgensen HH, Owen L, Neus A. Making change work. IBM Corporation; 2008. http://www-07.ibm.com/au/pdf/making_change_work.pdf. Accessed 8 July 2015.

Kahneman D, Lovallo D, Sibony O. Before you make that big decision. Harvard Business Review 2011 June.

Kaplan RS, Norton DP. The balanced scorecard: translating strategy into action. Boston: Harvard Business Press; 1996.

Kitching E, Shaibal R. 70% of transformation programs fail. AIPMM Webinar Series; 2013. http://www.aipmm.com/aipmm_webinars/2013/08/70-of-transformation-programs-fail---make-your-program-succeed-with-proven-strategies-to-generate-mo.php. Accessed 14 July 2015.

Kotter JP. Leading change: why transformation efforts fail. Harvard Business Review 2007 Jan.

McGrath R, MacMillan I. Discovery-driven planning. Harvard Business Review 1995 July-Aug.

Merck & Co. Vision. 2015. http://www.merck.com/about/home.html. Accessed 20 July 2015.

Moussa M. Making learning stick: the STAR model. Wharton @ Work Leadership series. 2015. http://executiveeducation.wharton.upenn.edu/thought-leadership/wharton-at-work/2015/09/making-learning-stick. Accessed 19 June 2015.

Nayar V. Employees first, customers second. Boston: Harvard Business Press; 2010.

Sull D, Homkes R, Sull C. Why strategy execution unravels—and what to do about it. Harvard Business Review 2015 March.

Part II

Case Examples of Institutional Change: Hospitals, Treatment Centers, and Provider Groups

The Pursuit of the Integrated Multidisciplinary Service Line

6

James Andrews

Abstract
The integrated multidisciplinary service line (IMSL)—horizontally aligned business units within institutions—is often viewed as offering the promise of flexibility to adapt to a rapidly changing, uncertain healthcare world. The challenge, as healthcare leaders contemplate adopting an IMSL model, is that with counterbalancing any improved flexibility comes the variability of the organization model. If not fully integrated, institutions can create more bureaucracy through evermore complex organizational structures, with no gain in efficiency or patient satisfaction. Based on the experience of Brigham and Women's Hospital, this case outlines the opportunities and challenges to transforming institutional structures.

Introduction

There is no panacea when it comes to a patient's health; the same principle applies to the viability of your healthcare institution. Despite this fact, the "magic pill" label has been used for decades to describe the impact of implementing an integrated multidisciplinary service line (IMSL). Known throughout the years as "service lines," or "centers of excellence," these horizontally aligned business units assume ownership for the people, finances, clinical infrastructure, and processes that fall within their disease-based scope. These clinical operating structures have been utilized by organizations for such lofty goals as transcending traditional academic and/or healthcare silos or maximizing synergies and care continuity across merging

J. Andrews, B.S., E.M.H.L. (✉)
Brigham and Women's Hospital Heart and Vascular Center, Boston, MA, USA
e-mail: jrandrews@partners.org

J. Austin et al. (eds.), *Leading Strategic Change in an Era of Healthcare Transformation*, Management for Professionals,
DOI 10.1007/978-3-319-30776-3_6

organizations. Today's IMSLs offer the promise of institutional flexibility to adapt to a changing healthcare landscape.

Recently, healthcare institutions have faced sweeping changes: compliance with the Affordable Care Act, shift toward Accountable Care Organizations, a greater prevalence of at-risk reimbursement contracts, and a growing number of consumer assessments based upon "triple-aim" fundamentals of cost, quality, and access. If implemented correctly, an IMSL model offers a unique opportunity for institutions to restructure resources and create value as providers attempt to lower costs, encourage preventative health, coordinate care, maximize clinical quality, and increase access to care. However, as many have discovered, if implemented without structure and context, an IMSL can reduce flexibility, create hierarchical ambiguity, and reduce accountability. Despite these risks, more and more institutions continue their pursuit of the IMSL. This case examines my hospital's efforts to transform its own IMSL, specifically across the cardiovascular disease spectrum.

Heart and vascular care at Brigham and Women's Hospital (BWH) in Boston, Massachusetts, is widely recognized for pushing the frontier of clinical practices and outcomes. Prior to 2008, each specialty area provided clinical services across several locations at BWH and its distributed campuses. Collaboration among physicians and surgeons toward the best treatment plans for patients had always been valued but the physical separation between practices, particularly amongst the ambulatory clinics, proved challenging. To address this issue, BWH geographically co-located all heart and vascular disciplines into a state-of-the-art building, the Shapiro Cardiovascular Center. The Center's design promoted interdisciplinary, patient-focused care and comfort. At the time, the hospital's executive leadership generally accepted that this move would strategically align the heart center's principal resources: brilliant faculty in all relevant cardiovascular specialties; a sterling reputation (US News 2014) for excellence in clinical care and scientific discovery; a supportive senior leadership team; and completely integrated facilities (Brigham and Women's 2008) including every procedural and imaging modality available. Despite the new building, several significant challenges remained:

- Disparity between medical and surgical resources, compensation, and volume targets
- Inefficient patient coordination and hand-offs, especially regarding care transitions
- Lack of transparency on financial, operational, and quality metrics between cardiovascular specialties as well as professional and hospital units
- A culture which did not organically foster interdisciplinary programming and inter-professional clinical collaboration
- Vertical administrative reporting alignments preventing accountability and visibility across the newly created horizontally orientated clinical areas

In 2012, the executive leadership of the hospital made the decision to take a more proactive, service line approach. This decision coincided with the healthcare system participating in the Pioneer Accountable Care Organization pilot program.

Service Line Key attribute	Cited 2010 Industry Leader	Brigham and Women's (pre-HVC)	U. of Michigan	Cleveland Clinic	Mayo Clinic	Johns Hopkins U.	Vanderbilt U.	Northwestern Memorial
New governance structure	S. Miami Hospital	W	E	E	W	E	E	E
Eliminated physician / surgeon competition	Presbyterian Hospital NC	N	W	E	W	E	W	E
Profit sharing	U of Michigan	N	W	W	W	W	N	N
Restructured physician compensation	U of Michigan	N	W	E	E	W	N	W
Shared work spaces	Shady Grove Hospital	E	E	E	E	E	W	E

Fig. 6.1 Summary of peer benchmarking analysis. *N* not yet in place, *W* work in progress, *E* established

Collectively, these two moves marked a transformational shift toward building infrastructure that promotes quality improvements and an enhanced patient experience in defined populations and disease categories. To address this shift, the organization commissioned a group of leaders to develop and implement a BWH Heart and Vascular Center (HVC) strategic plan charged with integrating six cardiovascular stakeholder areas and aligning the organization with the changing needs of patients, clinicians, and the American healthcare landscape.

The group tasked with the creation of the Heart and Vascular Center included the President, Chief Operating Officer (COO), Chair of Medicine, Chair of Surgery, Senior Vice President of Surgical Services, Senior Vice President of Clinical Services, and other key physician and administrative thought leaders. Based on extensive peer benchmarking (see Fig. 6.1), expansive industry research, and in-depth internal analyses, it became clear that the legacy organizational model, developed over the last 100 years, required modernization to create the integration and oversight necessary for effective stewardship of our portfolio of services.

While all interest groups were in agreement that a new model needed to be undertaken, the degree of integration was an actively debated topic. Full integration represented a culture change, the potential introduction of new species of stakeholders into the previously autonomous ecosystems of the existing units. At the end of the day, with several of the key elements (space, research, academics, revenues, and staff) on the line, compromises were made to balance the organizational

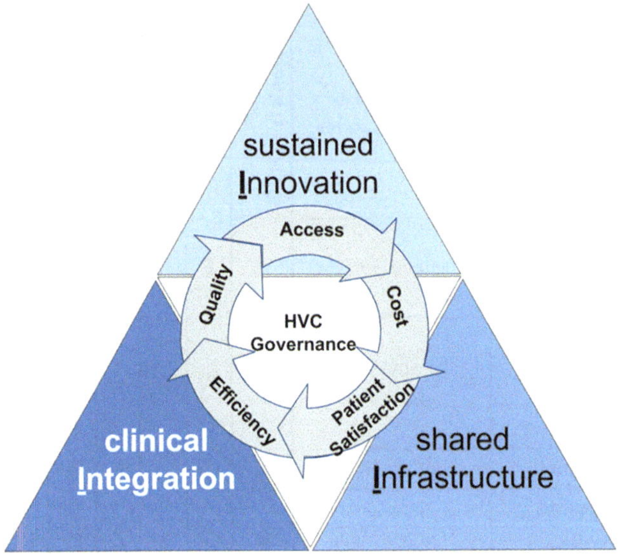

Fig. 6.2 3-I strategic model

requirements of the HVC while maintaining the integrity of the academic departments. The HVC was chartered with the following objectives and parameters for success.

1. Vision: Deploy the "3-I" (innovation, integration, infrastructure) strategic model.
2. Alignment: Reorganize the governance structure.
3. Transparency: Standardize metrics dashboards and define communication channels to adopt a theme of "five core competencies": cost, access, quality, patient satisfaction, and efficiency.
4. Accountability: Define clear roles and responsibilities within a matrix structure of horizontal clinical areas and vertical disease-based collaborative centers (CCs).
5. Innovation Incentives: Create a sustainable integrated financial model that monitors costs and incentivizes CC leaders/staff by funding their research, teaching, or clinical initiatives.

1. **Vision: Deployment of the "3-I" Strategic Model**
   BWH Heart and Vascular Center attempted to align the clinical infrastructure with the organization's own vision to "transform the future of healthcare, through science, education and compassionate care, locally and globally." The self-developed, 3-I strategic model (see Fig. 6.2) focused on the shared *i*nfrastructure, proposed clinical *i*ntegration, and sustainable efforts in *i*nnovation.

The practical application of the 3-I model aimed to achieve balance among all components while maintaining the hospital's strategic mission "serving the needs of our local and global community, providing the highest quality healthcare to patients and their families, expanding the boundaries of medicine through research, and educating the next generation of healthcare professionals." The 3-I model focused on the areas of the hospital the service line had immediate oversight and impact over:

- Shared Infrastructure: Leverage the institution strength that all HVC disciplines were already geographically co-located in a state-of-the-art building.
- Clinical Integration: Implement a new HVC organizational structure, detailed below, to oversee the integration of clinical care. Focusing on disease-based care, HVC leadership further divided the organizational structure between two primary components: clinical units and collaborative centers. This effort promoted collaboration and the cross-pollination of ideas between physician, nursing, and administrative stakeholders. To advance these subgroups into formal business units and create accountability for performance, the HVC designed and developed a charter system, communication structure, and dashboard infrastructure to monitor progress. The ultimate goal for all of these centers was to bridge the traditional gaps between the academic silos while simultaneously achieving quality clinical outcomes and advancing scientific discovery.
- Sustained Innovation: Without a fully integrated financial model and sustainable revenue stream, the center required a mechanism to incentivize buy-in and promote a culture of innovation without the institutional and administrative hurdles typically encountered by faculty members during their pursuit of a landmark finding, procedure, or trial. As such, seed funding dollars were contributed to the center from the hospital and departments and an investment strategy (detailed below) was enacted to reward those clinical units and collaborative center leaders who achieved their annual targets.

2. **Alignment: Reorganization of the governance structure**
   A SWOT (strengths, weaknesses, opportunities, threats) analysis of the current departmental leadership structure led the institution to select a co-director model (see Fig. 6.3). The newly appointed HVC leaders quickly created a balanced, flexible, empowered, and responsible leadership structure to address deficiencies in communication and collaboration. Their efforts resulted in a three-tiered organizational model, with each level designed to govern aspects of the HVC while interacting across shared services and seamlessly communicating up and down the chain of command.

   - HVC Oversight Committee provides guidance to the HVC service line, approves HVC budgets/major investments, and reviews leadership appointments put forth by HVC leadership.
   - HVC Executive Leadership provides overarching leadership and strategic direction to the entire HVC enterprise. This group orchestrates and communicates initiatives to ensure transparency, alignment, and execution. Through

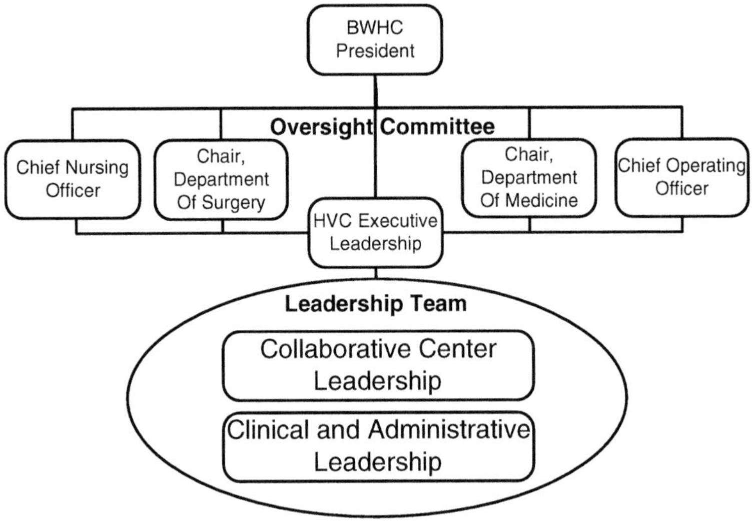

Fig. 6.3 Co-director governance model

the inclusion of key leaders across all stakeholder groups, this team creates an open forum for discussion and collective decision making.

- The HVC Leadership Team oversees strategic planning, implementation, and outcomes across the horizontal organizational units while ensuring the primacy of the "five core competencies" of cost, access, quality, patient satisfaction, and efficiency.

3. **Transparency with a standardized metrics dashboard**
Once assembled, the BWH HVC created a list of finite metrics and a defined data collection plan rooted in their five core competencies. This foundation strategically aligned the center's goals and provided a common measuring metric not only for the center as a whole, but also for all of the HVC stakeholders, centers, clinical units, and quality improvement initiatives.

Executive Dashboard: Given the size of the organization, their portfolio of initiatives was quite large but tracked and communicated upward through the organization via a three-dimensional dashboard system (see Fig. 6.4). The HVC developed a dashboard reporting structure emulating one of organic chemistry's basic fundamentals: the strongest and most sustainable structures are built in fractals. This philosophy ensured that the smallest pieces of the organization were infused with the same structure, metrics, and communication strategy to easily aggregate into the whole.

Deploying the HVC 3-D approach to data collection and data dissemination allowed leadership to maintain general oversight but also gave the operational areas the flexibility to customize those quality metrics important to their area. The guiding principles for this initiative were for each metric to fit within the construct of the overall five core competencies. Having a consistent set of reliable metrics,

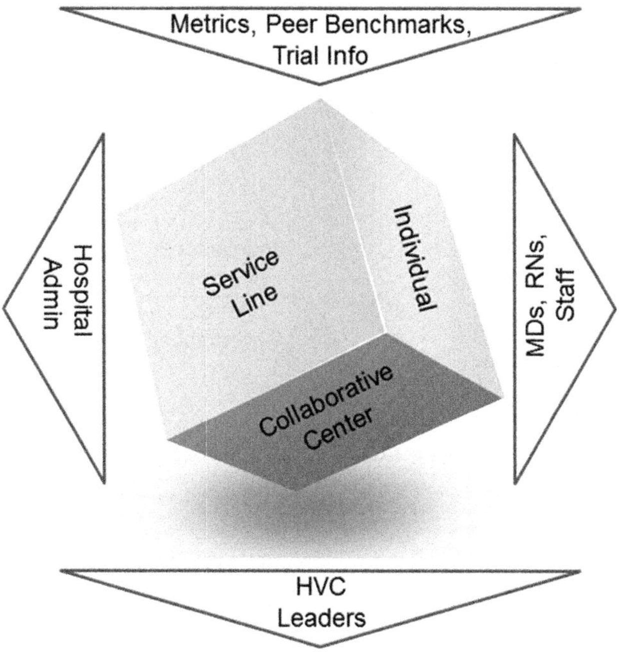

Fig. 6.4 Three-dimensional dashboard

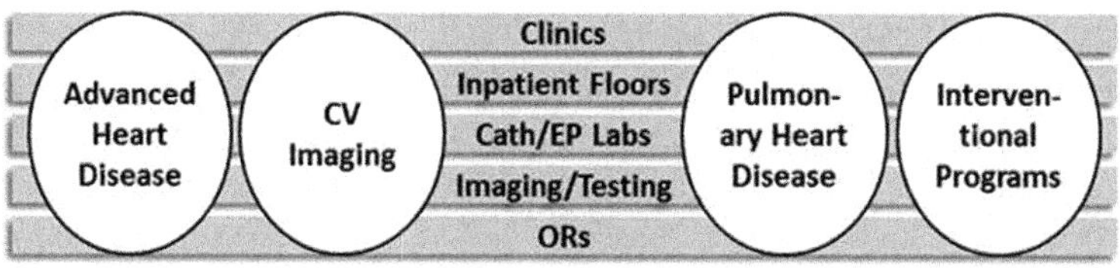

Fig. 6.5 Interwoven clinical units and collaboration centers

defined data collection plan, and reporting transparency allowed the HVC systematically to approach measurement of outcomes across all areas and reward high performers.

Operational Dashboards: The BWH HVC Leadership Group members, Clinical Units, and Collaborative Centers set annual performance targets within the five core competencies, as well as at least three quality improvement initiatives to be overseen and directed by the HVC Executive Team. Delivering value, defined as (quality + patient satisfaction)/outcomes, is at the heart of the service line. Monitoring the daily operations of the HVC, given the size and complexity of the business model, would become a full-time job if not for a system of intricate dashboards created in partnership with the BWH Center for Clinical Excellence. Operational dashboards at the subunit and program levels ensure

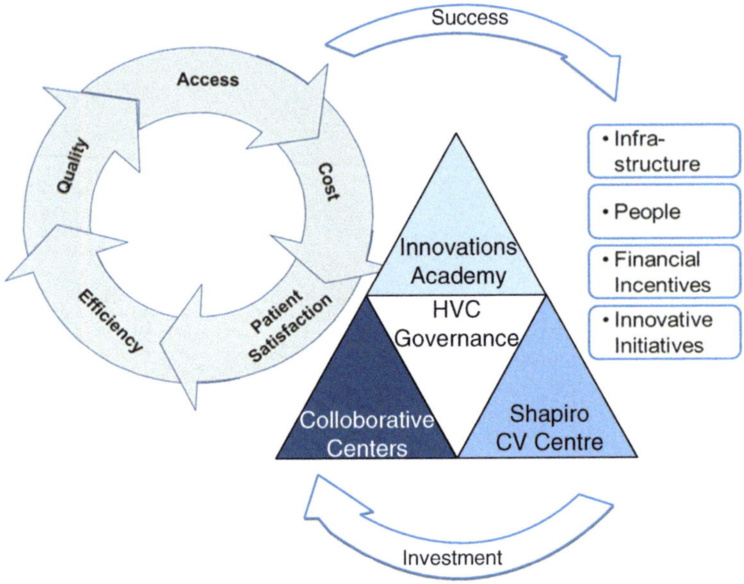

Fig. 6.6 Integrated success model

that the quality improvement activities at all levels of the organization are supported with timely and accurate information.

4. **Accountability Within Horizontal Clinical Units and Vertical/Disease-Based Collaborative Centers (CCs)**

   Building upon the foundation of standardized metrics and quality improvement, the BWH HVC has started promoting patient centeredness and disease-based patient pathways by creating an interwoven tapestry of horizontal *clinical units* and vertically aligned, disease-based, *collaborative centers* (see Fig. 6.5).

   This infrastructure maintains accountability at the lower levels of the organization in addition to providing frontline leaders with clear channels of communication to drive quality and operational improvement initiatives from the ground up. Focusing on standardized patient pathways, centralized protocol development, and targeted patient communication/education, the HVC coordinates these efforts and goals through a shared set of metrics and dashboards.

5. **Innovative Incentive Programs and Financial Sustainability**

   Steps 1–4, outlined above, enabled BWH leadership to entrust the HVC with funds for targeted financial interventions such as incentives, equipment/devices, and FTEs to areas of the organization it deems most appropriate. This HVC investment "seed" pool was provided by the hospital, Department of Medicine, and Department of Surgery to be utilized at the discretion of the HVC Executive Leadership Team (under the broad supervision of the HVC Oversight Committee) as a means for the institution to "forward invest" in non-recurring/non-operational expenses. Such an incentive program could be perceived as biased by our stakeholders if not for our alignment to a single mission, clear objectives and

Metric	FY12 (Pre-launch)	FY13 (Year 1)	FY14 (Year 2)
Volume			
Procedural (OR/EP/Cath)	8,787	8,941	9,155
Imaging	38,880	39,650	42,368
Office Visits	40,580	43,972	43,519
Discharges/ATOs/RPPRs	7,189	7,403	7,365
Efficiency			
ALOS	6.39	7.10	7.50
CMI	4.65	4.89	5.29
CMI Adjusted LOS	1.37	1.45	1.42
30-day Readmmission	11.9%	11.4%	11.2%
Quality			
Observed/Expected Mortality	1.11	1.09	0.98
Patient Satisfaction Percentile	99%	99%	99%

Fig. 6.7 Results and outcomes, FY12–FY14

measurement tools, and accountability/ownership across the organization. HVC reinforced its position by utilizing these funds to garner buy-in of faculty, nurses, and staff that encourages collaboration and improvement activities grounded in the five core competencies (see the integrated success model in Fig. 6.6). HVC hopes that their selected investments build innovative programs that add value to the HVC brand, ultimately drawing more patients and generating incremental financial margins.

Results and Outcomes

Two years into the transformational change, BWH saw positive results across three key metric areas of volume, efficiency, and quality (see Fig. 6.7).

Targeted efforts to increase access and market presence created a steady rise in office visits and procedural volume while a focus on population management has helped to curtail the rising inpatient discharge totals. Although length of stay increased due to an increased case mix index (CMI), the decreasing CMI-adjusted length of stay (LOS) and 30-day readmission rates reflect efforts to improve efficiency across the 136-bed, inpatient facility. Perhaps the biggest area of improvement is the observed/expected mortality rate of our patient population. While only a snapshot of the work invested to date into the Heart and Vascular Center, these metrics demonstrate the positive returns an institution can expect when they restructure themselves into an organizational structure aligned with quality, value, and outcomes.

Lessons Learned Through the Development of Growth Assessment Tools

Transformational change cannot occur in an institution without stumbling and a retrospective review on the lessons learned, obstacles faced, and market shifts throughout the process. As BWH discovered, not all service lines are created equal nor are all service lines designed to achieve a common result. In a recent survey (Advisory Board 2014) of 126 Advisory Board Cardiovascular Roundtable hospitals, a mix of community and academic institutions, 70 % of respondents had an integrated heart and vascular service line. Despite a prevalence of service lines in the industry, a great degree of variability exists in practice and application when the term "service line" is utilized.

The largest issue facing BWH and other organizations attempting to create a service line is the variability of integration. As a matrix governance structure spanning existing strong academic departments, the BWH HVC continuously encounters challenges pertaining to scope, influence, and ownership. Often the HVC leadership helps adjudicate governance issues in high-impact areas with influence as opposed to direct control over the particular subject matter. While it is internally perceived a success, compromising on the depth and breadth of the center during the scoping phase and creation of the 3-I strategic plan created a structure that has ambiguity in asset ownership, personnel management, and operational control. To better assess their integration progress, BWH created an *Integrated Multidisciplinary Service Line Asset Grid* as well as an *Integrated Multidisciplinary Service Line Scorecard* (see Figs. 6.8 and 6.9) that outline the assets and decisions necessary to create, sustain, and improve the HVC and other institutional IMSLs.

IMSL Asset Grid: This tool (see Fig. 6.8) outlines the ownership of assets important to any IMSL and tracks the progress, if desired, as the service line expands into areas outside of the originally designed scope.

IMSL Scorecard: The IMSL Scorecard (see Fig. 6.9) outlines the ten key components of an IMSL based on BWH and benchmarked institution's best practices in management, organization, and care. Each key component includes an associated critical question and one to several attributes that will help in assessing the strength of integration on a three-part (low, medium, high) scale. Scores are applied to each of the cells in the Scorecard. By quantifying the key component scores, the IMSL Scorecard attempts to serve as a baseline grading system for IMSL integration effectiveness.

Next Steps

In developing the *IMSL Asset Grid* and *IMSL Scorecard*, BWH created two management tools to track progress of the HVC and other to-be-created service lines for the institution. While their own IMSL pursuit represents a transformational change

Service Line	Strategy*	Operations^	Finance~
Hospital Assets			
Nursing	◇	◇	◇
Ambulatory Clinics	◇	◇	◇
Procedural - Cath/EP Labs	◇	◇	◇
Surgical ORs	◇	◇	◇
Imaging	◇	◇	◇
Inpatient Beds	◇	◇	◇
Administrative Space	◇	◇	◇
Technical Revenue	◇	◇	×
Departmental Assets			
Physicians	◇	◇	×
Physicians Admin Support	×	×	×
Departmental Administration	×	×	×
Professional Revenue	×	×	×
Clinical Mission			
Procedure Portfolio/Patient Mix	◇	◇	◇
Clinical Leadership/Organization	◇	◇	◇
Clinical Activity/Operations	◇	◇	◇
Academic Mission			
Housestaff Direction/Deployment	◇	◇	×
Medical CMEs	×	×	×
Grand Rounds	◇	×	×
Research Mission			
Sponsored Research	×	×	×
Clinical Trials	◇	×	×
Innovative Internal Programs	◇	◇	×
Thought Leadership/Publications	◇	◇	×
Administration			
Development	✓	✓	◇
Marketing/Communication	✓	✓	◇
Website/Electronic Patient Access	✓	✓	◇
Centralized Call Center Access Hubs	✓	✓	◇
Networking	✓	✓	◇
Integrated/Leadership Reporting	✓	✓	◇
External Contracts/Alliances	✓	✓	◇

Key: ✓ = Control, ◇ = Influence, × = Out of scope

* Strategy = Portfolio of services and procedures; appointed leaders; communication methods; subcommittees

^ Operation = Quality; Access; Cost Effectiveness; Patient Satisfaction; and Volume

~ Finance = FTEs; Operating Budgets; Investments, Funds Flow; Capital Investments; Compensation Models

Fig. 6.8 IMSL Asset Grid

Key Component	Critical Question	Attributes	Strength of Integration		
			Low	Medium	High
Services **(1-10 pts)**	What services will be integrated?	Example: Heart & Vascular = CV Med, Cardiac Surgery, Vascular Surgery, Nursing, CV Anesthesia, CV Imaging	Limited (3 pts)	Majority (6 pts)	All (10 pts)
***Mission** **(1 pt each)**	What activities will be included in the center's *value proposition?	*Clinical: Quality *Clinical: Cost Clinical: Patient Satisfaction Clinical: Access Clinical: Volume Education: Teaching Education: CME Research: Sponsored Research Research: Clinical Trials Research: Publications	Limited focus on an ad hoc basis (0 pts each)	Full focus but out of alignment with institutional goals (.5 pts each)	Full focus in alignment with institutional goals (1 pt each)
Leadership Model **(1-10 pts)**	Who will lead the center?	1.) Single Leader 2.) Dyad Model (Co-Leaders) 3.) Triad Model or Multi-leader	Strength dependent on ability/respect of leader, cohesiveness of team, and alignment of goals/participation		
Reporting Structure **(1-10 pts)**	To whom will the center report?	1.) An overlay of services 2.) Parts of the existing silo structure 3.) Independent governing body	Virtual overlay of services (3 pts)	Matrixed into existing academic or clinical silos (6 pts)	Vertically aligned independent body (10 pts)
Collaboration and Central Coordination **(1 pt each)**	How will collaborative efforts be encouraged and supported?	Clinical: Care teams *Clinical: Quality Review Clinical: Service portfolio decisions *Administration: Marketing Administration: Development Administration: Access Center Administration: Networking *Administration: Finance *Administration: Management of external influences (Regulations/Policy/etc) *Administration: Information Technology	No admin structure or resources (0 pts each)	Limited admin support and resources (.5 pts each)	Empowered admin support and control over resource base (1 pt each)
***Funding & Financial Sustainability** **(1-10 pts)**	How will funds flow to the center?	1.) No backstop 2.) Institutional backstop 3.) Institutional + departmental backstop 4.) Self sustaining model	Reliance on backstop, no or partial visibility into funding (3 pts)	Reliance on backstop but virtual P&L and visibility into financial health (6 pts)	Independent in chart of accounts with a defined financial sustainability model
Equity, Incentives, and Compensation **(1-10 pts)**	How will you establish equity in pay and incentivize individuals?	1.) Department based compensation 2.) Salary + Department incentives 3.) Salary + Center incentives	Variable, department-based compensation (3 pts)	Aligned, department-based compensation (6 pts)	Center determined salary and incentives (10 pts)
Physical Infrastructure **(1-10 pts)**	Where will center activities be located?	1.) Virtual 2.) Co-located 3.) Stand alone building	Virtual (3 pts)	Co-located (6 pts)	Stand alone building (10 pts)
***Internal and External Communication** **(1-10 pts)**	How will you engage stakeholders?	1.) Ad hoc basis 2.) Frequent communication 3.) Defined bi-directional communication	Ad hoc (3 pts)	Frequent (6 pts)	Defined bi-directional communication (10 pts)
Patient Experience & Standardization of Care **(0-2 pts each)**	How will you create a seamless patient experience?	Standardized patient pathways Centralized protocol development *Integrated reporting/dashboards Patient Communication/Education Consistent metric tracking	One-off efforts (0 pts each)	Centrally coordinated efforts (1 pt each)	Cultural adoption of vision and practices (2 pts each)

** Indicates an element featured within the EMHL curriculum*

Fig. 6.9 IMSL Scorecard

for BWH, as is the case with most service lines, it remains unique and specific to the implementing institution. In using the above tools of assessment, BWH has reassessed their Heart and Vascular Center goals for the upcoming year to include:

- Continued integration across the clinical care spectrum by building upon the collaborative areas, and leveraging their comprehensive heart and vascular physical plant.

- Working within the traditional academic silos to identify ways to influence and contribute to departmental finances and incentives.
- Further promote buy-in and adoption of the HVC vision across all of its constituents: While the BWH HVC remains visible to all of these stakeholders, further efforts to expand employee support need to be made so these individuals can truly identify with the center's leadership and mission.

The above BWH HVC case demonstrates the value of the IMSL approach to care. A center of excellence structure can create institutional flexibility to meet the demands of an ever-changing healthcare landscape. However, as your own institution contemplates the adoption of an IMSL model, remember that the benefits of improved flexibility are often counterbalanced with the injection of variability in your organization model. If not fully integrated, institutions can create more bureaucracy through evermore complex organizational structures, with no gain in efficiency or patient satisfaction. Understanding the impact of how your institution handles each critical question measured in your scorecard, and your institutional commitment to integration—especially the ability to relinquish assets to the service line—will improve your chances for a successful implementation of an IMSL model, better preparing for the uncertainties that lie ahead of all of us.

Chapter Summary

This case study explores the organizational transformation of the Brigham and Women's Hospital (BWH) Heart and Vascular Center (HVC) to a more efficient IMSL. This excellent chapter further explores the opportunities for transformational change in healthcare delivery. As indicated by Mr. Andrews, it was not a simple process. In fact, early on various stakeholders were undecided on the degree of control to bestow upon the new entity—a critical determinant of future success. Only with committed leadership from the larger institution, agreement on the overall vision of patient-centric care, and scaled back expectations did the project move forward. Implied is that the effort quickly shifted from strategic discussions to execution: measuring progress and building on accomplishments. Detailed execution then was critical, as evidenced by the extensive IMSL Asset Grid and Scorecard. As summarized in this book's concluding chapter, what is critical in successful transformational efforts is the translation of strategic objectives into operational objectives that guide the performance of all organizational levels.

Interestingly, while not specifically mentioned, the IMSL evidenced many attributes of the high-performance organization (see Chapter 3) in building from a unique vision to embracing the leadership culture of BWH and the HVC, specifically. One area, Mr. Andrews, implies, is still a work in progress: engaging all levels of the organization. As he writes, in the near term they will be focusing on promoting the "buy-in and adoption of the HVC vision across all of its constituents." Presumably, without such support, as well as the resources to incentivize the transformed behaviors and clear operating metrics, efforts to create comparable service line entities in other institutions may only lead to "more bureaucracy through ever more complex organizational structures, with no gain in efficiency or patient satisfaction."

Finally, in Chapter 4, the tool of SWOT analyses is outlined as being more static than dynamic and thus not typically well suited for challenging, uncertain environments. Here, it does make sense as a quick means for assessing the current departmental organizational structure. The framework provided insights into the issues behind the changes enacted. This points to another facet of the article: the homegrown nature of the BWH efforts. While it may be tempting to seek "drop-in frameworks" for strategic change, as this chapter makes clear, real change begins when leaders become actively involved in hammering out solutions that are relevant to their situation, culture, and resources.

In summary, before beginning a comparable transformational change in one's organization, the following questions should be reviewed:

- Is senior leadership truly committed to engaging in the strategic development process and enacting necessary changes?
- What will be the scope of such an effort: subspecialty, group, or institutional?
- How will the lessons learned be shared throughout the broader institution?
- What resources will be redirected in the newly formed organization so that incentives clearly match the vision and strategic priorities?
- How will all levels of the organization be engaged in the development and implementation of the plan?
- Was there flexibility in priorities agreed, and what are the "non-negotiables"?
- Is the effort focused more on strategic idea generation or is there a bias for action, and thus more emphasis on execution?

Acknowledgment The author wishes to acknowledge the valuable contributions of his colleagues, Dr. Mandeep Mehra (Medical Director of the Heart and Vascular Center) and David McCready (Senior Vice President of Surgical, Procedural, and Imaging Services), for their inputs and advice on the creation of the HVC Strategic Plan and the analysis of benchmark data.

References

Advisory Board. Outlook for integrated cardiovascular services. 2011. http://www.advisory.com/research/cardiovascular-roundtable/cardiovascular-rounds/2011/04/benchmark-your-heart-and-vascular-program-strategy. Accessed 30 Dec 2015.

Brigham and Women's Hospital. Shapiro cardiovascular center details. 2008. http://www.brighamandwomens.org/about_bwh/locations/main/shapirocenter/AboutOverview.aspx?sub=0. Accessed 30 Dec 2015.

US News and World Reports. Best hospitals: cardiology and heart surgery. 2014. http://health.usnews.com/best-hospitals/rankings/cardiology-and-heart-surgery. Accessed 30 Dec 2015.

7 Creating Ever Better Ways to Provide Cost-Effective Care for Our Community: The Coastal Medical Journey

Meryl Moss

Abstract

Coastal Medical is a major primary care provider group in the New England area. Run by physicians, it is committed to delivering high-quality, accessible, cost-effective care. What to do when ideals clash with reality? This case is about the journey from a committed, patient-focused organization to a primary care practice of the future. This required the group to envision a completely different primary care practice, one that fundamentally, not incrementally, changed their traditional model. Such change is not easy. Coastal created their change through pilots—not one, massive shift, but a series of smaller efforts, with the lessons learned then embedded in the broader organization. Unsurprisingly, not all staff members agreed on the new path forward. There was employee turnover. But, the majority moved ahead. And the impacts are impressive across multiple dimensions: quality, efficiency, patient support, and employee satisfaction.

Introduction

Change is hard. Transforming healthcare organizations requires visionary leadership, consistently clear communication, and execution. Importantly, as in the case of Coastal Medical, it requires flexibility and the willingness to adjust—while never losing sight of the overall reasons for initiating change.

Coastal Medical is a large, successful primary care group in Rhode Island with a history of highly committed physician governance. In 2009, the executive management team, led by Dr. Alan Kurose, Coastal's President and Chief Executive Officer

M. Moss, M.P.A., E.M.H.L. (✉)
Chief Operating Officer, Coastal Medical, Providence, RI, USA
e-mail: mmoss@coastalmedical.com

J. Austin et al. (eds.), *Leading Strategic Change in an Era of Healthcare Transformation*, Management for Professionals,
DOI 10.1007/978-3-319-30776-3_7

(CEO), in collaboration with the physician board made the strategic decision to implement the new patient-centered medical home model in each primary care practice. The aim was to deliver a higher level of cost-effective care to patients by augmenting primary care visits with ancillary clinical staff, such as nurse care managers, pharmacists, and medical assistants.

In 2012, it became clear to both executive management and the board that the patient-centered medical home model was only the first step in allowing Coastal to transition from traditional, fee-for-service medicine to a model based upon population health management.

Many organizations discuss the need to move towards the Institute of Healthcare Improvements' triple aim: improving the patient experience of care, improving the health of populations, and reducing the per capita cost of healthcare (Stiefel and Nolan 2012). Maybe the triple aim can be achieved through incremental steps. At Coastal, to create the primary care practice of the future required us to envision a completely different primary care practice, one that fundamentally, not incrementally, changed our traditional model.

This case study discusses the background and reasons for our transformational change, as well as the ways we approached it at Coastal. The outcomes are greater than we hoped. However, we are not finished; the journey of creating ever better ways to provide cost-effective care for our community is a never-ending quest.

Background

Coastal is a primary care group practice in Rhode Island that cares for approximately 120,000 patients at over 20 medical offices throughout the state. The company was built on a culture of participation and inclusion. Physician shareholders are also practicing physicians, so their input in all aspects of the company is essential. Physicians drive the values and direction of the company and consistently confirm their commitment to offering the highest quality of care to patients.

The executive team, consisting of Dr. Alan Kurose (President and CEO), Dr. Edward McGookin (Chief Medical Officer), and me (Meryl Moss, Chief Operating Officer), enjoyed an open and transparent relationship with the physician board. In addition, there was unity around the common values of providing the highest quality of care possible to Coastal patients.

In 2012, Coastal developed a vision to provide highly differentiated patient care and to be paid based upon value, rather than volume. The goal was to lead healthcare transformation by creating positive, disruptive change. In essence, Coastal sought to transition the traditional business model away from fee-for-service medicine to value-based reimbursement with the dual aims of meeting a myriad of robust quality measures while reducing the total cost of care.

To execute this vision, Coastal entered into shared savings contracts with multiple commercial payers and became a US Centers for Medicare and Medicaid Services (CMS) Accountable Care Organization (ACO). These contracts had differing degrees of financial incentives for meeting quality targets. In addition, Coastal's executive team felt strongly that the primary care organization should be held to the highest standards of quality measures and therefore had made the decision to seek NCQA III patient-centered medical home recognition as well as achieve meaningful use for all Coastal physicians.

It was therefore not a stretch for the organization to focus its efforts on quality measures. Coastal physicians are known for providing high-quality service for their primary care patients. We had been reporting on a limited number of quality metrics for our patient-centered medical home contracts and had participated successfully in NCQA and meaningful use. However, the new shared savings contracts brought quality reporting to a much higher level. Data now needed to be captured in a standardized fashion and the number of quality metrics increased exponentially. But physicians, executive management, and the board felt that we couldn't achieve what we couldn't measure. So we made the decision together to forge ahead.

Payers and accrediting organizations developed measures, connected to financial rewards, as incentives for physician organizations to create patient-centered medical home care, or accountable care organizations. Coastal realized that in order to build the clinical infrastructure an ACO required, we had to meet these new quality standards. As quality was consistent with our values and the standards that we wanted to achieve, it was easy to commit to work on quality in order to gain financial incentives that would allow Coastal to further develop a much-needed clinical infrastructure.

Defining the Problem

While easy to articulate, institutionalizing these new quality standards posed a multitude of challenges. Every Coastal practice operated differently. The individual units, or "pods"—individual primary care practices—were proud of their unique identities even as they felt connected to the larger Coastal organization.

Also, each payer contract had different quality measures. Blue Cross had similar but different metrics than United than CMS/Medicare. "Meaningful use" articulated different targets than NCQA. In total, Coastal was to report on 142 quality measures, many similar, but with slightly differing targets (see Fig. 7.1).

For example, recording an individual patient's body mass index (BMI) and then, if out of range, following up with a documented educational discussion is a quality measure in almost every contract. However, follow-up requirements differ.

Office managers initially requested, with support from their practice physicians, that each practice be allowed to determine the best way to meet these expanded quality targets. They emphasized the uniqueness of each practice and felt that practice leadership could create their own solutions. Management supported this approach, believing that it was best for solutions to come from the practices, rather than be imposed by the corporate office.

After 6 months of effort, quality reports were uniformly produced across the organization—and the variation between practices was astounding, with *no* practice achieving at a high level. Now the management team was facing a crisis. If we did

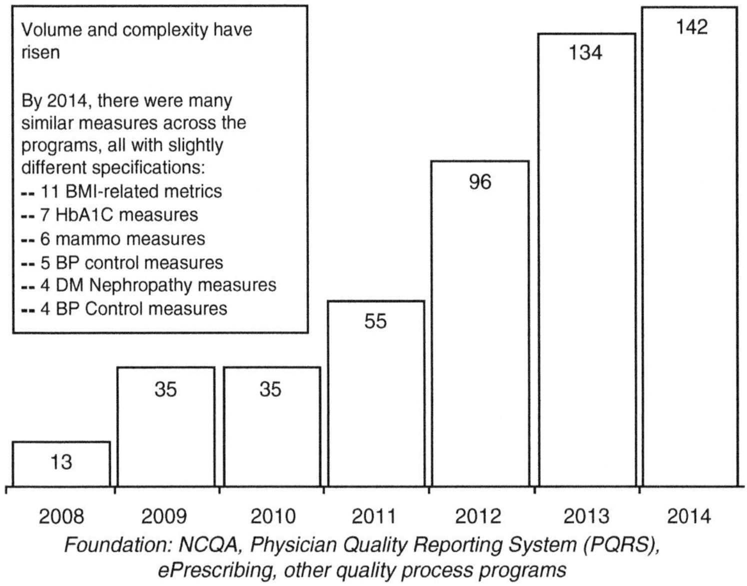

Fig. 7.1 Number of performance-based measures

not meet quality targets, we could not achieve the financial rewards that would support both the medical home transition and our envisioned population health work. In addition, one quick fix resorted to—reassigning the quality work to nurse care managers in each medical site—reduced their ability to work directly with patients. This caused a major disruption in the practices. Executive leadership could tell that the nurse care managers were unhappy about being re-tasked. Physicians were unhappy about losing a vital patient care resource. Office managers were unhappy about the overall disruption to their already busy offices.

Over the next several months, through intensive discussions, in-office reviews, and general "gnashing of teeth," Coastal achieved all its quality metrics. However, no one felt good about the process. It caused undo stress and, while meeting the expanded quality measures, we had reduced the resources available for our highest risk patients. All agreed that the process was inefficient, extremely stressful, and unsustainable.

Coastal's executive management became concerned about the level of pressure imposed upon the practices to meet quality targets. We wondered if both physicians and staff alike were having misgivings about our commitment to patient-centered medical home care and quality. The management decided to survey the entire organization and, most importantly, be open to the feedback.

The results of the survey were generally very positive. Employees really did understand the vision and direction of the company. They felt that patient-centered care made a difference for patients. Staff also said that through these new efforts they had been elevated to a greater role on the care team and felt better about their

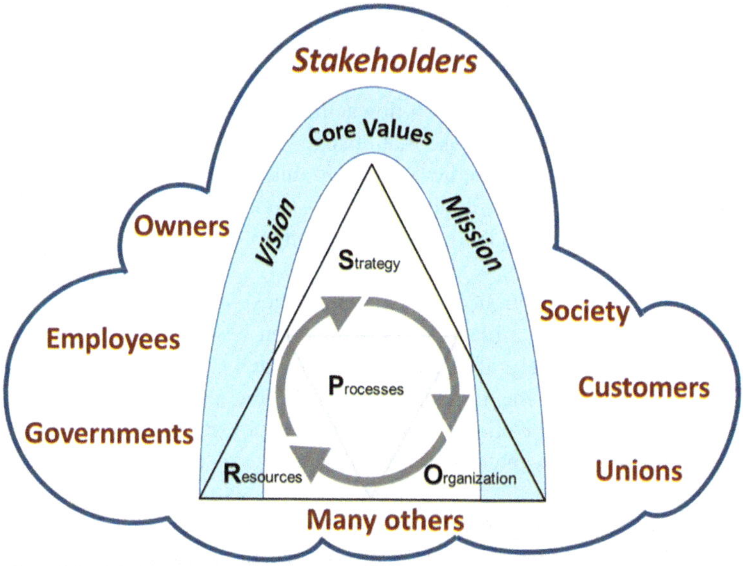

Fig. 7.2 Elements of the high-performance model

jobs. Employees stated that they felt more important … they wanted to continue in the new direction.

Physicians believed that overall care had improved and that both their patients and staffs were happier in the patient-centered medical home model. They supported the vision, direction, and strategy of the organization.

However, it was also clear from the surveys that both physicians and staff felt overburdened by the amount of quality-related work added to their already busy schedules. They did not like nurse care managers being removed from working directly with patients once a week to do quality work at a central location.

Staff felt burdened by the new quality work. These were busy primary care practices with serious and committed individuals caring for patients. How could they do more? It was not that we did not have support for the overall effort, but the work seemed overwhelming.

In late 2013, I entered Brown University's Executive Masters of Healthcare Leadership (EMHL) and was introduced to the high-performance model (HPM) for organizations (see Fig. 7.2).

I was pleased to see that Coastal had aspects of the HPM in place: a participatory culture; strong leadership; and a linked vision, mission, and strategic plan. However, it had become uncomfortably clear through the physician and staff surveys that neither the right processes nor resources were in place to support the expanded quality work and efforts to move to an ACO. How could Coastal actualize its strategy when old processes, systems, and procedures were the foundations of the existing primary care practices? The individuality and autonomy, so foundational to our physician's sense of independence, were becoming barriers to systematizing new and complex processes. What and how to change to reach over 140 new quality measures that underlie the effort to be a patient-centered medical home?

Management recognized that a top-down, directive approach to change would be poorly received, especially because that change had to occur at both the corporate office and the various, local medical sites. Up until this time, the corporate office functioned largely as a support to the practices—consolidating administrative functions such as accounting, credentialing, IT, and payroll—not to intervene directly in their daily operations.

We needed a broad discussion with all employees—MDs, nurses, office managers and staff—to develop a plan for transformation based on everyone's input. In January 2014, immediately after submitting the quality targets for that year, we called a "brainstorming" meeting and asked each practice to send a representative. We invited members of the clinical team, including physicians and office managers, as well as line staff. We wanted everyone to feel their voice counted and they should be part of the solution.

The executive team did not have to impart a sense of urgency. Office managers, physicians, nurse care managers, and staff had felt the stress and pain of the prior year-end. Everyone agreed that we had to solve the problem and solve it together.

First Brainstorming Session

The invitations to the brainstorming session were well received and 45 individuals volunteered to participate, many of them physicians. As I facilitated the group, it became clear that everyone had specific and clear idea of how "the new primary care office of the future should operate." Office managers wanted to create a welcoming and unhurried environment with open access to patients. Nurse care managers wanted the time to work directly with their highest risk patients, effortlessly identifying these individuals. They wanted to know when their patients were in the emergency room or hospital in real time. They did not want to be distracted by administrative tasks if the office was short staffed or overly busy. Nurse care managers wanted to practice at the top of their licenses, truly impacting the sickest and neediest patients.

Physicians wanted the new primary care practice of the future to run well, with the aim of preventing—not just curing—health problems. They wanted to impact the health of their patients, not episodically, but over the long term. As a result, MDs felt that all Coastal patients should routinely receive basic preventive care from mammograms to colonoscopies. MDs hoped that their staffs would be fulfilled in helping keep their communities healthy. Physicians truly wanted to make a difference in healthcare outcomes.

All of these desires we pulled together to outline the "Primary Care Practice of the Future," as summarized below:

- Telephone answered on time, no busy signal.

- Patients feel welcome and are engaged by staff.
- Patients have open same-day access.
- Primary care physicians are able to book directly into specialty schedules to get real-time consults.
- Patients are able to schedule appointments directly through the patient portal.
- Diabetics, CHF patients, and COPD patients are able to get a differentiated level of service that eliminates unnecessary visits to ER and hospital.
- Practice received real-time information on all emergency room (ER) and hospital admissions.
- All mundane administrative work does not interfere in direct patient care.
- Data team is able to produce accurate predictive modeling reports on highest risk patients for practice.
- All busy work is eliminated from the practice.
- Quality measures are systematized and institutionalized in day-to-day workflows.
- There is a high level of efficiency and patient needs are addressed in a timely fashion.
- Physicians are performing to the top of their licenses and doing only work that physicians should do.
- There is enough staff to do the work so that practices are not always in crisis.
- Staffs are performing to the top of their licenses and contributing to the clinical team.

After we compiled the characteristics of a high-performing primary care practice, we conducted the "mirror, mirror" exercise from the book, *Employees First, Customers Second* (Nayar 2010), again introduced in the EMHL program. This exercise asks any leadership team to reflect on the following question: Are we truly operating like the future operation we aspire to be? Our brainstorming group agreed that while we wanted to function as the high-performing primary care home with all the associated characteristics listed above, we were falling short in many areas.

Why? The answer lay in our history: most of our practices were functioning in the traditional primary care model. We had just *layered* the patient-centered medical home and quality work on top of already busy practices. Our total processes and resources were *not* supporting the vision or strategy. We had garnered buy-in but fell short in execution. Worse, we had not made fundamental trade-offs. Physicians and employees alike said that they wanted to provide patient-centered medical home care and understood its importance, but did not have the time or resources. We were not being challenged by the "why," but the "how." That was a great place to start.

Second Brainstorming Session

Our second brainstorming session, one month after the first, was equally well attended. Pointedly, several physicians asked how the corporate office could alleviate some of the work and provide the practices with "breathing room." Many attendees felt that if corporate could remove tasks that did not need to be accomplished in the offices, practices could really focus on our evolving new model for direct patient care. The group recommended the following:

- That a centralized team does all document scanning and fax inclusion into the electronic health record
- That a new quality team be formed to provide auditing services, education, and hands-on help to the practices to help each practice meet their quality measures
- That the pharmacy team process all prescription refills and drug prior to authorizations
- That a new centralized transitions-of-care team be developed to work with all patients who have been in the emergency room or hospital
- That a new centralized diabetic team be formed to work directly with diabetic patients and physicians on insulin management, medication adherence, pre-visit planning, and diabetes education
- That minimum staffing standards be developed for each office so that there is enough staff to do the job
- That workflows to support the PCMH and quality metrics be standardized across all offices
- That Coastal develop a floating pool for medical assistants and secretarial staff so that the offices can fully function when staff is out sick or on vacation

This approach was a complete departure from how the organization traditionally operated. Coastal had provided limited clinical services centrally which included the "Coastal 365-Urgent Care Clinic" so that patients could access a physician at night and on weekends. It was a little intimidating to imagine providing direct patient care in terms of physician refills and other clinical services at a central location, but we agreed.

Coastal historically tested new initiatives on a small scale, so pilots were developed for each of the programs listed above. Physicians made the recommendation that every Coastal practice be required to be in at least one pilot, thereby spreading out the work of testing, and evolving these new programs. Each practice signed up for one of the pilots and agreed to not only be part of the pilot, but to participate in a quality improvement team, ensuring that none of these new programs would be scaled until we "got the bugs out."

Executive management, while pleased at the progress made, felt that practice physicians needed to agree. We were not looking for unanimous agreement, but wanted to air any concerns or reservations. Dr. Kurose together with Dr. David Fried, Coastal's Chairman of the Board, called a shareholder meeting and Dr. McGookin and I framed the problem. Since every practice had felt the pain and stress of reallocating staff to meet the quality measures, the problem was easily communicated and understood. We shared the recommendations of the two brainstorming groups. Overall, there was general support for the direction recommended, especially because most practices had representatives at the brainstorming sessions

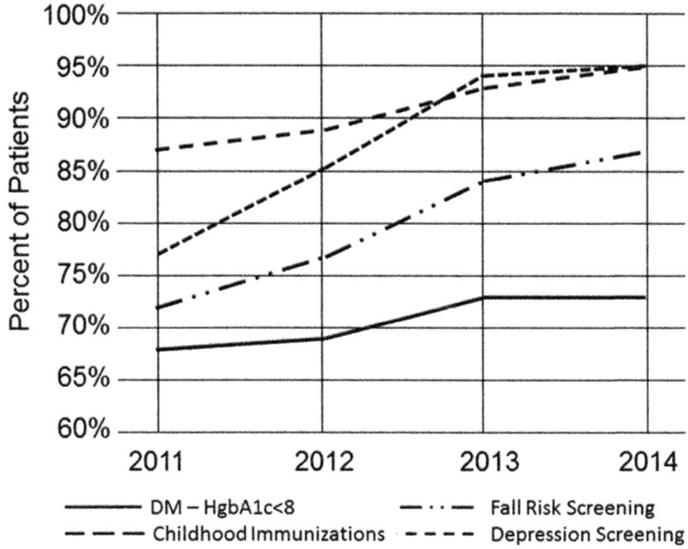

Fig. 7.3 Blue Cross Blue Shield RI Quality Measures, Coastal Medical, 2011–2014

and thus an understanding of the proposals. In particular MDs liked the idea that to give practices "breathing room," certain services could be centralized.

Standardizing processes caused the most concern. Again, these practices had prided themselves on their independent thinking and bristled to think that they would have to conform to a "top-down" way of operating. However, there seemed to be no other way. Standardizing workflows, simplifying processes, and creating structured data fields within the electronic medical record to support the quality measures were just too appealing. Physicians voted to accept and support the brainstorming groups' recommendations, to participate in each of the pilot projects and quality improvement work groups, and to conform to minimal staffing requirements/responsibilities to achieve change.

Results

The results are better than expected. In 2014, Coastal ranked in the top 1 % of *all* CMS Medicare Shared Savings Program (MSSP) ACOs in quality. We met or exceeded quality benchmarks for all other shared savings contracts and easily renewed our NCQA III patient-centered home status (see Fig. 7.3).

Coastal is in the process of scaling all the pilots because every one was a success. Office managers and physicians collaborated closely with corporate staff to modify and improve the pilots in real time. The quality team was so successful in helping practices achieve our quality measures that physicians asked them to take on new projects and expand their scope.

Most importantly, physicians feel that this new quality work is really making a difference in the healthcare outcomes of our patients. At our most recent board meeting, Coastal's CEO asked the physician board members to discuss our new population health work. As one physician so beautifully summarized: it has been tough work changing the way that primary care practices traditionally functioned, but patients are getting much better care. She added, "And that's why we all go to work every day."

This was a major group effort. Coastal received shared savings from most major contracts. We needed to thank everyone. Although a major portion of earned shared savings was reinvested to fund clinical infrastructure, Coastal distributed a portion to every single employee, including physicians, advanced practitioners, office managers, corporate staff, secretaries, phlebotomists, imaging technologists, and medical assistants. The executive team, with support from the board, visited each office personally and handed a check to every single employee with a thank you and recognition that this new model of care is truly a team sport.

Lessons Learned

We learned many lessons. The first was that our overall strategy had to be consistent with our vision and our values. The executive team reassured the board, physicians, and staff that we would not attempt to achieve any quality measure that we did not believe was clinically important. There was no "jumping through hoops" simply for the sake of scorekeeping.

In addition, we elicited direct feedback from stakeholders within the organization. We could have assumed that we were not achieving the initial quality targets because the practices did not support the overall plan. But we asked all employees and were open to the feedback, learning that execution, not buy-in, was the issue. Had we assumed the opposite, we might have tried to solve the wrong problem, creating further misunderstandings, raising additional barriers to change.

The most important lesson of all was to include stakeholders at all levels of decision making. We did not need to create a false sense of urgency, because it already existed and everyone collectively wanted to improve our patient care. I do not believe that we would have achieved our excellent results if physicians, office managers, or staff had not helped craft solutions. In fact, management would have gone in a different direction and we would have received less than optimal results.

Once the stakeholder group developed the recommendations, we needed to communicate and obtain support from the rest of the medical staff. Skipping shareholder meetings where concerns and objections could be openly aired would have delayed our efforts and possibly raised additional barriers to change. Allowing everyone to have a voice was essential.

Piloting is a great way to engage stakeholders and it worked for us. Every practice had to participate in a pilot. Since stakeholders were direct participants on the pilot's quality improvement teams, they wanted it to work. More importantly, their contributions to the work were invaluable. Had we attempted to develop these pilots without input from the practicing physicians and their staffs, the results would have been subpar.

We learned that we had to audit to make sure that our intentions were actualized. The shift from traditional medicine to an ACO is complex, directly affecting patients. We learned through auditing that everyone wanted this work to succeed, but we needed to raise the level of education and training. If a practice was struggling with meeting a quality target, it was usually because of a misunderstanding in documentation.

Mostly, we needed to be resilient. Change is so hard and we needed to find ways to support and renew each other. I believe that this is hardest of all. It is easy to be worn down. Motivating and sustaining this very important work means reminding everyone, every day, that our efforts change patient lives.

Since this new work requires participation and engagement from every single employee in the organization, we needed to thank them for achieving our goals. We also needed to remind them that they are integral to our success and the care that we provide to patients. Having line staff share in the distribution, with an emphasis on meeting the quality measures, acknowledged their role and helped them to feel that what we do at Coastal can really make a difference.

Chapter Summary

Coastal Medical's transformational journey is instructive at many levels. The organization was doing well, but something was missing. As Ms. Moss writes:

> Coastal achieved all its quality metrics. However, no one felt good about the process. It caused undo stress and, while meeting the expanded quality measures, we had reduced the resources available for our highest-risk patients. All agreed that the process was inefficient, extremely stressful and unsustainable.

What to do? First, they opened up a dialogue across all levels of the organization around the fundamental question: What do we want to be? While the answers initially varied, they soon coalesced around creating a "new primary care practice of the future ... with the aim of preventing—not just curing—health problems."

What then occurred is also instructive: they tried one approach and it did not work. Coastal initially, building on its decentralized structure, devolved the responsibility for transformation to their individual delivery points. And they were simply overwhelmed in trying to cover current operational necessities while "layering on" becoming a patient-centered medical home.

As a result, Coastal leadership made a strategic retreat. They engaged in further all-employee discussions, deviated from the past model, and centralized certain activities at corporate, giving more scope locally to develop new models of patient care. Importantly, management worked at engaging critical stakeholder groups; as Ms. Moss explains, "Allowing everyone to have a voice was essential." And change was developed through pilots—not one, massive shift, but a series of smaller efforts, with the lessons learned then embedded in the broader organization. Unsurprisingly, not all staff members agreed on the new path forward. There was employee turnover. But, the majority moved ahead.

The transformational change impacts were "better than expected. In 2014, Coastal ranked in the top 1 % of *all* CMS ACOs in quality. We met or exceeded quality benchmarks for all other shared savings contracts and easily renewed our NCQA III patient centered home status," writes Ms. Moss.

To summarize, in beginning a transformational change effort comparable to the journey Coastal started, several questions must be answered:

1. Why undertake the effort to change at all? What is the "itch" and how urgent the need to change?
2. How are management and all levels of the organization working together? Is there good communication? Are senior leaders "hearing" the concerns of all staff, and engaging in a constructive dialogue to develop strategic options?
3. Is there flexibility in developing options for future growth? Is the organization willing to experiment, to pilot, and to learn from the outcomes of these efforts … even if it means pulling back to reconsider, readjust, before moving ahead again?
4. How might the organizational culture and structure have to change to realize transformational change? And can this be managed while continuing with current operations?
5. How will success be measured? Is there a "finish line," or is this part of a never-ending effort to become ever better?
6. Is leadership sufficiently resilient to bend with the challenges any major change effort entails while maintaining the focus on the longer term goals behind the transformational effort?

References

Nayar V. Employees first, customers second: turning conventional management upside down. Boston: Harvard Business Press; 2010.

Stiefel M, Nolan K. A guide to measuring the triple aim: population health, experience of care, and per capita cost. IHI Innovation Series white paper. Cambridge, MA: Institute for Healthcare Improvement; 2012.

Transforming the Facility Master Planning Process: How to Manage Risk in Times of Uncertainty

8

David H. Deininger

Abstract

How might the architectural profession help healthcare leaders deal with future uncertainty and risk? This case, based on multiple master planning efforts, argues that the physical planning process should utilize similar ideas and frameworks as the business or strategic planning process. Specifically, employ scenario planning to challenge existing orthodoxies and traditional master planning approaches. From this, develop flexible options that can be contracted, expanded, or re-configured based on evolving models of care. Cross-discipline transformational efforts as outlined in this case may create a more common language for embracing uncertainty, expanding the sensitivities and impacts of architects, financiers, planners, as well as healthcare leaders.

What's the Problem?

In the last 10 years the healthcare context changed significantly; relying on the typical "tried and true" facility master planning process is not going to yield sustainable results. There is simply too much uncertainty involving all the stakeholders: providers, payers, regulators, and patients. "Uncertainty confounds the planning process by invalidating the rules of the game under which the industry has operated, without revealing obvious new rules," write healthcare strategists Margo Kelly and Dennis V. Kennedy (Jennings 2000). By embracing uncertainty, the planning process can develop strategies to succeed even in the midst of change.

D.H. Deininger, AIA, LEED AP, EMHL (✉)
2dplanning, Brookline, MA, USA
e-mail: ddeininger@2dplanning.com

J. Austin et al. (eds.), *Leading Strategic Change in an Era of Healthcare Transformation*, Management for Professionals,
DOI 10.1007/978-3-319-30776-3_8

> Although related, uncertainty and risk differ. *Uncertainty* is defined as the condition of being uncertain, or doubt; *risk* is the probability of loss. In true uncertainty, it is impossible to imagine all potential outcomes or assign probability to any one particular outcome. With risk, it is quite possible to assign a probability to a particular outcome. *Information* [and *data*] can help one move from uncertainty to risk; from being in doubt to knowing the odds (Jennings 2000).

Specifically related to facility master planning there is one fundamental question: *How will this "new normal" influence the delivery of care and its relationship to the built environment*? Other questions will logically follow. Where will services be located? How should they be configured to emphasize population health? Will increased access require more space in the acute care setting? Or will it be balanced by a more robust primary care network? Clearly *one must remain flexible*, ready to adapt to a very dynamic situation going forward.

Why the Need for Change?

It is here that the well known fable, The Blind Men and the Elephant is instructive. In various versions of this tale, a group of blind men touch an elephant to learn what it is like. Each touches a different part, but one part only, such as the side, trunk, leg, ear, or tusk. They compare their observations ("it's a wall," "it's a snake," "it's a tree," "it's a fan," and "it's a powder horn") and learn that they are in complete disagreement. Each has felt a part of the elephant but believes that they understand the whole elephant (Wikipedia 2015). Like the elephant, a *hospital campus is without question a complicated organism.* Often the strategic plan is prepared by the planning department or the facility plan is done in isolation by the hospital's engineering group but neither is linked to service line business plans, the CFO's financial analysis of debt capacity, or the CEO's vision for the future. This attitude permeates the master planning decision-making paradigm today as well; each player is so focused on their area of expertise, their department, or their unit that the whole becomes lost in the parts. The resulting effort is myopic, disjointed, and unrelated to the bigger picture.

What's the Transformational Process?

What is needed is a new way of approaching planning: a comprehensive one that drives towards a totally different definition of success. The present landscape that healthcare institutions will be forced to navigate is going to require different and innovative answers to fundamental strategic business questions: Where to play and how to win? What are my future ways of making money (my financial "engine")? Who are my business partners? What are my operational and clinical models? This will require collaboration between all aspects of the enterprise, in other words an integrated model. As outlined earlier in this book, the challenge is to create a high-performance organization, an integrated model, where:

> ... seeking high performance is an exercise in optimization. Myriad forces are at work in organizations, pushing and pulling them in different directions. The challenge is to align those forces to the extent possible so that they are all moving in the same direction ... [and] sustaining high performance involves ensuring the continuity of that alignment as situations change and the vision and mission evolve.[1]

Today's healthcare master planning problems require a diverse assembly of expertise—*strategy, operations,* and *facilities*—that can all work together, concurrently in real time across all facets of the system. Master planning is all about taking a step back to look at the big picture, to gain context: an overall, comprehensive framework that can provide clarity and guidance to the decision-making process.

Strategy: Where Are We Going?

Before any provider can embark on a comprehensive planning process, they must determine how they will differentiate to win in their chosen markets. In times of change, resources must be conserved, directed to highest impact areas. Healthcare providers can no longer be all things to all people, but must determine a deliberate value proposition. Healthcare thought leaders Brett Spencer, MD, Igor Belokrinistsky, Szoa Geng, and Neil Patel at Strategy& (part of Price Waterhouse Coopers) summarize the current context:

> ...some systems are moving with a purpose and a clear set of priorities, but many others appear to be stuck, as if waiting for their competitors, regulators, and payers to tell them how to define themselves. With a different way of thinking about function and form, hospitals and health systems can regain control of their destiny (Gamble 2015).

A sustainable business model requires evaluating what they are best at and how to leverage these abilities in their chosen markets. The authors at Strategy& identify the following possible ways to win or differentiate:

1. R&D Leader: These health systems invest in research and development to build world-class service lines that attract patients from all over the world. The treatment and expertise available are innovative, cutting edge, and may be experimental in nature for those patients who desire a second opinion or have limited future options. Cleveland Clinic is an example.
2. Clinical Specialist: These health systems focus their resources on a specific clinical niche or specialty and brand themselves as such becoming market leaders and the preferred destination for patients, employers, and payers due to the consistent excellence of their clinical outcomes. MD Anderson Cancer Center is an example.
3. Convenience King: These health systems provide easy access to reliable and consistent care and are "an alternative to the gold standard." This can be particu-

[1] Presentation by L. Chait at Brown University, August 2013.

larly valuable to payers who may want to exclude premium, high-cost providers. They offer a solid package of services to the community and are connected to a network of partners who can provide specialty care if the need arises.
4. Integrator: These health systems understand the notion of population health by providing a coordinated array of services across the entire continuum of care and especially by focusing on wellness/prevention and post-acute care. Geisinger is an example.
5. Premium Property: These health systems provide the highest standard of care both clinically and from a patient satisfaction perspective by focusing on patient and family amenities. Their experience is similar to the hospitality industry: privacy, luxury accommodations, personalized care, and alternative holistic services.
6. Value Maximizer: These health systems provide value, an affordable product with quality outcomes. There are no unnecessary extras. They practice continuous quality improvement by removing waste, increasing efficiency, and providing pricing transparency.
7. Price Cutter: These health systems provide the lowest cost on a particular treatment or service at "reasonable quality levels." With patients responsible for an ever-increasing amount of the bill, this strategy allows for some treatments to occur in lower cost ambulatory environments with physician assistants or nurse practitioners providing care when appropriate. The Healthcare Clinics at Walgreens and the Minute Clinics at CVS are examples.

More than ever, the current economic climate as well as the Affordable Care Act will require and reward providers who think and act in an integrated and coordinated manner, in other words for *thinking in systems*. Pioneering system analyst Donella H. Meadows (2008) describes a system "as a set of things—people, cells, molecules, or whatever—interconnected in such a way that they produce their own pattern of behavior over time." Historically, hospitals and physicians worked in virtual isolation, typically defined by subspecialty, sometimes at cross purposes, and the resulting delivery construct is a three trillion dollar annual industry that is 18 % of our national gross domestic product (GDP) (Wayne 2012). This is clearly not a sustainable path. The healthcare industry has responded to the ACA with an ever-increasing number of hospital mergers and acquisitions, some 76 in 2010, rising to 100 in 2014, with a peak of 107 in 2012 (Ellison 2015a) as hospitals attempt to gain financial strength by eliminating the weak players, increasing market share, reducing redundancy, improving efficiency, and creating scale. This merger and acquisition (M&A) activity impacts the built environment, which results in reshuffling services within the system to provide for optimal access for patients.

Only 13 % of hospitals surveyed in 2013 indicated that they intend to maintain independence from alignment with other hospitals or systems (Yanci et al. 2013). That means that the vast majority of hospitals may consider a change in status, which should be a mandatory discussion topic during the master planning process. As a result:

> Whether they are an acquirer, acquired company, or an organization pursuing a potential deal, virtually every hospital and health system will be touched by the unfolding wave of healthcare M&A [activity]. Even if the system is not involved in a deal, consolidation among hospitals, health systems, and physician practices can upend traditional market dynamics, leaving existing systems with new and bigger competitors (Barnet et al. 2014).

There are a variety of transactions ranging from affiliations to acquisition, and reasons for entering into some form of agreement include "seeking economies of scale, drawing on a partner's unique clinical or managerial strengths, or gaining geographic strength to better serve the patient and community need." The following are the types of transactions and their characteristics as outlined in Yanci et al. (2013):

1. **Affiliations**: This is the most flexible form of consolidation. It is usually undertaken to increase footprint, gain economies of scale, create referrals, add to an already successful set of services, and exchange best practices. These transactions do not necessarily alter the management or governance.
2. **Joint Venture**: There still is some flexibility with this arrangement. JVs expand the capability of the two parties, whether inpatient or outpatient services, beyond what each could achieve on its own. There is usually shared governance as well as some form of profit/risk sharing.
3. **Joint Operating Agreement**: This is referred to as a "virtual merger" where assets may be separate but services integrated and coordinated. A new umbrella board structure is created, but hospitals maintain their independent boards as well. Similar to a JV, but larger, agreement extends beyond a specific set of services allowing the new entity to pursue capital.
4. **Merger**: This is a mutually agreed-upon decision to legally combine two (or more) independent businesses; the hospitals absorb each other's assets and liabilities. Leadership and governance are usually a combination of each hospital. The reasons to merger are to increase scale, improve quality, and expand market share.
5. **Acquisition**: This is an outright purchase of one hospital by another, most frequently a smaller hospital by a larger hospital (or system). The acquired hospital sometimes has some degree of autonomy depending upon the situation. The goals are to increase market share, gain operating efficiencies, add new services, and improve financial stability.

As outlined earlier in this book, *scenario planning* is a structured, disciplined way for hospitals to think about the future. Senior leadership should utilize this tool to develop a number of scenarios: stories about how the future might unfold and how different futures might affect them. Peter Schwartz describes scenario planning as:

> Stories that can help us recognize and adapt to changing aspects of our present environment. They form a method for articulating the different pathways that might exist for you tomorrow and finding your appropriate movements down each of those possible paths (The Economist 2015).

Scenarios deal with two worlds: the world of facts as we know them and the world of perceptions, assumptions, and ultimately best guesses. The art of scenario planning lies in the ability to blend the known and the unknown into a limited number of internally consistent views of the future that spans a range of possibilities.

Case Example 1

A 450-bed Mid Atlantic community hospital was deciding how best to proceed as an independent entity in a mature market. Three potential future scenarios were developed: first, the *shrink option* which assumed the status quo, a gradual decline in market share, and a reduction to 325 beds. Second, the *sustain option* which develops a more robust ambulatory strategy and a reduction to 425 beds. Third, the *strengthen option* which assumes a proactive alignment with physicians, volume growth in disproportionately high margin procedures, and an increase to 515 beds. This exercise and the subsequent selection of the final option provided hospital leadership with a strategic roadmap for all future decision making.

Operations: What Are Our Models of Care?

As our healthcare industrial complex slowly makes the transition from volume-based to value-based care models, the financial incentives will dramatically reduce the *need for acute care inpatient space*. Ezekiel Emanuel, MD, PhD, former health policy advisor to the Obama Administration, questions the need for the some 5000 hospitals existing in the USA today (Becker 2014).

Case Example 2

A 150-bed community hospital in New England went into bankruptcy in 2014 before being acquired by a local large regional health system. As part of this transaction the state determined that the site was no longer feasible for inpatient services. The question was this: How to repurpose this former inpatient campus? The preferred redevelopment option reused a medical office building as an integrated community wellness and education center; expanded the emergency department to include treatment spaces for observation and infusion patients; created a new, clear public wayfinding sequence reducing from three separate entrances to one, consolidating ambulatory surgery and endoscopy prep and recovery; and "land banked" space for 20 inpatient beds in the event that they are required on site at some future date.

Minoo Javanmardian, Vice President of Booz|Allen|Hamilton's global practice in Chicago, says that consolidation is not a strategy. Instead, "mergers are the result of a strategy that [organizations] define and are meant to leverage the differentiating capability systems of the partners" (Rosen 2015). Mergers or acquisitions only make sense if there are truly combining complementary skills and services that improve patient care, rather than simply trying to achieve economies of scale. Within the inpatient arena there are a number of forces at play: a national inpatient utilization rates dropping from 123.2 hospital admissions per 1000 people in 1991 to 111.8 per 1000 in 2011 (Adamopoulos 2013); internal operational consolidations of services away from the historic departmental silos to more collaborative arrangements such as procedure platforms that locate all invasive treatment (surgery, cardiac catheterization, interventional radiology, endoscopy, and minor procedures) in one location with universal operating and recovery spaces; and technological advances that drive care into the outpatient setting. As a result, theoretically institutions should free up space. As facilities configure their current space more effectively, they may be able to offload aging, maintenance-intensive, obsolete structures. Many foresee the future of the inpatient hospital as the setting for only the sickest patients: trauma, highly complex intensive and cardiac care, perinatal, and NICU services. Identifying and embracing these shifts allow for the implementation of a long-term tactical planning process: *making the most of what you have and supplementing with targeted new construction projects.*

Dramatic changes are happening on the outpatient side through population health initiatives engaging the patient within the wellness/prevention/patient-centered medical home context. As a result, there is a need for more outpatient space. These additions need to be located in an easily accessible, community-based, and cost-effective environments. Affecting all areas of care is the advancement of medical devices/technology that allows for virtual/remote monitoring, planning, treatment, and follow-up of patients without the need to set foot in the acute care hospital. The same goes for the providers; they too can be in a variety of locations. "As inpatient care becomes increasingly complex, providers will become more specialized meaning more disciplines involved in the care of the patient in conjunction with more challenging care coordination needs," says Siva Subramanian, PhD founder and Chief Operating Officer (COO) of CareInSync, a mobile care collaboration platform. According to Dr. Subramanian, "In the hospital of the future, we're going to see this reversal of telehealth, where the patient is immersed in a virtual world and has a care team virtually connected surrounding that individual at whatever location and time" (Adamopoulos 2013).

Whatever the future, both hospitals and systems will need to *develop a comprehensive, system-wide plan for the efficient distribution of inpatient and outpatient services.* The plans will include sharing staff and managers, times of operations, load balancing volumes, integrating electronic medical record (EMR)/communication tools, education and marketing campaigns, and branding opportunities. Unfortunately, the definition of a comprehensive plan in the days of fragmented, fee-for-service medicine is radically different in the "outcome-based," population health model envisioned in the ACA. The question from the built environment is as follows: What legacy systems/structures can be reconfigured to meet the needs of the future and where are whole new built environments required?

Case Example 3
A southern New England hospital was able to expand geographically onto an existing ambulatory site. This shifted emergency volume from the maxed out main campus and added new market share with the establishment of a new 24/7 emergency department (ED), directly accessible from the highway. As a result, overall system-wide ED annual visits increased from 100,000 to a projected 125,000.

The delivery of care is rapidly evolving away from the disciplinary silos of the past to a more integrated, efficient, and effective *continuum-of-care infrastructure*. All providers regardless of their role and place in the process are partnering to better understand the needs of the patient (and their family) in order to provide a comprehensive care model, "one that is transforming the delivery system from hospital-centric sick care to a super outpatient model that will emphasize community-based care" (Jarousse 2014). To achieve this new vision, hospitals are expanding horizontally through M&A activity to gain scale, prioritize services and programs, increase purchasing power, and cut costs. But another critical, complementary avenue is through vertical integration: partnering with or purchasing physician groups, primary care practices/PCMHs, care management systems, EMR integration, ambulatory services (emergency, imaging, or surgical), home care services, wellness companies, long-term care (assisted living, post-acute, and nursing home), and finally insurance vehicles to improve the health of a defined population. Realizing the triple aim (improving the health of a population, reducing costs, and enhancing the patient experience) is often the goal, in large part through information technology to inform decision making. Judith Pearlson, RN, MS, CPHQ writes, "healthcare organizations will need to shift from investing in buildings and facilities to developing integrated clinical and analytics information technology (IT) platforms that can be accessed by providers across the healthcare enterprise" (Pearlson 2014).

Presently, 10 % of all patients account for 65 % of the total spent on healthcare in the USA (AHRQ 2014). These patients are typically dealing with chronic diseases and/or end-of-life issues. For example, 30–90-day post-acute Medicare costs account for a majority of the total cost of treatment: 72 % for heart failure, 68 % for renal failure, and 63 % for COPD (Gage et al. 2011). As providers respond to the ACA, they will create new integrated models of care that will subsequently require new physical models (patient-centered medical home) that will eliminate redundancy and support collaboration through accountable care organization relationships. Patients will be seen and cared for over the entire spectrum of their life lives—from primary care, acute care, post-acute care, and nursing home to end of life—necessitating new architectural and operational solutions.

Facilities: How Are We Configured?

This question is especially relevant, now that most hospitals are no longer "standalone" entities, but part of multi-campus systems that require facility solutions to optimize their physical assets in a coordinated manner. This requires a systems thinking approach to create a *flexible framework for facility development*. In 1974, federal legislation was passed which required all states to have a Certificate of Need (CoN) program on the premise that by regulating the number of hospital and nursing home beds, expensive medical equipment, and ambulatory facilities, excess capacity could be managed, reducing healthcare costs. In 1987, this law was repealed leaving it to states to decide their regulatory course. As a result, some states eliminated CoN while others strengthened its purview.

The following seven drivers of change are essentially evaluation criteria used as best practice guidelines to steer the master planning process towards a successful and consensus-driven outcome:

- Long-range vision
- The hospital reassembled
- Consolidation
- Circulation
- Highest and best use
- Growth opportunities
- Clinical industry benchmarks

Long-Range Vision

So often hospital planning and the subsequent building projects that result are at best ad hoc efforts. Over time such efforts can negatively affect a campus's ability to redevelop itself. So, it is important to take a comprehensive look at existing physical assets to determine what the site might look like at some future date as a guide to facility decision making. It is of utmost importance to identify a flexible long-range plan that can be implemented in a staged, incremental way that aligns with available capital and market realities. Instead of projecting from the past, reverse the thinking by developing future scenarios and work backwards.

Case Example 4

A 550-bed community hospital in the Mid Atlantic developed a multi-year plan comprised of a phased, on-site replacement of outdated facilities. Most importantly, this plan allowed for the logical redevelopment of the site with no expensive enabling projects or unnecessary disruption. Site improvements included the following: clear and identifiable public/patient access and wayfinding, separation of public and service traffic, maintenance of existing curb cuts, and improved parking. Zoning relief was negotiated with the local officials concerning building height, floor area ratio, lot coverage, and setbacks. The proposed plan includes three phases:

(continued)

Case Example 4 (continued)

Phase 1: A new public lobby/atrium that provides a multistoried organizational element for clear patient access to various service portals and introduces natural light into the interior of the hospital complex. The critical care area will be reconfigured to accommodate volume growth and higher industry planning standards covering surgery, diagnostic imaging, cardiac catheterization, imaging, and M/S beds. On the service levels there will be a new loading dock, energy plant, dietary, and CSS. The Woman's and Infants Pavilion will be rebranded, consolidating obstetrics (antepartum, LDR, postpartum), NICU, PICU, and pediatric beds. As for parking, an additional 1000 car spaces will be added to accommodate the overall parking shortage, comprised of a 600-car off-site garage for employees and a 400-car on-site garage for patients, visitors, and physicians. This phase also includes the demolition of the oldest building on campus.

Phase 2: A new critical care building adjacent to the public atrium including emergency, observation beds, and intensive care unit (ICU)/critical care unit (CCU) beds: This phase allows for the demolition of the next oldest building on campus.

Phase 3: This last phase provides potential future flexibility for the hospital, including additional inpatient beds, ambulatory expansion, or an unforeseen specialty program.

The Hospital Reassembled

This planning philosophy refers to the separation of clinical and public spaces. In this separation, clinical spaces—those that generally require change ahead of public spaces—can be better accommodated to meet future needs. To create a flexible design, take components that are usually rigidly integrated with each other (clinical functions, public spaces, infrastructure, and circulation systems), isolate them, and reassemble them as separate, identifiable parts. Different attitudes towards space, one orthogonal and modular that can evolve and expand with the changes in clinical patient care delivery, and the other organic and unique that expresses the existing, external site context and internal, community programs. Taken together, the "clinical box" serves as an armature for the major public spaces, a rectilinear counterpoint to the detached composition of identifiable objects.

The "*clinical box*" is a framework for flexibility. It is derived from the need to consolidate and house all diagnostic and treatment functions within a flexible enclosure. By using of a universal 30′-0″ planning grid and 15′-0″ minimum floor-to-floor ceiling heights, the space within the box can accommodate future needs plus new technologies with the minimum of physical changes. Vertical elements such as elevator cores and egress stairs are pulled to the perimiter of the box, while mechanical shafts and electrical closets are grouped together, thereby minimizing their impact and providing larger, unencumbered floor plates for clinical flexibility.

Separate from the clinical box is the *public sequence* or *wayfinding network*. While the clinical box is similar in concept from project to project, public spaces for each project are different and provide a wonderful opportunity to place the building within its unique site context. Because they are separated from the clinical components, the design team can creatively explore multiple solutions to respond to views, natural light, and other buildings. These programs can include lobbies, atrium space, "medical malls," gift shop, cafeteria/snack, auditorium, conference, community, meditation, and education/resource rooms. The linking of these objects in a wayfinding system helps to orient the patient and family, from parking to entrance, to lobby, to elevator, and to point of service.

Consolidation

Consolidation allows for clinical synergies to occur. For example a procedure platform can group all interventional procedures (inpatient and outpatient surgery, cardiac catheterization, endoscopy, and interventional radiology) and the corresponding prep/recovery in one location. This then aligns ICU/CCU with telemetry and/or step down beds on the same floor for a more seamless transfer of the patient. It also allows for a more efficient nursing support by co-locating all emergency treatment beds (trauma, urgent, fast track, behavioral health) and observation beds.

Case Example 5

This northwestern hospital improved imaging efficiency by centralizing all imaging services in one location adjacent to new emergency department. The existing geographically scattered modalities resulted in the need for radiology rooms: one magnetic resonance imaging (MRI), three computed tomography (CT), and five basic radiology rooms. By aggregating all modalities, the number of machines required was based on actual patient demand, not location. As a result, the hospital reduced modalities to one MRI, two CT, and four basic radiology rooms.

Circulation

Navigating a medical campus can be a stressful, confusing experience. One must create a wayfinding strategy that starts with a clear path from the major local arteries to the hospital, and then from parking to point of service. This requires the separation of different traffic flows (patient, visitor, staff, physician, emergency, and service vehicles). Once in the building, an internal separation of public and service functions needs to be respected within the corridor and elevator network. The site should be organized by *quadrants* for there are many subsets of activity and circulation flows that need to be identified within the public and the private zones. For example, the site could be divided into four quadrants: *Q1*: Receiving/Energy Plant, *Q2*: Emergency, *Q3*: Flexible/Specialty, and *Q4*: Main Patient/Visitor. This delineation will determine site entry points, internal campus circulation, parking, and building entry points—helping clarify wayfinding and avoid circulation bottlenecks. In order to maximize development and expansion flexibility, it is important to identify a Flexible/Specialty zone (*Q3*) on site. Once the internal site zones are determined, then each specific functional quadrant requires its own circulation strategy: how and where the site is accessed, its relationship to parking, and how it is connected to various building entry points. Incorporating public transportation/bus traffic can also be an issue. Ambulance and truck traffic should ideally have their own dedicated pathway from the edge of the site.

Highest and Best Use

Aligning the building with the appropriate use is critical for optimal real estate asset management. Having all the services on campus is being reevaluated to incorporate off-site opportunities for ambulatory services, support services, and affiliated physicians. Many hospital sites are overcrowded with older, high-maintenance structures that are obstacles to inpatient redevelopment. While the tendency is to remove such buildings, those with flexible, well-maintained systems can be repurposed for suitable support functions.

Case Example 6

On many sites, planners ask: What to do with the older nursing units? In the case of a building organized by double-loaded corridors, the structure might be a good candidate for support services, physician office space, or administrative functions. If the building is organized by a "race track" configuration, the structure becomes more valuable for potential, continued patient use. If the total number of patient rooms is enough to create an all-private environment and there is adequate support space available, there may be an opportunity for reuse as a smaller specialty nursing unit. And as institutions face financial penalties for hospital readmissions within 30 days of discharge, seamless coordination between hospital and post-acute care is critical. This may mean taking in-house control of the entire continuum of care through the repurposing older nursing units for either a skilled nursing unit or long-term acute care (LTAC) unit.

Growth Opportunities

Growth strategies must include both short- and long-range priorities. Where is the next expansion project located? Does it integrate into a future vision for site development? How best to utilize older buildings? What additional space is required? By using the various site quadrants for planning purposes, flexible strategies can evolve that support and build upon the changing healthcare environment. There may be older buildings that have outlived their useful life and are therefore candidates for removal, thereby opening up valuable real estate. Other options to explore include vertical growth on existing structures, the purchase of abutting property, or working with local officials to close adjacent streets.

Clinical Industry Benchmarks

These metrics are very useful to determine the size of a particular department based upon certain volumes. Importantly, such industry benchmarks aid leadership in working through competing agendas and embedded fiefdoms to make an objective assessment of a particular problem or issue. Whether decisions are based upon market forces, competitive advantage, operational savings, relocation of services, or a revenue enhancement opportunity, being able to access objective data allows for more meaningful discussion.

Case Example 7

A typical emergency department should be able to see about 1500–1800 patients per treatment space per year depending upon acuity levels (the more behavioral health patients the lower the number becomes). With this information, hospital planners can divide the total annual visits by 1500–1800 to get the total treatment spaces required and then multiply by 750 square feet to determine the departmental square feet required for that particular hospital (75,000 annual visits/1600 (47 treatment spaces) × 750 sf = 35,200 sf for the ED). Armed with this information, one can compare the existing square footage against the benchmark and adjust accordingly.

What Are the Takeaways?

What concerns institutional care leaders most today? According to the American College of Healthcare Executives' 2014 survey of top issues confronting hospitals, "financial challenges ranked No. 1-above healthcare reform and patient safety and quality" (Ellison 2015b). While it seems that the market is headed towards value-based purchasing, "as long as there is substantial fee-for-service reimbursement, the Chief Executive Officer (CEO) dilemma is how to prepare for the future while not creating an adverse financial situation in the short term," writes Andrew Ziskind, MD, managing director of Huron Healthcare Consulting (Mosquera 2014). Additional angst concerns the pace of change:

> … move too fast and hospitals risk losing revenue and implementing a strategy the market does not support. Move too slow and they may lose partnership opportunities, experience, and time that could have been spent modifying clinician's behaviors and transforming practices (Barnet et al. 2014).

In summary, practical facility planning processes should attempt to:

Stay Flexible: The only certain thing in healthcare is change. In order to accommodate change over time one needs to build in flexibility. First, ensure that each new building has a universal structural grid and reasonable floor-to-floor heights. These simple moves ensure that future changes in clinical operations can be mirrored by internal changes to the facility. Second, foresee the need to expand by building in the vertical structural capability and capping off a first phase with an interstitial mechanical floor that provides a buffer for future construction. Third, medical planning must eliminate functional solos and consolidate programs, thereby "blurring the lines" between clinical departments and providing flexible enclosures that are highly adaptable for the inevitable physical and operational changes that will occur in the future. And fourth, zone the entire site in a broad manner (inpatient, outpatient, support) that will allow for downstream modifications to the vision.

Simplify the Amount of Data: There is an increasing proliferation of data. It is of paramount importance to use the "right" data. Vilfredo Pareto was an economist and sociologist interested in land ownership and the distribution of wealth in nineteenth-century Italy. After collecting and analyzing the available data he found a curious pattern: over 80 % of the land was owned by less than 20 % of the population. The ownership was not distributed evenly or in a bell-shaped distribution curve as many people had assumed. Instead wealth was concentrated among a relatively small group of individuals. What was going on? In answering this question he created the Pareto Principle: in any complex system a minority of the inputs produce the majority of the output (Reh 2015). This nonlinearity may not always be literally 80/20, but there are many examples of this phenomenon; for example 20 % of customers typically account for 80 % of the revenue, 20 % of employees do 80 % of the work, and 80 % of one's time is spent communicating with roughly 20 % of one's personal contacts, and closer to healthcare, 64 % of the overall cost of healthcare in the USA is spent on 10 % of the population (Conwell and Cohen 2005). With all the data available today, one can fall prey to "analysis paralysis." Understanding which data are critical, where the true inflection and decision points are, should be the foundation of any strategic facility master planning process.

Use a Range of Values: One means to manage future uncertainty is to accept range estimates, rather than trying to identify specific targets or "point" estimates. After all, the chance of hitting every planned number is remote. Instead of seeking certitude, try to group key variables, comparing *a range of values* or outcomes. This is the idea of testing and comparing multiple options based upon a scenario analysis—challenging assumptions and priorities across multiple futures to assess estimate "robustness" (these assumptions hold up in multiple futures) vs. fragility (priorities are only relevant in one or two futures).

Case Example 8

What if a hospital was trying to determine how many inpatient beds it needed in the future? Based upon market and demographic analysis, there could be reasonable assumptions made as to the use rate (a range of +3 to −17 %), market share (a range of +7 point gain to −5 point loss), and average length of stay (a range increase by 10 % to decrease by 10 %). With these ranges, create different scenarios comprised of various combinations of these factors/variables and the resulting number of beds. The outcome of this exercise is a range of total beds required (131–221) that aligns with the various scenarios from wildly optimistic to drearily pessimistic. Then the planning team can proceed with an increased sense of confidence by ensuring that any facility solution will accommodate the likely range of values/beds.

Simplify Complex Functional Relationships: As the buildings on a campus have grown in an ad hoc fashion, so has the development of all the various functional departments, in amount of space, location, and condition. It is important not to get mired in the details here, but observe the overall hospital's functional relationships and interdependences from a high-level perspective whereby these services can be assessed for their highest and best use, whether clinical care, inpatient beds, specialty care, support services, or outpatient. By grouping all the various departments into three simple categories, their interrelationships to each other are more easily understood and therefore connected.

1. **The Diagnostic/Treatment Platform**: The diagnostic/treatment platform consists of the major clinical components that intersect directly with the delivery of patient care (both inpatient and outpatient) including emergency, observation, testing, and all procedures (inpatient, ambulatory, endoscopy, interventional radiology, and cardiac catheterization).
2. **The Inpatient Bed Platform**: The inpatient bed platform consists of all beds within the hospital including medical, surgical, ICU, CCU, and specialty (obstetrics, pediatric, NICU, PICU, rehabilitation, behavioral, substance abuse, and geriatric).
3. **The Support Platform**: The support platform consists of all those departments that serve both the D&T and inpatient bed platforms including dietary, loading dock/material management, linen, housekeeping, biomedical engineering, central sterile, administration, physical plant, and maintenance. As the delivery

model shifts from fee for service to population health, physicians and wellness/prevention components will become that much more integrated and at the center of care.

Implement No-Regret Moves: It is important as part of the any strategic analysis to include a baseline option that maintains the status quo. After all, "doing nothing" is a choice with repercussions as well. Unfortunately, this is often the only option decision makers investigate, implicitly or explicitly. As argued above, developing multiple scenarios and assessing different initiatives or development options across those varied futures, it should be evident that certain choices are more "robust" than others. These "no-regret moves" should be undertaken with confidence. Investing in options that work today and across multiple futures allows for a multi-phased development program that optimizes future opportunities while lowering risk—keys to transforming the master planning process in times of uncertainty.

Chapter Summary

This chapter takes the various frameworks and approaches outlined in Part I and applies them to the process of developing master plans for healthcare institutions. At the macro level, while the other chapters explore transformational change in the context of operational or management structures, Mr. Deininger asks a provocative question: In planning for physical buildings and facilities that should last generations, how can such efforts embrace uncertainty? While financial assessments such as risk-adjusted NPVs or capital expenditure "hurdle rates" conceptually adjust for the risks of rapidly evolving external markets, is that sufficient when planning for medical facilities? As Mr. Deininger concludes: No.

What to do? First, use the framework of scenario planning to challenge existing orthodoxies and traditional master planning approaches. From this, develop flexible options that can be contracted, expanded, or re-configured based on evolving models of care. Thus as Chapter 4 outlines, do not plan for a "point future," but rather a possible range of futures, creating a portfolio of initiatives in the built environment that meet short-, medium-, and longer-term requirements. Not surprisingly, the further out one plans, the greater an "option" mentality should prevail. And with the scenarios developed, seek those "no-regret" physical investments that seem to make sense across a range of possible futures.

As with several other chapters, a critical question is how to break down subspecialty or functional silos, seeking systemic responses, not unit- or time-dependent ones. In a way, Mr. Deininger is seeking to bring the physical planners together with healthcare strategists, united in a common approach to systems thinking, breaking down the barriers between these disciplines. While not typical in the field, such transformations may create more common language around embracing uncertainty, expanding the capabilities and sensitivities of architects, financiers, planners, and healthcare leaders. To do this, several questions flow from this case chapter:

1. How narrow or broad is the master planning process being envisioned? Specifically, should different scenarios of the future be constructed to challenge existing templates and historical design solutions?
2. How are different stakeholders—especially nontraditional ones such as healthcare theorists and technology gurus—being engaged with architects and physical planners in the master planning processes?
3. What flexibly, smaller scale solutions are possible vs. large footprint, massive new buildings that typify past expansion practices?
4. Are community-based solutions that embrace population health, ACOs, and cost-effective modalities such as telemedicine part of the master planning process?
5. How is success being defined ... the most cost-effective solution from a community perspective or a more narrow "institutional physical needs assessment"?
6. How are master planners learning from past successes, and failures?

References

Adamopoulos H. The future of hospitals: visions of the healthcare landscape in 2035. Becker's Hospital Review. 2013 Nov 27. http://www.beckershospitalreview.com/hospital-management-administration/the-future-of-hospitals-visions-of-the-healthcare-landscape-in-2035.html. Accessed 29 July 2015.

AHRQ (Agency for Healthcare Research and Quality). Analysis of 2008 medical expenditure panel survey. 2014. http://meps.ahrq.gov/mepsweb/. Accessed 10 July 2015.

Barnet S, Gamble M, Punke H, Rappleye E, Rizzo E, Rosin T. 10 challenges and opportunities for hospitals in 2015. Becker's Hospital Review 2014 Dec 30. http://www.beckershospitalreview.com/hospital-management-administration/10-challenges-and-opportunities-for--hospitals-in-2015.html. Accessed 10 June 2015.

Becker S. 8 of the most interesting things we are seeing in healthcare. Becker's Hospital Review 2014 March 19. http://www.beckershospitalreview.com/white-papers/8-of-the-most-interesting-things-we-are-seeing-in-healthcare.html. Accessed 6 June 2015.

Conwell LJ Cohen JW. Characteristics of people with high medical expenses in the U.S. civilian noninstitutionalized population, 2002; Statistical brief #73, March 2005. Rockville, MD: Agency for Healthcare Research and Quality; 2005. http://meps.ahrq.gov/mepsweb/data_files/publications/st73/stat73.pdf Accessed 7 April 2006.

Ellison A. For-profit vs. nonprofit: a breakdown of hospital deals over the past 5 years. Becker's Hospital Review 2015a April 27. http://www.beckershospitalreview.com/hospital-transactions-and-valuation/for-profit-vs-nonprofit-a-breakdown-of-hospital-deals-over-the-past-5-years.html. Accessed 6 June 2015.

Ellison A. The community hospital survival guide: strategies to keep the doors open. Becker's Hospital CFO 2015b June 15. http://www.beckershospitalreview.com/finance/the-community-hospital-survival-guide-strategies-to-keep-the-doors-open.html. Accessed 20 July 2015.

Gage B, Morley M, Potelle J, Ingber M. Post-acute episodes: expanded analytic file. RTI International, RTI Project Number 0208824.002.007. 2011. https://innovation.cms.gov/Files/x/Bundled-Payments-for-Care-Improvement-Chart-Book-2011.pdf. Accessed 10 June 2015.

Gamble M. 7 strategies for health systems to distinguish themselves. Becker's Hospital Review 2015 Feb 12. http://www.beckershospitalreview.com/hospital-management-administration/7-strategies-for-health-systems-to-distinguish-themselves.html. Accessed 3 March 2015.

Jarousse LA. Take a look at how market forces will impact healthcare. American Hospital Association 2014 Sep 8. http://www.hhnmag.com/articles/4012-take-a-look-at-how-market-forces-will-impact-health-care. Accessed 29 July 2015.

Jennings M. Healthcare strategy for uncertain times. San Francisco: Jossey-Bass; 2000. p. 4.
Meadows D. Thinking in systems. Vermont: Chelsea Green Publishing; 2008. p. 2.
Mosquera M. 5 challenges facing health systems. Healthcare Finance News 2014 Jan 6. http://www.healthcarefinancenews.com/news/5-challenges-facing-health-systems. Accessed 20 July 2015.
Pearlson J. Creating a care coordination infrastructure to achieve triple aim goals. Becker's Hospital Review 2014 Nov 10. http://www.beckershospitalreview.com/hospital-management-administration/creating-a-care-coordination-infrastructure-to-achieve-triple-aim-goals.html. Accessed 10 July 2015.
Reh FJ. Pareto's principle—the 80-20 rule. 2015. http://management.about.com/cs/generalmanagement/a/Pareto081202.htm. Accessed 10 Aug 2015.
Rosen T. 5 key lessons to prevent your hospital from going the way of Radio Shack. Becker's Hospital Review 2015 Feb 10. http://www.beckershospitalreview.com/hospital-management-administration/5-key-lessons-to-prevent-your-hospital-from-going-the-way-of-radioshack.html. Accessed 29 July 2015.
The Economist. Idea: scenario planning. 2008. http://www.economist.com/node/12000755. Accessed 30 July 2015.
Wayne A. Healthcare spending to reach 20% of US economy by 2021. Bloomberg Business 2012 June 12. http://www.bloomberg.com/news/articles/2012-06-13/health-care-spending-to-reach--20-of-u-s-economy-by-2021. Accessed 10 July 2015.
Wikipedia. Blind men and an elephant. 2015. https://en.wikipedia.org/wiki/Blind_men_and_an_elephant. Accessed 10 July 2015.
Yanci J, Wolford M, Young P. What hospital executives should be considering in hospital mergers and acquisitions. Charlotte, NC: Dixon Hughes Goodman LLP; 2013. p. 3. Winter.

Part III

Case Examples of Population Health Change

9 Buprenorphine Integrated Care Delivery Project: Genesis of the Howard University Urban Health Initiative

Chile Ahaghotu

Abstract

Population health initiatives are notoriously difficult to realize for reasons of scope and their often cross-functional support requirements. This case, initiated in Washington, DC, targeted the fragile patient population of chronic opiate addicts (and their families). It reveals a number of the themes from Part I, particularly the power of a vision, the need for strong leadership, the flexibility to manage through expected/unexpected challenges, the importance of current capabilities, and the need to develop tactical (short-term) as well as transformational (long-term) initiatives.

Introduction

Approximately one million people in the USA are addicted to heroin, and more than three million people over the age of 12 years have used heroin at least once (SAMHSA 2005). An additional 1.4 million are dependent on opiate prescription drugs. The annual cost of opiate dependence in the USA exceeds $21 billion (Mark 2001). Medical care, including drug treatment and indirect consequences such as IV transmission of diseases (23 %), lost productivity (52.6 %), and crime (23.9 %), accounted for the largest portion of these costs. Annual costs for prescription opiate medication abuse in the USA are an estimated $4.6 billion in the workplace, $2.6 billion in healthcare, and $1.4 billion to the criminal justice system (Birnbaum 2011). Misuse and abuse of opiate pain killers account for roughly 475,000 emergency room visits each year in the USA (Caron 2014).

C. Ahaghotu, M.D., M.B.A., F.A.C.S., E.M.H.L. (✉)
Howard University, Washington, DC, USA
e-mail: ozondu@me.com

J. Austin et al. (eds.), *Leading Strategic Change in an Era of Healthcare Transformation*, Management for Professionals,
DOI 10.1007/978-3-319-30776-3_9

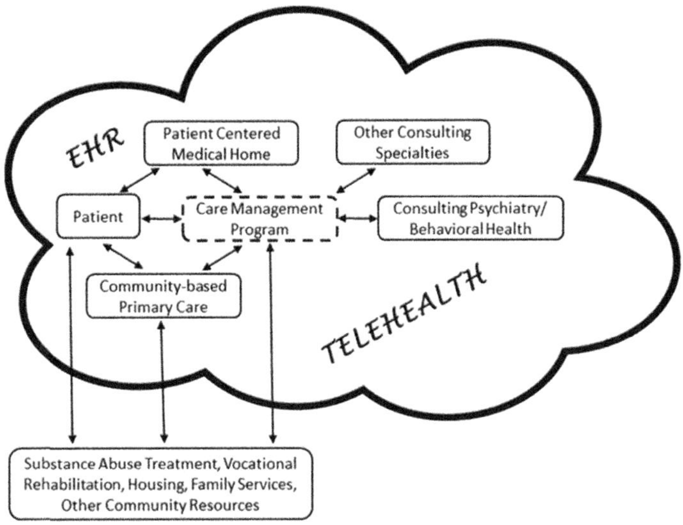

Fig. 9.1 Buprenorphine integrated care delivery model

Howard University's Urban Health Initiative (HUUHI) decided to tackle this crisis in its Washington, DC, neighborhood by launching the Buprenorphine Integrated Care Delivery Project. This multidisciplinary collaborative between Howard University and a vibrant community-based medical practice focused on linking patients receiving buprenorphine therapy for chronic opiate addiction (and their families) to comprehensive healthcare services via (1) care coordination/ patient navigation, (2) telehealth services, and (3) a common electronic health record (EHR) platform. This fragile patient population represents a substantial risk to community health due to disproportionately high healthcare expenditure, suboptimal access patterns (e.g., emergency department (ED) over utilization), maternal and child health effects, and other collateral consequences (community violence, communicable disease transmission, etc.). This innovative care delivery model (see Fig. 9.1) leverages the clinical and functional efficacy of buprenorphine to facilitate improved clinical outcomes, reduced chronic disease burden, enhanced health-seeking behavior, and improved family and community health dynamics. Figure 9.1 illustrates the model of care.

The Buprenorphine Integrated Care Delivery Project received considerable support from both external and internal stakeholders. The project evolved from discussions about how to promote healthcare innovation at Howard University Health Sciences. Participants included clinicians from Departments of Community and Family Medicine, Psychiatry and Behavioral Health, Maternal and Child Health, hospital leadership, pharmacy managers, research coordinators, and administrative staff. Key community stakeholders also actively participate in the initiative, including members of Washington, DC's Ward 8 Health Council, community advocates, and community physicians who provide primary and behavioral healthcare in medically underserved areas of DC. The project leverages

Howard University's strong ties to the community, aligning its resources with the medical and psychosocial needs of a population with traditionally poor health outcomes and high healthcare costs.

Strategic Preparation for Transformation

The Howard Urban Health Initiative (HUUHI) is committed to develop and implement a healthcare delivery system that focuses on community enrichment and leverages Howard University's unwavering commitment to high-quality patient care, medical research, and education in diverse populations. Creating a community-centered healthcare delivery system is a paradigm shift from the traditional philosophy driving most academic health centers that principally focus on training healthcare professionals, performing medical research, and advancing healthcare technology. Despite these valuable contributions, academic health centers have often been characterized by complex hierarchy and convoluted organizational culture (Keckley 2009). Creation of a patient-focused, team-based integrated system refocuses the organizational objectives to the unmet needs of the patient population. Taking this approach in the context of "the community" repositions the organization to be optimally responsive to those needs. The "medical home" model places organizations closer to critical healthcare community stakeholders (nursing homes, home health services, community-based organizations, primary care networks, etc.), creating opportunities for cross-functional synergies, shared resources, and creation of shared value across organizations. This strategy results in a robust patient-oriented healthcare delivery system that uniquely interfaces with the community across the continuum of care.

One of the key challenges for this project was realistically defining its scope based on available resources and organizational priorities. Restructuring care delivery at a large academic health center is an ominous undertaking. Over roughly 18 months from 2013 to 2014, we were able to focus the project scope to a collaborative initiative between Howard University and a community-based medical practice that links patients with chronic opiate addiction (and their families) to comprehensive healthcare services via care coordination/patient navigation, telehealth services, and a common EHR platform. This approach increased feasibility of implementation while providing the opportunity to develop high-functioning team-based performance with substantial scope and scale expansion potential. The Buprenorphine Integrated Care Delivery Project is the first step towards the vision of the Howard University Urban Health Initiative.

Patient Care and Wellness Promotion Process

Care Coordination: In collaboration with the HU Department of Community and Family Medicine and the HU Faculty Practice Plan (FPP), the HU Department of Psychiatry and Behavioral Sciences established protocols to provide coordinated comprehensive primary and specialty care services annually to approximately 700 individuals receiving buprenorphine-based medication-assisted therapy (MAT) for opiate addiction from a community-based primary care practice in a medically underserved section of the District of Columbia. To meet the needs of these individuals, the project includes an initial wellness assessment process to identify and prioritize their medical and psychosocial needs. Care managers engage patients during their MAT visits using tools that capture data essential to create a relevant and actionable 90-day care plan. Every week, a multidisciplinary team that includes clinicians, care coordinators, and social service professionals vets and finalizes these care plans. This strategy fosters shared accountability for each unique care plan with meaningful integration of patient-centered, family-oriented, and culturally sensitive support.

The care management and social services team assesses each person's ability to self-manage daily living activities, earn a living in a living wage job, and function independently. Care managers and navigators coordinate support services such as transportation assistance, childcare, and housing. They maintain contact with the patient between visits to help them prepare for tests, find the right location on the day of their appointment, connect them to training and vocational resources, and teach them self-management skills that promote greater independence and adherence to their wellness plan.

Telehealth Services: Telehealth, and particularly telebehavioral health, has been identified by the Substance Abuse and Mental Health Services Administration (SAMHSA), Health Resources and Services Administration (HRSA), US Centers for Medicare and Medicaid Services (CMS), and other healthcare agencies as a significant technology driver for healthcare transformation through access innovation, clinical integration (quality), and downstream reduction in the cost of care (SAMHSA-HRSA 2014). The two basic modalities for telebehavioral health services include the following:

1. **Telebehavioral health consultation**—Conducting a distance-based consultation between a non-behavioral health provider and a behavioral health specialist to collaborate in planning a patient's mental health needs
2. **Telebehavioral health encounter**—Conducting a videoconference session between a patient and behavioral health specialist

Telebehavioral health is one of the more successful applications of telehealth across the spectrum of clinical services as outcomes and patient acceptance for telebehavioral health are comparable to face-to-face visits (Hailey 2008). HUUHI relied on telebehavioral health as a foundational element of the Buprenorphine Integrated Care Delivery Project. The majority of the project's target population requires behavioral health services for substance-abuse therapy and concomitant diagnoses such as depression, bipolar disease, and schizoaffective disorders. Appropriately selected patients stabilized on buprenorphine-based MAT therapy receiving care in community-based practices, as well as on a campus-based patient-centered medical home, have access to behavioral health specialists via the telebehavioral health platform. The system also facilitates online consultations between providers for care coordination and optimizes the management plan across specialties. Care managers are key participants in these web-based consultative sessions that facilitate effective exchange between patients and providers, documenting their role in the process. This service will eventually be rolled out to other appropriate specialties such as dermatology, oncology, and hematology. Expanding the scale and scope of telehealth services will enhance its financial viability and integrative impact on the project.

Health Information Exchange: In an effort to comply with regulatory requirements as well as quality and efficiency demands of the changing healthcare market, physician practices across the country are making efforts to implement EHR systems while maintaining viable business operations. These efforts have created opportunities for novel partnerships between smaller, community-based practices and larger health systems. The Buprenorphine Integrated Care Delivery Project capitalized on this opportunity by linking a community-based practice in a medically underserved sector of Washington, DC, to the Howard University Clinical Enterprise. Incorporating the community-based practice into the Howard University EHR network provides bi-directional information exchange and links the practice to the university's information technology resources, which include patient and physician portals, applications for remote prescription writing, medication reconciliation, evidence-based practice guidelines, computerized physician order entry, as well as IT security resources. The EHR system also provides access to key performance indicators and customized provider dashboards through a practice management database. Community and on-campus providers share telebehavioral health notes, lab reports, and additional valuable health information via secure messaging, facsimile, and DC's regional health information exchange (CRISP-1 2010).

Measuring Performance

The Buprenorphine Integrated Care Delivery Project adapted the *Whole System Measures* model to measure the overall quality of a health system and to align improvement work across a hospital, group practice, or large healthcare system (Martin 2007). One attractive feature of this model is its ability to assess performance at different points in the patient care process and across the continuum of care. This attribute makes the model a great fit with the integrative nature of the project. Figure 9.2 illustrates our adaptation of the *Whole System Measures* model for the Buprenorphine Integrated Care Delivery Project.

The model also monitors events associated with how patients engage the healthcare system when presenting with an ongoing need. It incorporates several process and outcome measures, such as the *number of ED visits* per unit time, which provides considerable insight into resource utilization, treatment compliance, and health-seeking behavior changes. The model also relies on *30-day readmission rate* as a measure of care received in both the acute and post-acute care settings.

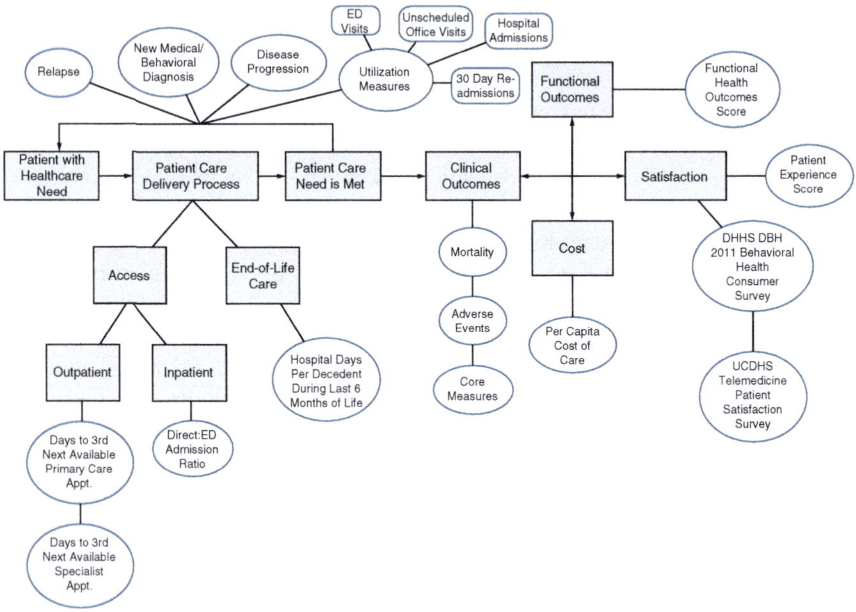

Fig. 9.2 Buprenorphine whole systems measurement model

Our system performance model also measures access to care with metrics such as the *days to third next available appointment* and *direct-to-ED admission ratio*, which is the proportion of hospital admissions that occur in the elective setting without utilization of ED resources. The measure reflects the efficiency of utilizing emergency room resources. *Hospital days per decedent during the last 6 months of life* (*MOL*) is defined as the number of days spent in the hospital during the last months of a patient's life. Although this data has traditionally been reviewed from the regional or hospital perspective (Dartmouth 2015), the measure can be applied to targeted populations (e.g., patients receiving buprenorphine in a community-academic collaborative setting) as a method for assessing utilization of services and disease burden during the process of delivering end-of-life care.

The model also incorporates outcomes and cost. The two domains of outcome include the following:

1. **Clinical outcome**, measured by mortality rate, clinical quality measures (CQMs) as defined by the National Quality Forum (CMS 2014), and *outpatient adverse events* using the IHI outpatient adverse event trigger tool (IHI 2007)
2. **Functional outcome**, measured by the physical and mental health status score of a system's patient population (Martin 2007)

We chose *per capita cost* over time (PMPM) as the primary measure of health-care expenditure for the target population. Functional outcome measures capture the patient care experience. For this purpose, we administer the *patient experience score*, based on response to the statement, *They give me exactly the help I want (and need) exactly when I want (and need) it.*[8] We also use the Department of Health and Human Services' Division of Behavioral Health DHHS DBH Behavioral Health Consumer Survey, and the UC Davis Telemedicine Patient Satisfaction Survey measures the patient experience with telebehavioral health services (Callahan 1998; Nebraska 2011).

One of the challenges with designing comprehensive models for measuring system performance is ensuring that there are appropriate resources and capabilities to capture, analyze, and report performance data to appropriate internal and external stakeholders. In the context of this project, data sources include the practices' electronic health record and practice management system (clinical and analytics data); hospital data (ED visits, inpatient, ancillary services); utilization/claims data from the DC Department of Health Care Finance; and agnostic medical record and utilization data available through DC's regional health information exchange (CRISP-2 2015). Protocols are established to capture survey data (e.g., DHHS-DBH survey) as part of the patient care workflow, and a full-time data manager is responsible for organizing and reporting the data.

Filling Potholes and Project Milestones

Implementing an integrated innovative care delivery model for patients with chronic opiate addiction in a medically underserved community is not without its bumps in the road. Some of the major challenges encountered include (1) patient and provider engagement, (2) identifying adequate financial resources to support nontraditional care delivery functions, (3) establishing a culture of collaborative leadership, and (4) efficiently integrating new processes, such as care coordination and telehealth services, into existing clinical practice workflows.

Our care coordination model incorporates provider participation into the care planning process. This strategy ensures that we promote meaningful clinician buy-in during early development of the care management plan. The project design incorporates patient feedback throughout the care delivery process. This includes surveys related to their experience in general as well as their participation in telehealth and integrated behavioral health services. Team members review survey results regularly as part of our performance improvement process. The care management team underwent cultural sensitivity training and embraces a culture of patient empowerment.

Our efforts to address the challenges in funding nontraditional care delivery functions such as care coordination, telehealth services, and data management leveraged the growing interest for financing healthcare innovation that has moved to the center stage of policy-making efforts locally as well as nationally. Howard University Urban Health Initiative members engaged DC healthcare policy makers through roundtable discussions, town hall meetings, and council hearings, providing insight into the challenges and opportunities for implementing integrated care management for vulnerable populations such as those identified in the Buprenorphine

Integrated Care Delivery Project. A variety of agencies fund such efforts; our project received funding to support staffing and infrastructural development through the "Innovations in Ambulatory Care" grants by DC Community Health Administration (DC.GOV 2015).

Creating an effective strategy for integrating community-based initiatives into the operational framework of an academic health center has been a critical building block in the ultimate success of the Howard University Urban Health Initiative and its associated projects. Outlining and understanding the components of such a strategy must be done within the context of the strategic goals and objectives of the institution to form the foundation for a successful implementation plan. Howard University's long history of providing healthcare services to a vulnerable population and establishing meaningful community partnerships aligns closely with the goals of the project. This led to considerable interest and support for our efforts by institutional leadership. Early in our deliberations, project members agreed that collaboration was the key ingredient to the project's success. We embraced the concept of "Level 5 leadership" (Collins, 2001), characterized by shared vision, consensus building, and data-driven decision-making and workforce empowerment (Collins 2001).

Project Milestones

The Buprenorphine Integrated Care Delivery Project recently began enrollment and development of care plans. Community-based MAT practices and academic-based services have been linked using a shared electronic health record platform and secure messaging for out-of-network providers. A telehealth platform has been established that links participating providers and workflows for patient-to-provider encounters and provider-to-provider consultations.

The project has received considerable attention from internal as well as external stakeholders. The DC Department of Health committed to ongoing funding of the project and members have been invited to participate in the development of DC's state innovation model (SIM) funded by the Center for Medicare Medicaid Innovation. The project was also recently recognized by the National Center for Healthcare Leadership as part of their 2015 Leadership Challenge, *Leading Together*, for their pioneering work around enhancing leadership competencies and collaboration skills across stakeholders. Project performance data will be reported out early next year.

Keys to Success

Key success factors for the Buprenorphine Integrated Care Delivery Project include (1) sustained provider and patient engagement, (2) effective and efficient care plan management, (3) continuous commitment to staffing development and performance improvement, (4) a sustainable financing model that accounts for nontraditional care delivery and management functions, and (5) effective leadership. An important part of this approach is looking for opportunities to leverage existing high-performance processes that can enhance project development. Seeking these opportunities also creates avenues to identify underutilized and/or underperforming processes for redesign. This approach not only reveals key success factors for implementation but also enhances existing operations, which includes prioritizing resources to support the strategic objectives of the project. Leaders who utilize appropriate management tools along with rigorous data gathering will identify resource needs for implementation. However, aligning the strategic objectives of implementation with the overarching strategic priorities of the institution is by far the most important priority for ensuring appropriate resource allocation.

Future Horizons

The Buprenorphine Integrated Care Delivery Project has set the stage for a comprehensive behavioral health service provider that offers innovative healthcare financing for delivering integrated patient-centered care to behavioral health patients and their family members as part of a population-based healthcare system. Addressing the unmet healthcare needs of a population that adversely affects the health and well-being of the entire community creates a deeper connection to the community while improving the quality of the patient care experience and reducing unnecessary healthcare expenses associated with unmanaged use of healthcare resources. By focusing on the community, the organization positions itself to be optimally responsive to the needs of the community. The Howard University Urban Health Initiative will continue to strive towards establishing models of accountable care that collaborate with community health partners to provide high-quality, cost-effective population-based healthcare for diverse communities locally and globally. The Buprenorphine Integrated Care Project is the first big step in that direction.

Chapter Summary

This chapter reflects a number of the themes from Part I, specifically:

The Need for an Aspirational, yet Practical, Vision: Without a clear vision of what could be accomplished between Howard University and the different communities, little would have been accomplished.

The Importance of Strong Leadership: As indicated in all of the case examples, without strong leadership, projects flounder.

The Journey Is Never Smooth: While it would be nice to think that once a plan is put in place, the "seas open up." In fact, in every example profiled in Parts II, III, and IV, there are setbacks. The question is the following: Are there the leadership and resource commitments to see the team through the inevitable downturns?

Build on Capabilities: This project pulled together existing resources, tying them together in new ways, in a grand, uplifting experiment. But the effort did not depend on competencies and resources that were not available.

Leverage Existing and New Initiatives: On the one hand, this project was all about personalized outreach and support for society's most at-risk populations. In that way, it utilized established programs for helping those most at risk and their immediate families in making more informed, cost-effective decisions. On the other hand, this project also utilized newer technologies such as electronic health records and telemedicine to expand the options offered. Creating a portfolio of initiatives that combine short-term (readily available) with long-term, more transformational (and riskier, more experimental) efforts is this book's central theme for dealing with uncertainty and rapidly changing environments.

In summary, the questions that should be asked in developing comparable community-based, transformational support systems for at-risk or underserved populations are as follows:

1. How are we defining success?
2. What is the target population and why do we think we can impact them?
3. What resources do we have … and might we need: financial, organizational, other?
4. What are the specific product and service offerings and how much will they cost to provide?
5. Who is the target—the community, the family of at-risk patients, the at-risk individual themselves?
6. What is the "value proposition" and why will payers/providers/patients embrace it?
7. Can this be extrapolated to other groups or is it essentially an effort to help a very defined population and situation?
8. Where will this go from here … how can whatever is developed flexibly respond to future challenges?

References

Birnbaum H. Societal costs of prescription opioid abuse, dependence, and misuse in the United States. Pain Med. 2011;12:657–67.

Callahan EJ. Patient satisfaction with telemedicine consultation in primary care: comparison of ratings of medical and mental health applications. Telemed J. 1998;4:363–69.

Caron. Heroin & opiate stats. 2014. http://www.caron.org/knowledge-library/statistics-outcomes/heroin-opiate-stats. Accessed 5 Nov 2014.

Collins J. Good to great. New York: Harper Business; 2001.

CRISP-1 (Chesapeake regional information system for our patients). http://www.guidestar.org/organizations/27-0332436/chesapeake-regional-information-system-our-patients.aspx. 2010. Accessed 12 Oct 2015.

CRISP-2 (Chesapeake regional information system for our patients). 2015. www.crisphealth.org. Accessed 30 Dec 2015.

CMS.Gov. Clinical Quality Measures basics. 2014. https://www.cms.gov/Regulations-and-Guidance/Legislation/EHRIncentivePrograms/ClinicalQualityMeasures.html. Accessed 15 April 2015.

Dartmouth. 2015. Dartmouth atlas of health care. http://www.dartmouthatlas.org/. Accessed 30 Dec 2015.

DC.GOV. Community health administration. 2015. http://doh.dc.gov/page/community-health-administration. Accessed 30 Dec 2015.

Hailey D. The effectiveness of telemental health applications: a review. Can J Psychiatry. 2008;53:769–78. CMS.Gov. Clinical Quality Measures basics. 2014. https://www.cms.gov/Regulations-and-Guidance/Legislation/EHRIncentivePrograms/ClinicalQualityMeasures.html. Accessed 15 April 2015.

IHI. Outpatient adverse trigger tool. 2007. http://www.ihi.org/resources/Pages/Tools/OutpatientAdverseEventTriggerTool.aspx. Accessed 17 July 2014.

Keckley P. Academic medical centers: the tipping point. Washington, DC: Deloitte; 2009.

Mark TL. The economic costs of heroin addiction in the United States. Drug Alcohol Depend. 2001;61:195–206.

Martin LA. Whole system measures. Cambridge: IHI Innovation Series; 2007.

Nebraska Department of Health and Human Services Division of Behavioral Health. Behavioral health consumer survey. 2011. http://dhhs.ne.gov/behavioral_health/documents/nebraska-2011behavioralhealthconsumersurveysummary.pdf2011. Accessed 17 Aug 2014.

SAMHSA. Results from the 2004 national survey on drug use and health: national findings. Office of Applied Studies, NSDUH Series H-28, DHHS Publication No. SMA 05-4062; 2005.

SAMHSA-HRSA Center for Integrated Health Solutions. 2014. http://www.integration.samhsa.gov/operations-administration/workflow. Accessed 14 Nov 2014.

Transforming Cancer Survivorship Care 10

Doreen Wiggins

Abstract

Population health efforts typically reach across subspecialties, ideally filling in healthcare management gaps from the patient's or community's perspective that should lower costs, improve access, and bolster quality. This case is a good example of the many differences between theory and practice. In 2012, Lifespan Healthcare System launched the Women's Medicine Collaborative to address the gender-specific healthcare concerns of women. The aim was to develop an evidence-based, integrative cancer survivorship program to serve the needs of female cancer survivors and their families. This case examines the progress made, as well as the remaining development issues, as the program seeks to fulfill multiple stakeholder needs for improving gender-specific survivorship care. It is a classic case of more experimental initiatives that hold transformational promise, but must adjust to the realities of ongoing financial constraints and existing treatment paradigms.

Introduction

In 2005, the Institute of Medicine (IOM) published the groundbreaking report, "From Cancer Patient to Cancer Survivor: Lost in Transition," examining the medical and psychosocial issues faced by cancer survivors (Hewitt et al. 2005). According to the IOM report, cancer survivorship care is deficient in two areas: (1) providers are too often ill equipped to help manage the long-term side effects of the disease, and (2) ongoing screening and disease prevention options. This case study

D. Wiggins, M.D., E.M.H.L. (✉)
Brown University, Providence, RI, USA
e-mail: dlwig@Center-OBGyn.com

J. Austin et al. (eds.), *Leading Strategic Change in an Era of Healthcare Transformation*, Management for Professionals,
DOI 10.1007/978-3-319-30776-3_10

summarizes our attempt to expand cancer survivor care modalities, focusing on the needs of the patient, but in ways that should lower overall care costs and improve outcomes.

In the developed world, the leading cause of death after cardiovascular disease is cancer. Part of the problem is the growth cycle of many cancers: it is estimated that 15–20 % of initial cancer survivors will be diagnosed with a second malignancy (Hewitt et al. 2005). In the USA the direct cost for cancer care in 2010 was estimated to be $124.57 billion; by 2020, given current trends, cancer treatment costs could rise to $158 billion (Mariotto et al. 2011).

These costs are typically greatest at the time of diagnosis and the last few months of life (Valdivieso et al. 2012). Congress targeted improving the delivery of cancer healthcare with the passage of several laws and regulatory changes: the Medicare Modernization Act (MMA) in 2003, the Health Information Technology for Economic and Clinical Health (HITECH) Act in 2009, and the Affordable Care Act of 2010 (ACA) (Levit et al. 2013). The ACA includes a number of cancer-specific initiatives, including (a) open access to cancer prevention; (b) provision of universal diagnosis and treatment; (c) clinical trial participation coverage; (d) programmatic support for shared decision making; and (e) development of specific outcome measures for different phases of survivorship (Ferris et al. 2010). The ACA guidelines outlined that access to cancer care will be determined by the patient's primary care provider (PCP) and will require meaningful quality and outcome measures (Spinks et al. 2011). Supporting these changes, the American College of Surgeons Commission on Cancer (CoC) mandated the Standard 3.3 Survivorship Care Plan Phase beginning on January 1, 2015 (ACS 2012). Requirements include that all patients completing cancer treatment be provided with a comprehensive cancer summary, a survivorship program, and a follow-up cancer surveillance plan.

Still, research indicates that despite advancements in cancer survivorship, the benefits are not being realized equally. Accessibility, affordability, and treatment deviations persist among different groups of cancer survivors, especially those who are poor, elderly, and an ethnic minority and/or lack health insurance. At the federal level, multiple agencies and societies (including the Department of Health and Human Services, Center for Disease Control and Prevention, National Program of Cancer Registries, National Cancer Institute, American Cancer Society, American Society for Clinical Oncology) (Levit et al. 2013) have designed programs and assistance for the overall treatment of cancer. However, long-term survivorship care is sadly lacking for the vulnerable and underserved populations.

Current Survivorship Care in Rhode Island

The state of Rhode Island provides free screening and treatment to women who are uninsured or underinsured through the Women's Cancer Screening Program. Income must be within 250 % of the poverty line and if a diagnosis of cervical or breast cancer is made, these women may qualify for medical assistance through the program to cover the entire cost of treatment (Department of Health 2014). However, once treatment is finished there is often a lapse in coverage for survivorship medical needs.

This case study focuses on the more transformative offerings developed by the Lifespan Healthcare System (Lifespan), with its four separate, multifaceted, and accredited cancer centers. In 2012, Lifespan launched the Women's Medicine Collaborative to address the gender-specific healthcare concerns of women. The aim was to develop an evidence-based, integrative cancer survivorship program to serve the needs of female cancer survivors and their families. This effort is now entitled the Women's Cancer Survivorship Program (WCSP); it fulfills multiple stakeholder needs, and has the potential to serve as a national model of gender-specific survivorship care.

In 2013, the National Comprehensive Cancer Network (NCCN) developed a guideline for survivorship care to address the broad needs of the 13.7 million cancer survivors living in the USA (NCCN 2013). The guidelines serve as the first published, evidence-based recommendations for screening, evaluation, and treatment interventions for cancer survivors, as well as outlining the consequences of the disease and its management.

Components of the NCCN Survivorship Guidelines are secondary malignancy screenings (estimated risk is 15–20 % for a second cancer); disease and cancer prevention; cancer-risk reduction strategies; and survivorship concerns. As the NCCN guidelines indicate, survivorship issues often include increased anxiety and depression; diminished cognitive function; general lassitude and fatigue; rising rates of infections; diminished sex drive and sexual dysfunction; and amplified sleep disorders.

The Lifespan program will expand survivorship concerns *beyond* the recommended NCCN guidelines to encompass areas such as genetics, fertility preservation and concerns, palliative and supportive care, physical therapy, nutrition, and community outreach and collaboration. Part of the rationale behind the Lifespan approach is the current lack of focus on the comprehensive delivery of cancer survivorship care. Programs that currently exist emphasize delivering a survivorship care plan (SCP) in accordance with the American College of Surgeons Commission on Cancer (CoC) requirements. But even here there are gaps: according to a recent study, the majority of cancer programs (56 %) do not use SCPs, few providers consult or create an SCP, and SCPs seldom reach the survivors and their PCPs (Birken et al. 2014). In fact, there appears to be no association between SCP use and cancer care quality improvement or adherence to guidelines.

Why? Concerns addressing the multifaceted aspects of survivorship care are (a) the number of appointments with different providers at many different locations; (b) the resulting higher patient costs by incurring multiple co-pays; (c) patient travel and appointment time commitments; (d) lack of dedicated survivorship programs; and (e) lack of survivorship training for primary care providers. The cumulative effect of these issues is that even with a survivorship care plan, compliance is low.

Integration of Shared Medical Appointments: The Lifespan Model

Cancer survivors, probably more than any other healthcare-related group, utilize support groups to promote psychosocial health and wellness. The reason is simple: individuals living beyond their first cancer diagnosis and treatment often have long-term side effects related to ongoing cancer management, personal health, and opportunistic illnesses. Unfortunately, most providers supply little information on these latent, but nonetheless, critical issues. Patients often feel isolated and many lack a broad range of medical and psychosocial support.

The Lifespan program—the Women's Cancer Survivorship Program (WCSP)—meets these issues head on. In particular, different than most cancer-survivor support programs, we created three components:

- Shared medical appointment (SMA)
- Fostering positive lifestyle change
- Palliative care

Shared Medical Appointment: The shared medical appointment allows providers to leverage patient visits effectively and efficiently by addressing and facilitating care for many survivorship concerns during one visit. It also builds on the support-group orientation of cancer survivors. Specifically, groups are formed of 8–12 patients with each group scheduled for a center visit in several hour increments. These encounters include staff appointments addressing all of the recommended NCCN initiatives as well as expanded patient concerns. In between provider-led medical sessions are non-scripted group discussions for the sharing of experiences, concerns, and personal stories. The SMA group dynamics has led to open discussions on sensitive topics such as fear of cancer recurrence and sexual dissatisfaction, enriching the before-and-after medical encounters. Preliminary results from our SMA demonstrate reduced levels of depression, increased physical activity, and overall improved quality of life. The SMA is a billable office visit, facilitates patient-centered care by bringing together multiple providers at each visit, and improves provider efficiency (1.5 h visit: SMA 8–10 patients seen vs. 3 patients in a traditional clinic setting). Patients typically schedule follow-up appointments every 6 months.

Fostering Positive Lifestyle Change: Emerging cancer survivorship evidence suggests that obesity and lack of physical activity increase cancer recurrence, overall morbidity, and mortality (Chan et al. 2014; Ballard-Barbash et al. 2013; Betof et al. 2013). However, lifestyle change promoted by providers alone seldom results in long-term behavioral adaptations by cancer survivors. The WCSP utilizes social media "group-me" and Facebook as avenues to remain connected to patients; through these connections—especially patients helping, encouraging their friends—behavioral change seems to be longer lasting. Specific support is expanded through virtual collaboration with community health promotion experts and cancer advocacy groups outside of Rhode Island. Again, leveraging social media, programs have included tying into a woman's cancer survivorship retreat in Sedona, promoting an evening of food and education events at a vegan juice bar, grocery shopping with a nutritionist, yoga instruction, stress reduction, and meditation events. Grant-supported research in collaboration with Brown University, to look at physical activity, meditation, and quality of life in female breast cancer survivors, is in the recruitment stage.

Palliative Care: A significant problem in the cancer survivorship continuum is the utilization of palliative and hospice care. There is underutilization of end-of-life integration of care with palliative and hospice services, overutilization of multiple providers, and too often costly in-patient interventions even in the face of patient-expressed wishes to be at home, with family members. Research has shown that palliative care and end-of-life discussions that allow for care delivery flexibility significantly improve quality of life for patients and their families (Wright et al. 2008). Recent research stresses how integration of palliative care and advanced directives at the time of advanced cancer diagnosis can improve outcomes and quality of care for patients and families and may translate to more cost-effective end-of life care (Greer et al. 2013; Chastek et al. 2012). As a result, Lifespan developed several initiatives including a palliative care fellowship to train postgrad doctors, and expanded staff with palliative and hospice expertise. Still, the program is underutilized. To date, there has not been strong synergies between Lifespan's survivorship programs and palliative care efforts. In part this may be due to the relative immaturity of the survivorship efforts; more fundamentally, the medical field generally lacks a deep understanding and established protocols for how to best facilitate end-of-life care.

Lessons Learned

Current focus on providing survivorship treatment summaries to patients and PCPs by "survivorship programs" is sadly lacking. These efforts have done little to instill patient-centered care, have not improved the cancer patient's understanding of disease, do not decrease long-term sequelae, and show minimal behavioral change in patients. At Lifespan, there are four independent (silo driven) cancer centers, each with components of survivorship care, but there is no comprehensive NCCN-based dedicated program except the Women's Cancer Survivorship Program. To build consensus within the entire organization, the WCSP has been marketing and promoting referrals for complex survivors—that is, patients with more than one primary cancer, gene mutation carriers, and unavailing problems and who are at high risk based on cancer diagnosis age and prognostic factors.

Looking ahead, there are several areas of opportunity and growth. First, we want to create a culture of change through teaching, by providing a cancer survivorship elective for medical students, residents, and fellows, and developing CME events for community primary care physicians/providers. Second, collaborative research has begun, with local and national presentations about the program to improve awareness. Third, we need to improve the financial support for this effort. Currently,

Lifespan is not in a financial position to place significant resources into the WCSP. However, there is support and creative commitment by leadership, including efforts to identify philanthropic resources for program expansion. In addition, we will be leveraging our internal resources, such as technology, to improve survivorship care. Lifespan recently implemented an enterprise-wide electronic medical record system (EMR). How can the EMR facilitate multidisciplinary care and coordination for cancer survivors and their families? Finally, we need to assess how best to liaise pediatric and adult oncology care such that there is a seamless transition in survivorship care.

In summary, cancer survivorship care is a relatively new area of expertise in medicine. Lifespan's transformative program—the Women's Cancer Survivorship Program—was not easy to initiate, as it is a new service line with national guidelines for screening survivorship concerns, yet little evidence-based data on treatments. Our long-term goal is to collect outcome data utilizing the NCCN evidence-based recommendations to determine best practice for patient-centered care. We expect that these data will guide the continuum of care for cancer survivors from ongoing quality-of-life issues to end-of-life palliative and hospice care. Only in this way will we be able to improve access, decrease costs, and improve the quality of care delivered to cancer survivors.

Chapter Summary

Population health efforts, by their nature, are integrative … combining disparate elements of care delivery into new, expanded models for healthcare delivery. They reach across subspecialties, ideally filling in healthcare management gaps from the patient's or community's perspective that should lower costs, improve access, and bolster quality.

This case is a good example of the chasm between theory and practice. As Dr. Wiggins outlines, existing cancer survivor summaries (the focus and crux of survivorship, rather than patient-centered survivorship programs) do little to "… instill patient-centered care … improve the cancer patient's understanding of [their] disease … decrease long-term sequelae and [realize] behavioral change …." To fill these gaps, taking a more holistic view of the continuum of care that cancer survivors must deal with, Lifespan is experimenting with potentially transformative care that creates communities of patients, leverages social media, reaches across provider subspecialties, and engages patients in innovative programs outside of the normal acute/chronic treatment arena.

As detailed in Chapter 4, Lifespan's efforts with its cancer survivorship program are classic "Wow" initiatives that should be part of any healthcare entities' strategic moves in dealing with future uncertainty, specifically: "*What are a few experiments or transformational opportunities that can be pursued? What are a few, wild ideas that are really only at the pre-feasibility stage, but could open up major new future possibilities?*" At the same time, the difficulties with such efforts are evident in this case: lack of good impact data, scarcity of financial resources, and balance between short-term/long-term concerns. Even related concerns, such as a lack of reimbursement for genetic counseling and risk assessments, mitigate against these broader, experimental population health efforts.

To summarize, any organization, for-profit or nonprofit, needs to explore the following issues as they engage in a transformational change effort comparable to this case study:

1. Why begin such an undertaking? What are the gaps, difficulties, or opportunities current care paradigms are not meeting?
2. What does it mean to be "patient" focused? And how does the new experiment or initiative differ from current care protocols?
3. What is the balance between "core, new, and wow" initiatives from the organizational perspective? How will each category be funded … managed?
4. What are the metrics for success? Over what time period?
5. How will current treatment protocols or subspecialty "silos" need to evolve for this effort to be successful? And what are the specific mechanisms or incentives to drive such change?
6. Can the initiative be quickly changed, even eliminated, if results do not meet expectations?
7. What capabilities does your organization have (or can easily acquire) to undertake such an effort? Are there options for sharing the risk (and reward) with other groups based on their capabilities? How will such an alliance, JV be managed?

References

ACS (American College of Surgeons). Standard 3.3 survivorship care plan commission on cancer program standards 2012. 2012. https://www.facs.org/~/media/files/quality%20programs/cancer/coc/programstandards2012.ashx. Accessed 27 Jan 2013.

Ballard-Barbash R, Krebs-Smith SM, Neuhouser ML. Potential to link dietary patterns in the food supply and populations to health. J Natl Cancer Inst. 2013;105(17):1265–66.

Birken SA, Deal AM, Mayer DK, Weiner BJ. Determinants of survivorship care plan use in US cancer programs. J Cancer Educ. 2014;29:720–7.

Chan DS, Vieira AR, Aune D, Bandera EV, Greenwood DC, McTiernan A, et al. Body mass index and survival in women with breast cancer—systematic literature review and meta-analysis of 82 follow-up studies. Ann Oncol. 2014;25(10):1901–14. doi:10.1093/annonc/mdu042.

Chastek B, Harley C, Kallich J, Newcomer L, Paoli CJ, Teitelbaum AH. Health care costs for patients with cancer at the end of life. J Oncol Pract. 2012;8:75s–80s.

Department of Health, State of Rhode Island. Women's cancer screening program information for healthcare providers. 2014. http://www.health.ri.gov/programs/womenscancerscreening/for/providers/. Accessed 17 Nov 2014.

Ferris LW, Farber M, Guidi TU, Laffey WJ. Impact of health care reform on the cancer patient: a view from cancer executives. Cancer J. 2010;16:600–5.

Greer JA, Jackson VA, Meier DE, Temel JS. Early integration of palliative care services with standard oncology care for patients with advanced cancer. CA Cancer J Clin. 2013;63:349–63.

Green McDonald P, O'Connell M, Lutgendorf SK. Psychoneuroimmunology and cancer: a decade of discovery, paradigm shifts, and methodological innovations. Brain Behav Immun. 2013;30(Suppl):S1–9. doi:10.1016/j.bbi.2013.01.003.

Hewitt ME, Greenfield S, Stovall E. Cancer patient to cancer survivor: lost in transition. Washington, DC: National Academies Press; 2005. http://www.iom.edu/Reports/2005/From-Cancer-Patient-to-Cancer-Survivor-Lost-in-Transition.aspx. Accessed 27 Jan 2014.

Levit LA, Balogh E, Nass SJ, Ganz P. Delivering high-quality cancer care: charting a new course for a system in crisis. Washington, DC: National Academies Press; 2013. http://www.nap.edu/catalog.php?record_id=18359. Accessed 16 Nov 2014.

Mariotto AB, Yabroff KR, Shao Y, Feuer EJ, Brown ML. Projections of the cost of cancer care in the United States: 2010-2020. J Natl Cancer Inst. 2011;103:117–28.

NCCN (National Comprehensive Cancer Network). Clinical practice guidelines in oncology—survivorship. 2013. http://media.wix.com/ugd/a2de8b_5e11db0e9da143e799174a98be61a0e1.pdf. Version 1.2013. Accessed 20 July 2014.

Spinks TE, Walters R, Feeley TW, Albright HW, Jordan VS, Bingham J, et al. Improving cancer care through public reporting of meaningful quality measures. Health Aff (Millwood). 2011;30:664–72.

Valdivieso M, Kujawa AM, Jones T, Baker LH. Cancer survivors in the United States: a review of the literature and a call to action. Int J Med Sci. 2012;9:163–73.

Wright AA, Zhang B, Ray A, Mack JW, Trice E, Balboni T, et al. Associations between end-of-life discussions, patient mental health, medical care near death, and caregiver bereavement adjustment. JAMA. 2008;300:1665–73.

Part IV

Case Examples of Market Transformation

Importance of a Vision: Licensure of Medical Dosimetrists

11

Brian Napolitano

Abstract

Advancements in technology place medical dosimetrists at the forefront of many new processes, increasing the demand for these professionals. However, demand must be tempered by clear practice standards and licensure as errors made by a negligent or inadequately trained medical dosimetrist can result in patient harm. This case summarizes an effort to obtain such licensure in Massachusetts. While not yet accomplished, this study highlights the need for a strong vision to unite various constituencies in driving transformational change, the first step of any High Performance Organization (see Chapter 3). It also outlines how difficult it is to sustain support without continual reference to overall goals, and the celebration of "small wins."

Introduction

Medical dosimetrists operate as part of the radiation oncology team, putting their clinical skills to use in preparing treatment plans for cancer patients undergoing therapeutic radiation. Most dosimetrists have the education and expertise necessary to generate radiation dose distributions and calculations to administer this therapy, but there are no formalized requirements that guide workforce competence in a manner similar to physicians, nurses, and most other healthcare professionals. Advancements in technology place medical dosimetrists at the forefront of many new processes, increasing the demand for these professionals. However, demand must be tempered by clear practice standards and licensure as errors made by a

B. Napolitano, C.M.D. (✉)
Department of Radiation Oncology, Massachusetts General Hospital, Boston, MA, USA
e-mail: briannapolitano@yahoo.com

J. Austin et al. (eds.), *Leading Strategic Change in an Era of Healthcare Transformation*, Management for Professionals,
DOI 10.1007/978-3-319-30776-3_11

negligent or inadequately trained medical dosimetrist can result in patient harm. This chapter summarizes an effort to obtain such licensure in Massachusetts. While not yet accomplished, this study highlights the need for a strong vision to unite various constituencies in driving transformational change, the first step of any High Performance Organization (see Chapter 3).

Why the need for state licensure? The American Association of Medical Dosimetrists (AAMD) and Medical Dosimetry Certification Board (MDCB) have developed the recognized practice standards by which medical dosimetrists are typically judged. MDCB certification evaluates a medical dosimetrist in areas such as critical thinking, judgment, and technical skill, with eligibility criteria that syncs with the constant integration of technology within the radiation oncology field (MDCB 2015a). There are approximately 3500 medical dosimetrists currently certified by the MDCB in the United States, representing roughly 80 % of dosimetrists in the workforce; within the state of Massachusetts, approximately 100 medical dosimetrists have attained certification (Robinson et al. 2014).[1] The problem is that MDCB certification is not required to practice within the field, though employers often cite certification as an ideal condition for employment. More fundamentally, dosimetry does not have any legal requirements for clinical practice (Zietman et al. 2012) as are required in many states for radiation oncologists, medical physicists, and radiation therapists.

At the Federal level, the Consistency, Accuracy, Responsibility, and Excellence in Medical Imaging and Radiation Therapy (CARE) bill—establishing formal practice standards for all subspecialists (such as dosimetrists) involved in radiation therapy—is slowly working its way through the US Congress (Whitfield 2013). To improve safety and allow for local medical treatment oversight, the CARE bill endorses licensure at the state level as a potential strategy to promote expanded competencies in the delivery of complex radiation oncology services.

Demand for Oncology Services in Massachusetts

Massachusetts currently employs various strategies to promote public health and safety under the broad Division of Professional Licensure that oversees a varied range of career paths from barbers to optometrists, electricians to podiatrists (MOCA 2015). The Department of Public Health and Human Services oversees physicians, nurses, and dentists in addition to most medical professions, including radiation oncologists and radiation therapists under the Department's Radiation Control Program (RCP) (MHHS 2015a, b). All of these licensure efforts promote the quality and safety of services provided to the public, with the state government enforcing minimum professional standards of education, experience, and competence. It is this standard by which medical dosimetrists should also seek to be measured.

[1] Also based on unpublished compiled data on medical dosimetry utilization nationally, 2015, by Boulter S and Robinson G.

The effort to license dosimetrists within Massachusetts through a thoughtful, measured approach to licensure quite simply seeks to improve the safety of cancer care provided by these professionals through building upon current licensure requirements for radiation oncologists and radiation technologists. It also replicates proposed medical physics legislation that would promote licensure to ensure appropriate professional qualifications. And the demand for medical oncology services is only going to increase.

It is estimated that almost 38,000 Massachusetts residents were diagnosed with cancer in 2014, driven by incidence rates from 2005 to 2009 already significantly higher than national rates (Gershman 2012; ACS 2014). As the median age of cancer diagnosis is age 66 and incidence rates increase past the age of 55, the maturing of the "Baby Boom Generation"—comprising 25 % of the US population—mean cancer occurrence totals will only grow (CNN 2013; NCI 2015). More than half of newly diagnosed cancer patients will require radiation therapy as part of their cancer care, so these demographics should increase the demand for qualified healthcare professionals to provide care (NCI 2010). While the population changes will drive the need for qualified professionals, there are additional market forces that will impact the profession regionally and nationally.

Many aspects of the Affordable Care Act (ACA) legislation will dynamically change the field of medical dosimetry. Under the ACA, more patients will have access to treatment coverage that had previously been beyond their financial reach. It is estimated that one in six cancer patients in 2011 were uninsured or roughly 12 million citizens nationwide (Schiller et al. 2012). As the ACA extends coverage to more uninsured and does away with limitations for preexisting conditions, these patients are likely to seek treatment. While Massachusetts has had universal healthcare coverage for residents since 2006, several large academic radiation oncology practices will continue to draw patients from outside the Commonwealth seeking treatment (Kaiser 2012). This potential sizable influx of previously uninsured patients into the national system will create increased demand for qualified Medical Dosimetrists, while also creating nationwide competition for those qualified individuals, at the local, state, and Federal levels. Unfortunately, simulations performed by the American Association of Medical Dosimetrists (AAMD) predict a shortage of qualified medical dosimetrists by 2020 without the expansion of more training programs (Mills 2012).

Licensure Efforts in Massachusetts

As can be imagined, multiple points of view arise when discussing licensure: some fear licensing might impede the immediate growth opportunities for accredited training programs, others emphasize patient safety above all other issues, and still others worry that licensure requirements might create geographic disparities in access to high quality cancer care. To start, an oversight committee was formed of various stakeholders in the delivery of therapeutic radiation within Massachusetts. As there was no formal organizational structure currently in place to start this process, efforts to develop the initial committee were based on "the old boy network," leavened by an ability to work with others. After a number of meetings, the committee realized it needed to create a unifying vision that could reach across, ideally unite, various perspectives in the oncology field. Specifically, the committee agreed upon the following:

> Through licensure, medical dosimetrists in Massachusetts will prevent harmful impacts of radiation and achieve quality patient care by adherence to highest professional standards.

While apparently simple, in practice, this vision statement—aligned with the missions of several radiation oncology oversight bodies—focused on improving the quality and safety of patient care, supported the need for continual professional development, emphasized the role of education in formal guidelines, and articulated the need for the profession's growth.

The defined vision guided the development of several strategic initiatives which will promote the value of competent medical dosimetrists in Massachusetts as overseen by this proposed licensure effort. The strategic initiatives are as follows:

- Communicate the vital role of the medical dosimetrist in the safe provision of therapeutic radiation to the general public in a manner that instills their confidence.
- Maintain scope of practice standards for medical dosimetrists that are equivalent with those published by the AAMD (AAMD 2012).
- Recognize the documentation of competence in medical dosimetry practice that is provided by the MDCB for encouraging a safe avenue for healthcare provision (MDCB 2015b).
- Uphold the formal educational standards for medical dosimetry as issued by the Joint Review Committee on Education in Radiologic Technology (JRCERT) (JRCERT 2014).
- Ensure that licensure does not impede access to healthcare in the Commonwealth of Massachusetts by recognizing the relevance of professionals not formally documented as competent.
- Ensure proper professional and public oversight of the medical dosimetry profession in the Commonwealth by creation of an Advisory Commission for Medical Dosimetry.
- Promote professional behavior of a medical dosimetrist in an open and objective manner through adherence to documented professional conduct standards.

The implementation of these strategies through licensure should both provide value for the many stakeholders within the radiation therapy care continuum, as well as improve the care of cancer patients in the state.

But strategies can quickly fail without metrics for success. As High Performance Organizations require operating metrics linked to strategic initiatives, the implementation of licensure for medical dosimetrists within Massachusetts will necessitate developing metrics for measuring licensure's impacts. First and foremost is to increase the utilization of qualified medical dosimetry practitioners in Massachusetts. The vision is quite simply that 100 % of individuals in Massachusetts holding job titles of medical dosimetrist will eventually meet competency qualifications as established by the AAMD (AAMD 2012).

Behind such efforts is the concern for patient safety. According to data from various states, the impacts of radiologic technologists' licensing are stark. Alabama, a state of approximately four million residents where there are no license requirements, reported 42 medical events to the NRC between 1981 and 1997 that involved radiation; in California, a state of approximately 30 million residents with strict licensing requirements, only 29 comparable medical events were reported (ASRT 2015). In the 10-year period prior to licensure in Massachusetts in 1990, the state witnessed 55 adverse medical events; whereas, post-implementation results saw that rate drop to 7 events over a similar timeframe (ASRT 2015).

On a related note, while the reporting of medical events is governed by regulatory requirements, the field lacks a central incident reporting structure prior to the implementation of ASTRO's Radiation Oncology Incident Learning System (RO-ILS). The governmental pressures brought about by the New York Times series entitled *The Radiation Boom* should result in more robust data accumulation by RO-ILS on rates of incidence where deviations from intended treatment occur (Bogdanich 2010; Lawton 2014). RO-ILS has just started its collection of clinical data in 2014; however, this national aggregate data will be useful for comparison to Massachusetts medical dosimetry practices as a measure of the impact of licensure on the state's safety record in the delivery of radiation therapy (Lawton 2014).

Keys to Success

The most essential step in any change effort is the delineation of a clear vision. Once stakeholders outlined the vision for dosimetry licensure, strategies and metrics quickly followed. Today, the Massachusetts State Legislature is reviewing licensure legislation. Given the diversity of positions and stakeholder beliefs, this legislation was not even contemplated until very recently. The key was engaging a diverse set of stakeholders within Massachusetts to ensure the resulting vision united, rather than divided. This diversity helped address issues that may have otherwise been missed, such as geographic difficulties in recruiting qualified professionals and ensuring continuity of employment for those not meeting the qualified standard after introduction of any licensure requirement. Identifying critical stakeholders up front and empowering them with the responsibility of developing a vibrant vision made them accountable for the project's success while also inspiring them toward the transformational change sought.

To gain stakeholder engagement, the effort's scope needed to be clearly and unambiguously conveyed early in the process: those ambivalent about participating readily agreed after further refinement of the scope and honing a strong statement of intent. Still, the potential exists that engagement may wane as the project's timeframe lengthens. Legislative action, by its very nature, is uncertain. Constant communication with key stakeholders on progress to expectations is critical to ensuring stakeholders support.

Finally, as with any major change effort, celebrating small wins builds excitement in the process and gives credibility to the effort. Many stakeholders may have chosen to withdraw their support without that early momentum from small wins, such as gaining access to crucial practice data from professional societies or having the licensure legislation introduced into the State Legislative process. In hindsight, what we did not do as well was to build broad public support. While we focused on the professional societies, our members and related medical subspecialists, we might have engaged patients and other constituents of legislators earlier in our efforts. Such broader community input has been shown to be a dynamic force in driving change in medical care.

Massachusetts, as the first state to provide universal healthcare coverage for its citizens, has shown it can be fertile ground for transformative healthcare initiatives. The medical dosimetry community has ample opportunity to flourish through licensing of professionals despite a lack of formal infrastructure. Alignment of the current processes, resources, and organizational elements to help grow the medical dosimetry profession will continue to provide value for the Commonwealth. This alignment is crucial for any project's success, so leaders should question whether their vision matches these elements while inspiring those stakeholders involved. Ultimately, this project should provide shared value to the various stakeholders in the cancer care community in Massachusetts as it progresses toward implementation of a licensure requirement for medical dosimetrists.

Chapter Summary

This case of the ongoing efforts to establish licensure requirements for medical dosimetrists in the state of Massachusetts raises a number of interesting issues. First, what are the practice issues that call for licensing? Could this be an example of the government unnecessarily intruding into the provision of medical services that is already being monitored by a number of government agencies at the state and federal levels? Second, maybe the legislation is simply an attempt by current providers to raise barriers to entry, restraining competition like the medieval guilds? As the author ironically writes, "…multiple points of view arise when discussing licensure…"

What in fact occurred is an excellent example of the aspirational and yet practical value of a strong vision: as the author argues, the organizing committee could not move forward without a "…unifying vision that could reach across, ideally unite, various perspectives in the oncology field." From the vision then came strategic initiatives, metrics for success, as well as the effort to develop in-state licensure requirements for medical dosimetry.

Also, while the development of a vision and the steps to realize this vision seemed to be working, communication and stakeholder support could have been broadened. The author specifically notes that while the focus was on the medical field, "...we might have engaged patients and other constituents of legislators earlier in our efforts. Such broader community input has been shown to be a dynamic force in driving change in medical care." As outlined in Chapter 4, strategic success is built on broad segmentation (Where to Play and How to Win?).

Finally, as Hambrick argues, the speed and sequencing of moves was essential for this case example's ability to continue moving forward. Legislative change, in particular, can be deadly as it is all-to-often slow, uncertain, and opaque. In this case, stakeholder support was maintained by celebrating "small wins"—tying achievements back to the vision of improved patient safety, a rallying cry that all could unite behind.

To summarize, any organization, for-profit or nonprofit, should discuss the following questions in beginning a transformational change effort comparable to this case study:

1. What are the specific reasons for engaging in this effort?
2. What are different stakeholder perspectives on the effort? How best to engage supporters, and overcome challengers?
3. Is there a unifying vision that will provide the aspirational, and yet practical, call to action internally and externally ... across all key stakeholder groups?
4. What is the timetable for action ... and how can the pressure for change be maintained by "celebrating small wins"?
5. What will be the metrics of success to assess the impact of strategic initiatives?
6. In the midst of change and uncertainty, how to maintain a "bias for action"?

References

AAMD (American Association of Medical Dosimetrists). Scope of practice of a medical dosimetrist. 2012. http://www.medicaldosimetry.org/pub/39731f93-2354-d714-5182-a342d50fd925). Accessed 10 May 2012.

ACS (American Cancer Society). Cancer facts & figures 2014. Atlanta: American Cancer Society; 2014.

ASRT (American Society of Radiologic Technologists). State and federal licensure issues. 2015. http://www.asrt.org/main/standards-regulations/federal-legislative-affairs/state-and-federal-licensure-issues. Accessed 15 May 2015.

Bogdanich W. Case studies: when medical radiation goes awry. New York Times 2010 Jan.

CNN Library. Baby boomer generation fast facts. 2013. http://www.cnn.com/2013/11/06/us/baby-boomer-generation-fast-facts/. Accessed 5 May 2015.

Gershman S. Cancer incidence and mortality in Massachusetts 2005–2009: statewide report. Boston: Massachusetts Department of Public Health; 2012.

JRCERT (Joint review committee on education in radiologic technology). Standards for an accredited educational program in medical dosimetry. Chicago: JRCERT; 2014.

Kaiser Family Foundation. Massachusetts health care reform: six years later. Menlo Park, CA: Kaiser Family Foundation; 2012.

Lawton C. Radiation oncology incident learning system congressional briefing. 2014. https://www.astro.org/uploadedFiles/Main_Site/News_and_Media/Media_Resources/Press_Kits/RO-ILS/ROILS%20Launch%20Briefing.pdf. Accessed 10 May 2015.

MDCB (Medical dosimetry certification board and Prometric Inc). Certification handbook 2015. 2015b. http://www.mdcb.org/sites/default/files/documents/2014/Exam%20Handbook_2015_FINAL_0.pdf. Accessed 15 June 2015.
MDCB (Medical dosimetry certification board). Certification exam information. 2015a. http://www.mdcb.org/certification-exam-information. Accessed 10 May 2015.
MHHS (Massachusetts health and human services). Certification, licensure & registration. 2015a. http://www.mass.gov/eohhs/provider/licensing/. Accessed 17 May 2015.
MHHS (Massachusetts health and human services). Radiologic technologist (RT) licensing program. 2015b. http://www.mass.gov/eohhs/gov/departments/dph/programs/environmental-health/exposure-topics/radiation/radiologic-technologist/radiologic-technologist-licensing-program.html. Accessed 3 March 2015.
Mills M. Technical report: future trends in the supply of and demand for medical dosimetrists. Herndon, VA: American Association of Medical Dosimetrists; 2012.
MOCA (Massachusetts office of consumer affairs & business regulation). License types, forms & requirements. 2015. http://www.mass.gov/ocabr/licensee/license-types/. Accessed 10 May 2015.
NCI (National Cancer Institute) (2010) Radiation therapy for cancer. http://www.cancer.gov/about-cancer/treatment/types/radiation-therapy/radiation-fact-sheet. Accessed 15 March 2015
NCI (National Cancer Institute). SEER stat fact sheets: all cancer sites. Washington, DC: National Cancer Institute; 2015.
Robinson G, Mobile K, Yu Y. The radiation oncology workforce: a focus on medical dosimetry. Med Dosim. 2014;39:127–204.
Schiller JS, Lucas JW, Peregoy A. Summary health statistics for U.S. adults: national health interview survey, 2011. National Center for Health Statistics. Vital Health Stat. 2012;10(256):218.
Whitfield E. Consistency, accuracy, responsibility, and excellence in medical imaging and radiation therapy act of 2013. H.R.1146 2013.
Zietman A, Palta J, Steinberg M. Safety is no accident: a framework for quality radiation oncology and care. Am Soc Radiat Oncol 2012. https://www.astro.org/uploadedFiles/Main_Site/Clinical_Practice/Patient_Safety/Blue_Book/SafetyisnoAccident.pdf. Accessed 15 May 2015.

Transforming Health Information Management: AHIMA and Scenario Planning

12

Linda Kloss

Abstract

The need for improved health information technologies from Electronic Medical Records to reimbursement systems is expanding rapidly. Coordinated and accountable care is only possible with information about individuals and populations that spans the continuum of care over time. Unfortunately, member organizations that support information technology (IT) personnel are often hesitant to outline future requirements for their members that may challenge existing relationships or capabilities. This case, based on the American Health Information Management Association (AHIMA), examines how a leadership team used scenario planning to challenge existing orthodoxies, thereby opening up transformational growth opportunities for members as well as the organization itself.

Introduction

Health information in digital form is both an enabler and driver of healthcare transformation. Digital information is a prerequisite for population health management, care delivery, and payment reform. Coordinated and accountable care is only possible with information about individuals and populations that spans the continuum of care over time. Digital information also has the potential to drive health and wellness transformation. People can make better health choices with access to understandable information about their health status, risk, and options. Communities can use health data to advance the health and safety of the public. Virtual communities educate people about effective self-management and scientific advances.

L. Kloss, M.A., RHIA, FAHIMA (✉)
Kloss Strategic Advisors, Ltd., Sister Bay, WI, USA
e-mail: linda@kloss-strategicadvisors.com

J. Austin et al. (eds.), *Leading Strategic Change in an Era of Healthcare Transformation*, Management for Professionals,
DOI 10.1007/978-3-319-30776-3_12

After decades of lagging other industries in deploying and utilizing information technology (IT), healthcare is quickly catching up. In 2009, the Health Information Technology for Economic and Clinical Health Act created a program of publicly financed incentives to support accelerated adoption of Electronic Health Records (EHRs). In just one decade, healthcare has largely replaced paper medical records with EHRs, as well as other types of information and communications technologies. This pace of adoption has had profound impact on all who must use IT to do their work. At the front lines, clinicians grapple with adjustments to their work processes resulting in unintended consequences such as changing interprofessional communications, increased time spent in documentation, and new types of errors. Great progress has been made, but most organizations have yet to optimize technology as a tool and are not yet satisfied that solutions meet healthcare's technology requirements for high reliability and safety. Having useful and trusted information to fuel decision-making at all levels across healthcare in the USA is still very much a work in progress.

The Case for Professional Transformation

In the era of digital health, useful and trusted information must be available when and where it is needed. It must be managed in a way that fully supports the patient care and business needs of the healthcare organization while upholding applicable legal requirements. And because health information has great value beyond supporting the mission of the healthcare entity, it must be safeguarded to uphold the rights and preferences of individuals and the public good.

It is tempting to look for a technology solution to all of these complex information management challenges. However, supporting the full range of transformative uses for health information requires a competent information management workforce to design and administer information policy and management processes and advance effective information governance and stewardship practices. In short, like all assets, information is a critical asset of healthcare organizations and must be proactively managed.

The adoption of IT has irrevocably altered the work of those who specialize in managing health information and data. The health information management (HIM) profession has served healthcare for close to a century. The historical role for HIM professionals was managing patient medical records as the record of patient care, a key legal "business" record of the healthcare organizations, and the source of data for operations management, research, and reimbursement. Records *in paper format* demand a set of centralized processes; thus HIM professionals managed record processing and archival functions including the completeness and accuracy of medical records and the management of access and disclosure of information from records. HIM organizational roles were fairly uniform and hierarchical with professionals moving from supervisory to department head roles and beyond.

HIM roles diversified in response to changes in the information ecosystem and introduction of new laws and regulations. In digital form, information transcends

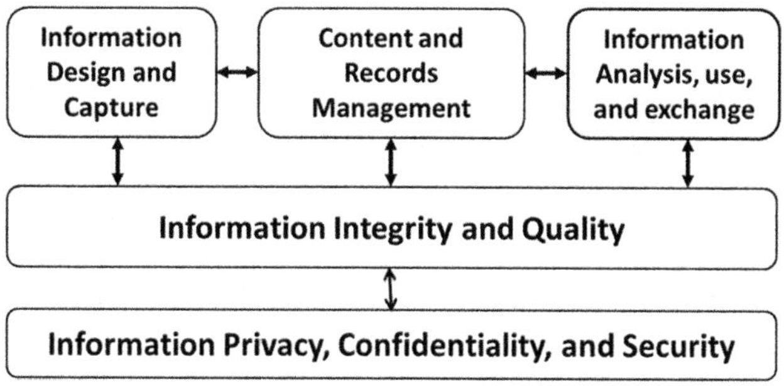

Fig. 12.1 Building blocks for enterprise information management. Copyright © 2013 Kloss Strategic Adivsors, LTD. Used with permission

physical controls and is not confined within a department or even within the enterprise. Information cannot be managed in silos by record type as data is being combined (e.g., clinical data combined with financial data) to support expanded uses not heretofore possible. Further, many record processing functions have been at least partially automated. As a result, the very nature of HIM work is changing from supervising trained clerical workers to performing in specialized knowledge work roles (such as privacy management, data integrity) and working collaboratively to solve enterprise-level information management challenges.

HIM in a digital health environment is a diverse family of functions that demands a systems view of managing information over its lifecycle and across the enterprise. As depicted in Fig. 12.1, information management requires policies, processes, people, and technology to manage the privacy, confidentiality and security, not to mention the integrity, and quality of information.

Information management begins with an assessment of information requirements and an agreement at the macro-level to acquire requisite data. Decentralized decisions about information collection leads to costly redundancy and inconsistency. Care in the design and capture of information is critical to downstream uses. While the historical core of HIM involved functions associated with managing patient records, contemporary practice involves lifecycle management of digital patient records and other high-value information that may be found in various media, including paper. It also extends to supporting the information needs through collection, display, and analysis of information to support quality-measures reporting and other analytic functions.

The regulatory environment contributes to transformation of health information management. For example, privacy and security management are important enterprise functions required under the Health Insurance Portability and Accountability Act of 1996 (HIPAA). HIM professionals often serve as the chief privacy officers for healthcare organizations and work in close coordination with IT security specialists and those responsible for legal and compliance functions. These roles are more challenging than they were pre-HIPAA for two reasons. First, the regulations expanded to include accountability for breaches of personal health information.

Second, medical identity theft and risks from hacking, as well as other threats, have clearly escalated.

Greater patient access to their health information is widely recognized as essential for patient engagement. Both the HIPAA and the Patient Protection and Affordable Care Act of 2010 (ACA) anchored patient access in public policy. The impact for HIM is that while once focusing on safeguarding the record and limiting access even to patients, HIM now actively *facilitates* patient access to information. Other information management trends, such as billing integrity and coding requirements, has embedded HIM in Revenue Cycle operations.

Scenarios to Support Professional Transformation: AHIMA

It is against this rapidly changing environment that the AHIMA utilized *scenario planning* to better understand and plan for plausible futures. AHIMA is a nonprofit professional membership association for HIM professionals established in 1928. Today, it has over 90,000 members that range from managerial to skilled knowledge work. Academic preparation for HIM roles include associate, baccalaureate, and Master's degrees from specialty accredited colleges and universities. Depending on the level of academic preparation, HIM professionals are also eligible to seek certification as a Registered Health Information Administrator or Registered Health Information Technician and may also add specialty credentials from AHIMA or other certifying bodies if, for example, their interests focus on information privacy and security management, data analytics, quality management, or technology systems management.

Anticipating and in support of computer-based medical records, in the early 1990s the field renamed itself from *medical record management* to *health information management*. While a prescient move, it would take another two decades to embrace the full impact of EHRs and other information and communications technologies on the roles and nature of the work of HIM.

The leadership team at AHIMA used scenario planning in 1996, and again in 2009, as part of its strategic planning process. The approaches taken were appropriate for the issues of the time. In each application, scenarios yielded results that could not have been achieved using traditional strategic planning techniques. In particular, scenario planning helps teams overcome the tendency to focus on what they are most comfortable with—incremental, operationally focused discussions—rather than longer-term, transformational strategy formulation.

In 1996, the focus of future scenarios was on understanding emerging professional roles across the HIM domains. For example, the HIPAA law had just been enacted in the USA, calling for formalization of privacy programs in healthcare organizations. In contrast, the 2009 scenario planning effort examined plausible futures for HIM in light of comprehensive health delivery and payment reform, as well as accelerating adoption of IT. These two experiences, a dozen years apart, demonstrated the unique value of scenarios for organizations like AHIMA assessing their professional futures:

- **Story telling**: Scenarios are plausible "stories" about the future, not predictions. In the articulation of possible futures, different perspectives on future challenges and resulting strategic choices can be freely debated.
- **Step Out of Today**: Rather than planning for a single future state, considering a range of plausible futures enables more creative discussion of options for large-scale systems and culture change. People are more open to alternatives when they literally step into different futures, envisioning alternative paths forward.
- **Stakeholder engagement**: The steps in developing different future scenarios supported strategic dialogue between a broad range of stakeholders. Specifically, by bringing together divergent yet related groups such as healthcare administrators, medical informatics communities, and AHIMA members, scenario planning helped expand greater understanding and support for future priorities across these groups as they grappled with how to gain the skills and competencies needed for the future.
- **Broaden perspectives**: The scenarios were a neutral foundation for identifying key success factors (KSFs) and strategic direction for the sponsoring organization. In this way, the scenario dialogue, rather than the opinions of a few leaders, inform the best paths forward.

The following case example focuses on the 2009 scenario planning efforts and results at AHIMA. Importantly, the utilization of scenario planning, in and of itself, does not guarantee transformational change. As AHIMA learned in its 1996 scenario planning efforts, scenario planning *must* begin with a clear-eyed assessment of external trends and uncertainties. While the 1996 scenario exercise did engage members in thinking about future professional challenges and their own career advancement, the strategies developed were aspirational, not embracing the changing healthcare and IT environments. The resulting strategies were too internally focused, reflecting what the profession wanted and what would be politically acceptable to most current members within AHIMA. As a result, AHIMA failed to take several critical, bold actions, such as elevating educational and certification standards that might have helped AHIMA members undertake more specific initiatives to advance their careers.

Scenarios to Inform Association Futures: 2009 Efforts

The 2009 scenario planning efforts consisted of the process steps shown in Fig. 12.2.

First, trends and uncertainties were developed for three interconnecting environments: the US healthcare industry, information management, and leadership/management of professional associations. To create the list of these trends and uncertainties involved literature reviews, extensive stakeholder interviews, and brainstorming sessions utilizing SWOT (Strengths, Weaknesses, Opportunities, and Threats) and STEEP (Social, Technological, Economic, Environmental, and Political factors) frameworks. AHIMA volunteer leaders participated in this phase,

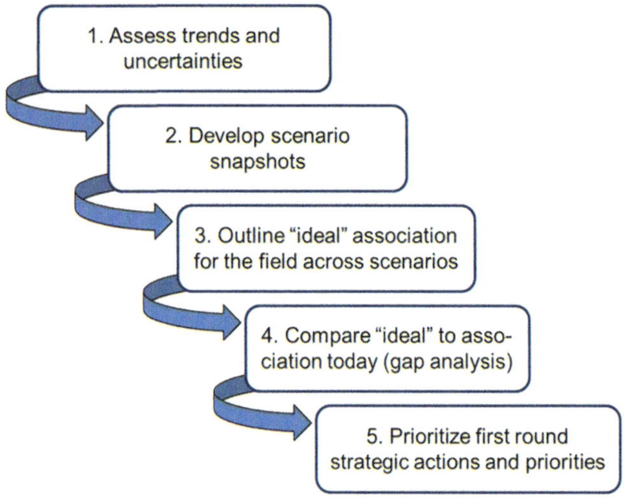

Fig. 12.2 Scenario development process

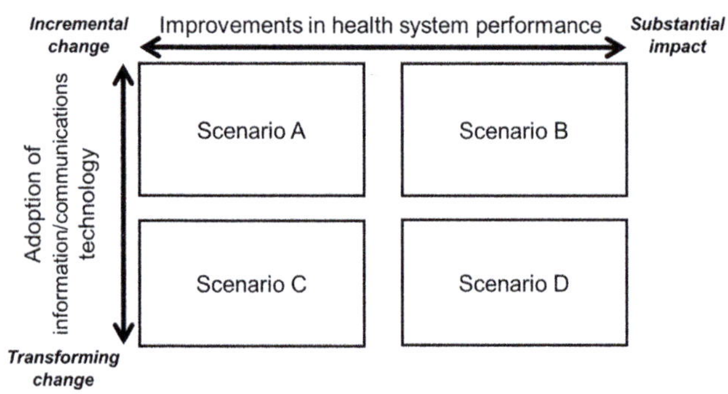

Fig. 12.3 Scenario snapshots

as did selected industry stakeholders and the Association's professional staff. The resulting list of key trends and potential uncertainties were presented to AHIMA members in an e-survey designed to test member's agreement with the importance, strength, and immediacy of each trend and uncertainty.

The compiled insights from this phase were utilized to construct scenario snapshots. Balancing the need to go far enough into the future that major changes could occur in the US healthcare system—but not so far out that literally everything could be different—the decision was made to use a 2015 timeframe for the scenarios (as our work was being done in 2009). The dominant uncertainties and drivers setting the "boundaries" or parameters of our scenarios were: (1) The extent of adoption of information and communications technology and its degree of optimization and (2) The state of improvements in health system performance.

As shown in Fig. 12.3, four scenario stories were constructed.

Each future was given a "title" that initiated the stories "explaining" different futures. Scenario A was "Groundhog Day" because it reflected a 2015 world in which technology adoption was still at the stage of implementation rather than optimization. Scenario B was called "The Little Engine that Could" reflecting the extraordinary effort required to realize health delivery improvement without an advanced information infrastructure. Scenario C was entitled "Free Market Baby" reflecting the uneven strategic advantage that some healthcare organizations would have if they could deploy rich information resources in an unreformed health system. And Scenario D—"A New World Order"—reflected an advanced future where information advancement and health reform were strongly progressing together.

The scenario stories included descriptions of HIM practice in each of these different futures. For example, in Scenario D, HIM would be working closely with clinical teams and be embedded in critical business units so information management skills and resources were directly supporting those who need information to do their jobs. Information management would be a value creator, rather than a cost center, because in this future organizations understand that information is a crucial strategic asset, and like other assets, it would be managed deliberately across the enterprise. There would be a collaborative learning environment committed to continually improving how information is managed and governed for value improvement and stewardship.

An important benefit of scenarios accrues when planners come to understand that aspects of *all* the futures could be in play in the future. They are not predicting the future, but are planning for a world that is comprised of a full range of plausible futures. To drive this point home, the AHIMA planning group discussed the proportion of healthcare organizations that might fall into each quadrant depending on how different uncertainties played out. This is an important strategic discussion because it reinforces the importance of unknowns, unknowables, and the key markers or indicators of external change that any organization should be monitoring over time.[1]

From the discussions about the scenarios, a clearer understanding began to emerge in the planning team of the trends, uncertainties, and the way they were likely to play out for HIM professionals. AHIMA could then consider what it must do to be successful in advancing its mission and vision. The planning group described the key association attributes for future success and considered *gaps* between these attributes and the current state AHIMA. Examples of identified gaps included the need to: advance a more contemporary definition of the HIM field, attract the "best and brightest" into the field, and utilize resources for mission critical rather than "nice to do" work. Identification of the gaps and KSFs provided the future-focused transition from scenarios to strategic prioritization. Ten KSFs for 2015 were identified as follows:

1. Agility: ability to adapt
2. Leadership development

[1] For more on monitoring and its role in strategy development, see Day and Schoemaker (2005).

3. Collaboration with stakeholders
4. Generate evidence-based research
5. Reputation as a trusted knowledge resource
6. High quality education
7. Effective accreditation and certification
8. Service support for members
9. A clear vision
10. Influence/shaping policy and leadership policy

In some instances, the analysis reinforced work underway within AHIMA; however, it also identified new work—such as leadership development and evidence-based research of best practices in HIM. The KSFs were analyzed for dependencies to identify those that were foundational to others. For example, because the environment was changing so rapidly, "agility" rose to the top as a priority. Speed of decision-making and execution of transformational priorities are not often characteristics of professional associations due to their tendency to favor tradition, stability, and current member needs.

Focusing on agility led to considerations of how to modernize the organizational and governance models of AHIMA. For example, the House of Delegates at AHIMA historically made many of the major, operational decisions for the association. Becoming more agile—more able to respond to a rapidly changing HIM future—required the House to transfer some of its authority to the Board of Directors (BOD). This level of governance change is risky if perceived as a "power grab" by the BOD. The 2009 scenario planning exercise helped build the case for this organizational change, creating a spirit of collaboration rather than confrontation.

But even as AHIMA embraced transformational change, certain structures and processes remained the same. Traditionally, AHIMA used a 3-year planning cycle, with an annual review and update process to incorporate lessons learned in executing the current strategy plus any unforeseen changes in the environment. KSFs were considered in laying out the portfolio of strategic initiatives for the coming year, as well as developing the metrics for success captured in AHIMA's balanced scorecard. These efforts continued, incorporating the broader set of strategic initiatives and metrics for success from the 2009 scenario planning efforts.

Lessons Learned

Strategy development is an art with no single conclusion or "right answer." This makes it an uncomfortable activity for many volunteer members of association boards of directors who come to their leadership roles with a deep commitment to the mission of the organization, but often limited experience in strategy formulation. For those leaders more accustomed to managing operations and optimizing short-term metrics, the framework of scenario planning helps such individuals deal with future uncertainty, formulating portfolios of strategic alternatives.

Scenarios consider a range of plausible futures, and in their articulation, reduce the tendency for "groupthink." Professional association boards are typically filled with members of the same profession and industry, often at similar stages of their careers. Such boards are fundamentally collegial in nature and may have difficulty with conflict, deferring to the opinions of the more vocal or senior group members. Constructive conflict leading to creative options is essential to transformational strategy formulation. Scenarios help shift the focus to future stories, not one's personal experience; they enable creative dialogue, not justifications of past efforts.

Professional association boards are also generally risk-averse, falling into the trap of rolling forward and tweaking strategies that by-and-large worked in the past. They favor incremental changes and are slow in abandoning approaches that are ill-suited for uncertain, rapidly changing times. Scenarios articulate the risks of business as usual in volatile times and help support broader discussions and articulation of not only what needs to be done in the short-term, but more fundamentally, what transformative changes may be required for longer-term sustainability.

Committing to a course of action that represents a major departure from past actions is challenging. It requires engaging members—who typically seek a stable refuge in their association from external changes—in a dialogue about the necessity of transformational change. Just as importantly, realizing transformational change requires a well-executed, ongoing member communications plan. Scenarios are very helpful in explaining the wisdom of such actions, maintaining the focus on "why" such changes are important for future success.

AHIMA used scenarios to engage members at many levels in envisioning alternative future states, assessing their ability to succeed in different futures, and thus, their growth opportunities for the future. Scenarios made different futures real and personal, helping gain support for transformational change. For example, AHIMA developed a roadmap to move the academic entry level for future professionals to a Master's degree (retaining certain technical roles at associate degree). For practicing professionals in or aspiring to leadership roles without a graduate degree, this is a major change. Scenarios helped make the case that the level of practice for new, future professionals could not be supported by undergraduate preparation alone.

Scenario planning also helps avoid a focus on operations improvement, often a more comfortable place for less experienced association board members. Starting with the external environment helps boards move beyond incremental changes to a focus on new programs and services that will improve the organization's fit with the evolving, external world. In times of organizational stress, association boards will often default to spending too much time on their operations oversight role, rather than focusing on the external environment and longer-term KSFs. Keeping scenarios as a part of the dialogue helps to preserve a more external, future-oriented focus. At AHIMA, it proved helpful to package the scenarios in way that kept the stories front and center. Figure 12.4 illustrates a shorthand summary, calling out selected characteristics that leaders of the HIM association world need to focus on in supporting current and future members.

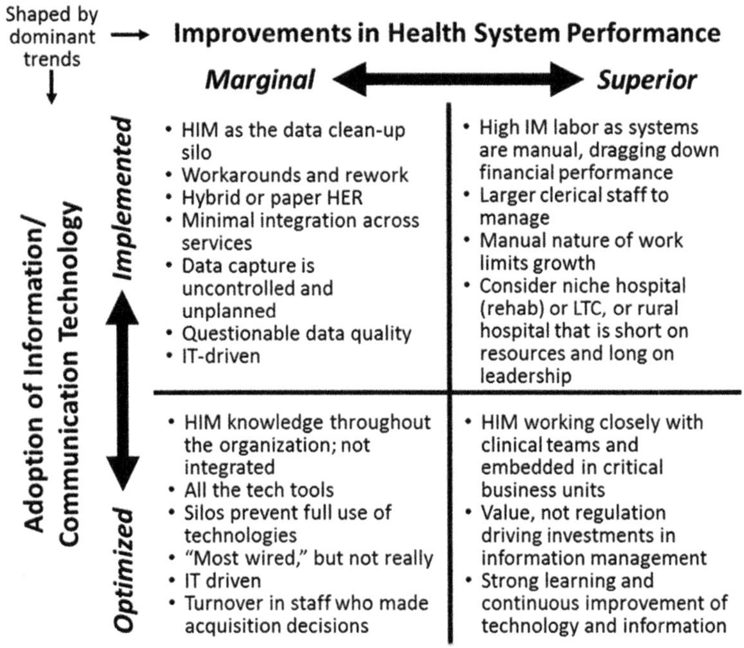

Fig. 12.4 HIM scenario snapshots

Impact/Results

Professional associations play an important and influential role in the US healthcare system. These organizations set professional standards and competencies. They help shape attitudes and aspirations of healthcare professionals at all levels. In short, they are fundamental to the overall delivery and quality of healthcare. The author has helped a number of healthcare professional association boards of directors use scenarios to strengthen their strategic capabilities. The challenges they face mirror those of AHIMA: most health professional roles are being profoundly impacted by the Affordable Care Act, evolving health delivery models and rapidly changing technology. And the pace of change has eclipsed the ability of most consensus-driven organizations to stay relevant, much less get ahead of the curve. Boards of Directors for most associations change each year with roughly a third of the members turning over. Learning to lead change is a continual challenge for the association's chief executive.

Scenarios have helped a number of health professional associations raise the level of strategic dialogue, get to the critical questions facing their members, and engage in transformational change. The lessons learned by association leaders are as follows:

- Transformational change addresses how the association in the future will deliver on its mission of service to healthcare and the profession, supporting the professional competence of its members.
- Leading change is more than a process to be managed: it is a way of thinking and acting. Leading change is the central role of the association board and chief staff executive.
- Effective systemic change happens when the association earns the trust of its members and engages them in a meaningful and personal way.
- Successful associations have a bias for action because leading change in challenging, uncertain time demands choosing among various options and a willingness to experiment, ever seeking a balance between current operations and new, transformative opportunities.

For members of the AHIMA community, the impact of technology, healthcare restructuring, and regulatory change are profound. For those with the leadership skills and professional competency, roles such as enterprise health information management have replaced department head roles. HIM departments are smaller as functions become embedded within business processes, such as revenue cycle management, quality improvement, and enterprise information governance. AHIMA is leading a healthcare industry initiative to improve the governance of health information. At the same time, it continues to grapple with how best to balance member engagement while trying to lead more aggressively. It is time for the association to develop new scenarios examining the world of HIM in 2022.

Chapter Summary

This case study explores the use of scenario planning to drive transformational change. Different than the other cases in this book, AHIMA utilized scenario planning twice: once in 1996 and again in 2009. The discussion of the differences between the two efforts is instructive: in 1996, the efforts were more internally focused, less about alternative external environments or futures. As a result, the strategies developed reflected "what the profession wanted and what would be politically acceptable to most current members within AHIMA." The point is, scenario planning is simply a framework; how it is utilized supports or undermines creative strategic planning.

In 2009, the effort was much broader. It began with an "environmental scan" developed through interviews, working teams utilizing SWOT and STEEP assessments, and then validated through an all-member, on-line survey. Perspectives on the future of healthcare, HIM, and leadership of nonprofit associations were the boundary conditions. But the primary focus was on implications for AHIMA. As outlined in the case, the scenarios helped spur discussions rather than rationalizations, clearing the way for strategic option development based on opportunities in the future, not justifications of the status quo. And, as Ms. Kloss writes, "most health professional roles are being profoundly impacted by the Affordable Care

Act, evolving health delivery models, and rapidly changing technology." The question is: what to do?

This case is also a good example of communication: using the scenarios to communicate with members throughout the process. More importantly, as outlined in Fig. 12.4, "HIM Scenario Snapshots," members and the broader healthcare community were engaged in challenging their own personal development for future success. This was strategy development that engaged the organization, for the benefit of the entire membership. Because of this outreach, even when the recommendations challenged existing organizational structures or educational pathways, they were accepted.

Finally, scenario planning was used by AHIMA to educate new board members on "playing for the long game," not simply focusing on short-term initiatives or operations management, best delegated to staff. The theme of how best to balance short-term necessities with longer-term opportunities is found in all of the case studies. Here, though, in the effort to develop greater institutional agility, leadership development was also a key outcome.

To summarize, any organization, for-profit or nonprofit, should explore the following questions in beginning a transformational change effort comparable to this case study:

1. Is the goal of the strategic planning process to better understand and succeed in an increasingly complex, external environment, or primarily to placate various internal factions for more immediate gains?
2. How will various stakeholders be engaged in the process?
3. What communication efforts will be engaged in throughout, and how can these ultimately enable key stakeholders to make better decisions for their own personal advancements?
4. Is the organization willing to learn from past strategic planning efforts … what worked, and what could be improved?
5. Once gaps between current capabilities and future requirements are identified, how will resources be (re-)allocated to close these gaps?
6. Overall, how will tough trade-off decisions be made, and then resulting strategic priorities embedded in operational processes to realize transformational change?

Reference

Day G, Schoemaker PJH. Scanning the periphery. Harvard Business Review 2005 Nov.

Transformation of Brand Planning to Embrace Future Uncertainties: A Pharmaceutical Company's Voyage

13

Brendan O'Brien

Abstract

The North American affiliate of a major, international pharmaceutical firm faced major change from increased market uncertainty with the Affordable Care Act to increasing competition. The case examines how the marketing department utilized the tool of scenario planning to help senior leadership move from short-term tactics to a discussion of future challenges and alternatives. Out of these discussions came future guidelines that enabled the brand teams to search creatively for new growth opportunities.

Introduction

The North American affiliate of a major pharmaceutical firm was facing a dilemma. Growth was currently strong, driven chiefly by sales within a single therapy area. Looking into the future, ever-increasing pressure from managed care payers and providers meant likely price compression, possibly even access restrictions primarily through higher patient co-pays. Clearly, portfolio diversification was needed. As a result, major investments in R&D and new strategic alliances to expand diversification and mitigate portfolio risk were made. The result? An impressive bench of planned new product launches over the foreseeable future.

However, executive leadership realized that the portfolio itself would not enable the company to reach its goal of sustainable competitive advantage. With the Affordable Care Act (ACA), new products could not be launched using simply the traditional "efficacy and effectiveness" criteria. With the ACA, pharmaceutical

B. O'Brien, M.B.A. (✉)
Decision Strategies International, Inc., Conshohocken, PA, USA
e-mail: obrien@decisionstrat.com

J. Austin et al. (eds.), *Leading Strategic Change in an Era of Healthcare Transformation*, Management for Professionals,
DOI 10.1007/978-3-319-30776-3_13

manufacturers would be pushed to demonstrate differentiated *value* for money for their treatments. This change in the healthcare environment and drive for evidence-based solutions required a transformation in capabilities in all areas of pharmaceutical companies. Gone were the days of push-oriented marketing campaigns. Instead, new launches had to provide explicit and evident demonstration of value to meet the often-unaddressed needs of patients.

This company faced a crossroad: continue to focus business as usual in the major therapy area where success had come in previous years, or take a new approach to challenge the deeply embedded organizational framing of opportunities in the external environment. With visionary leadership, the company dramatically broke from past thinking, and introduced a future-oriented, scenario-based planning process that revealed previously unseen sources of revenue and profitability.

Planning Approach: From Inside-Out to Outside-In

Traditionally, planning at the company was largely positioned as a financial exercise. There was great pride and emphasis placed on forecasting financial performance: meeting short-term numbers was key. The problem was this de-emphasized watching for and investigating possible changes in market drivers. The implication was that while there was a solid understanding of the correlation between low and high incremental investments in projects based on past results, future project estimates were fed through internally generated market assumptions. There was less stress placed on refreshing and challenging the understanding of changing environmental factors.

As a result, the US affiliate was not prepared for the unprecedented changes impacting the US healthcare market with the ACA. At a greater rate than ever, healthcare payers and providers expected more demonstration of the health economic impact from medicines. Increasingly higher discounting and rebates were demanded by pharmacy benefit managers (PBMs) when drug socioeconomic value was not clearly shown. But such broader data gathering required longer trial periods and greater pre-growth investments.[1] This placed pressures on gross margins of many pharmaceutical companies. By not anticipating the depth of investment needed to ensure future market access for products, the company risked missing its revenue projections, imperiling its ability to invest in new product development for future pipeline growth.

A change needed to occur. Just as these market tremors were occurring, a new president was appointed to the affiliate. The new leadership team recognized that the current approach to product forecasting based on past systems was myopic at best, and deceptive at worst. Incremental changes to the existing planning approach would not work. It was no longer sufficient to conduct a predominantly financial

[1] These pharmaco-economic trials are often referred to as Phase IV clinicals, as opposed to the FDA-mandated Phase I–III clinicals.

forecasting exercise as the foundation for future opportunity assessment. Not in the rapidly evolving US healthcare system.

The leadership team made the decision to transform the way business plans were made. For the first time, the entire affiliate would undertake a disciplined and concerted approach to identify and analyze the forces that will shape future market conditions. These would be used to define possible future operating worlds, critical for a holistic understanding of strategic options open to any company. Across the business, product teams would need to assess the best approach to succeed in these worlds to achieve commercial objectives.

The Process: Understanding and Aligning Around Future Market Forces

The first step in the planned transformation was to build an "outside-in" view of the future. This was accomplished through an objective environmental scan analyzing social, economic, technological, environmental, political, regulatory, and competitive forces that would impact the company over the next 6 years: far enough out that major changes could occur, but not so far away that literally everything could radically shift.

The executive team had conducted environmental reviews in the past. These provided useful snapshots of possible accelerators and obstacles for future performance. These perspectives were typically fed into a SWOT (strengths, weaknesses, opportunities, threats) analysis for strategic planning purposes. The plans were built using traditional tactical lenses: For example, how much larger could our market share be among existing competitors in a known therapy area? Challenges were superficial relative to questioning basic business assumptions. Existing strategies were deemed appropriate because they reflected past winning initiatives, assuming fairly constant, low-risk environments into the foreseeable future. Worse, the chief objective of these exercises was to inform the executive team. In each case, the work was used for boardroom presentations, and had little material impact through the rest of the organization.

The new affiliate president knew that more needed to be done. A break was required in the self-reinforcing thinking that pervaded the organization. A revolutionary approach to viewing future uncertainties was needed.

Working with the external experts over a 6-month period, the head of strategic planning conducted external and internal research through interviews with over a dozen senior company leaders at different levels across the affiliate. This was an important break from the past studies, which were limited to the views of the president's direct reports. The goal was to gain a diverse perspective on the environment, to pick up heterogeneous and multidisciplinary signals of future market dynamics. The fact that many more functions and roles were included in this environmental scan exercise broke from the past, and increased the inclusiveness and the lasting effect of the work throughout the company.

At first, the output seemed overwhelming: a total of over 50 possible, major forces were identified. Where to begin? Clearly these uncertainties—by likelihood and impact—need to be prioritized so choices for future direction could be made.

Executive Summit: Aligning Around the Future

The company had never tried to align around a view of the future, and how they were going to win. The executive team was comprised of veterans—leaders who had risen through the affiliate over many years—as well as recent external hires. Thus there was a natural tension between "prevailing wisdom" of deeply held beliefs internal to the company, and the external perspectives of those newer members to the executive team.

Pushed by the new president, the executive team took the bold step to tackle these differences directly through an intense one-day meeting to discuss the 50 possible forces. The objective was to select those uncertainties that were both highly likely and of major impact so choices could be made on how the affiliate was going to succeed in the future. In addition, the president included all department leaders in the summit—no longer would strategic planning be the task of just a few for the benefit of the board. The head of the pricing and contracting team remarked that "for the first time, absolutely everyone was at the table, no topics were filtered, and the view of the future was a blank canvas." The discussions developed a number of surprising outcomes; specifically market changes and players that had not been considered before were now given central focus.

The list of 50 possible forces were prioritized down to just four trends (those future forces where there was universal confidence of occurrence), and 12 uncertainties (those future forces where there was divergence of opinions in terms of future direction). Critically, the executive team went further. Through deliberate and intense dialogue, they agreed how the uncertainties would play out in the future, for the purposes of planning. They took a risk, and placed a "stake in the ground" on each of the 12 uncertainties, thereby universally and transparently declaring the united view of the executive team on each. This brought clarity, unprecedented in the organization. For the first time, the executive team's position on these challenging uncertainties was clear to everyone in the organization.

This transparency and inclusiveness was vital to succeed in the next stage—rolling out an aligned broader view of the future to the brand teams, and building a robust strategic plan from the bottom-up. Working with an outside consultant, the strategic planning team created a playbook summarizing the view of the executive team on all key trends and uncertainties, forming the planning assumptions about the future environment for all brand teams. Via workshops, the playbook was distributed and communicated to all brand teams throughout the affiliate. The result was a shared understanding of critical assumptions about the future environment, leaving it to the brand teams to determine their proposed routes for future growth.

Rollout to the Teams: Building the Brand Plans

Perhaps the greatest beneficiaries of this transformation in the company's approach to strategic planning were the brand teams. Most brand team leaders had a long and successful tenure with the affiliate. Most recognized, however, that the ACA and emerging evidence-based reimbursement requirements meant that past success were not good models for future decisions. A new way of marketing based on an emerging definition of value was needed. The past was not prologue.

At the same time that brand team frameworks were being challenged, the very process of reaching decisions on new initiatives was in trouble. The changes in the affiliate executive team meant that while veteran leaders shared an implicit understanding of the future based on the past, newer executive team members did not, slowing down decision making. For example, when product teams presented investment cases to the executive team, the opposing views about fundamental future market conditions among senior leaders stymied quick decisions, bringing new business initiatives to a halt.

These structural impediments largely subsided with the new planning playbook articulating the executive team's aligned view of the future. Now brand teams could focus on developing their plans, not trying to gain consensus among disparate groups of senior decision makers.

Specifically, brand teams developed a set of strategies for future growth given each brand's commercial objectives. Teams worked with the strategic planning group to lay out the strategic levers they could use, such as sales and marketing investment, pricing, and clinical studies. They then defined the various degrees to which these strategic levers were to be used, producing three plausible roads to success that comprised a series of distinct but credible strategic options. The advantage of this approach was that if the future world, as defined by the executive team, did not unfold as planned, there were other viable paths to success to choose from, thereby increasing organizational agility and preparedness.

The process was not an easy one. In workshops, the teams were challenged in their thinking with the help of the strategic planning group and outside consultants. As one brand team leader stated, this was the first time they methodically tried to understand the full range of strategic options that lay before them. In the past, the message was drive revenue and profits by relying on current approaches, making incremental changes only when really necessary. The process of creating strategic alternatives liberated thinking. Past marketing approaches were questioned. New and undiscovered markets were probed. Opportunities in unfamiliar areas that were previously considered only peripheral were re-framed as vital to future growth, and brought to the core of plans. All this was possible because for the first time teams were given the autonomy to create their own paths in a clearly framed view of future environments.

The teams were now ready to present each of their brand's three plausible roads, or "strategic pathways" as they came to be named, to the executive team for review and approval.

The Executive Team Strategic Plan Review Process

Traditionally, brand teams presented their proposed strategies and related investments within a single view of the future based largely on past trends. Less emphasis was placed on presenting a comprehensive review of possible future market conditions, and rarely was time spent challenging the viability of existing commercial models in future worlds. Similar to many pharmaceutical companies, the strategic plan review process was largely a financial review. Any scenarios that were presented were more likely to be upside/downside financial risk assessments than any fundamental discussion of external environmental uncertainties.

This worked well as long as the market conditions were stable and predictable, as had largely been the case over the past decade. However, with the changes brought by healthcare reform in the USA, as well as the rise in consumerism enabled by advances in healthcare technology, new approaches were needed. This was also advanced by the change in makeup of the executive team, with new members from outside the company encouraging different perspectives.

As outlined earlier, an important step for the executive team was their alignment around future trends and uncertainties. This shared sense of how future uncertainties could evolve provided a strong foundation for brand team strategic reviews. No longer were executive team discussions mired in debate about the possible evolution of external market conditions; rather, brand team strategic reviews focused on options and how best to reduce risk while improving growth opportunities.

The effectiveness and efficiency of this new review process were immediately apparent. In the previous year, it took almost three days to review the strategic plans for one of the major brand teams; this year, after the transformation of the strategic planning process, this same team's plans were reviewed in under three hours! With the clarity that came from an aligned view of future uncertainties, decisions were made quickly and confidently. Each brand team presented, and left with an approved strategic plan to guide their tactics for the coming year.

Across the brand teams, investment in innovation moved from a "nice to have" to being critical for future success. Early development product plans were given more attention, and there was greater understanding of what it would take to succeed in future markets. In some cases, longer term strategic initiatives were given precedence in funding over shorter term, tactical efforts—a clear change from past years. One overall result for the organization was a higher level of trust and transparency, and a greater sense of inclusion in the direction of the company.

Results: Lasting Impact

The executive team did not have to wait long for the transformation in strategic planning to be put to the test. Due to external market conditions, operating cost pressures heightened in the months following plan reviews. Within several months of the new fiscal year, it was apparent that tough trade-offs would need to be made to meet annual profitability targets. However, unlike previous years, the executive team now had a wide range of credible options for future growth, based on the alternative plans presented by each brand team. This brought greater agility to the affiliate, enabling relatively rapid investment reallocation decisions to be made, with a clearer understanding of likely future performance impacts. For example, in the past, early-stage development efforts were often sacrificed when times were tough. Now, even as growth slowed, the executive team protected key funding in several early-stage product development efforts due to an aligned appreciation of their strategic link to future growth.

Several lessons can be extrapolated from this case. First, change has to start with an unfiltered, objective view of future uncertainties. Entities need to ask themselves: Can future growth be realized from incremental changes to existing business efforts, or is more fundamental change required? And the tendency is to default to "Let's keep doing what was successful in the past." Unfortunately, in times of major change, as with the ACA and greater competitive pressures, the past is a poor guide to the future.

Which brings up the critical role of leadership. New leadership, willing to take a different look at future growth and external market assumptions, enabled the transformative realignment of the affiliate's brand planning processes. The executive team first aligned around key future uncertainties, and their resulting future external scenarios, thereby empowering the various brand teams to produce alternative growth plans. Brand team reviews were short, focused. And with the resultant options, the executive team was able to relatively quickly agree adjustments to the plan as external conditions evolved, meeting short-term requirements while not sacrificing longer term strategic investments.

Importantly, in the past, strategic brand planning was done on a pro forma basis, used primarily to present a plan to the board. Now the organization realized the value of focusing on future scenarios and how best to deal with critical uncertainties. Trade-off decisions became easier, as their context and implications were widely understood through the organization.

In short, different than past brand strategic planning, this pharmaceutical company took three steps to increase flexibility and lower risk in developing future growth plans:

- Started the strategic discussion "in the future," developing a reasonable range of alternative futures.
- Across those futures, asked the following question: How will our strategic brand initiatives fare?
- Finally, what portfolio of initiatives—short-term, medium-term, and longer term—will succeed in a range of possible futures, not just the one we hope to encounter?

Chapter Summary

This case study highlights the challenges every organization faces in managing short-term vs. longer term requirements. As Clayton Christensen writes:

> … a company's strategy is determined by the types of initiatives that management invests in. If a company's resource allocation process is not managed masterfully, what emerges from it can be very different from what management intended. Because companies' decision-making systems are designed to steer investments to initiatives that offer the most tangible and immediate returns, companies shortchange investments in initiatives that are crucial to their long-term strategies (Christensen 2010).

The tool of scenario planning, beginning with prioritization of key uncertainties, offered a framework for the leadership team to move from short-term tactics to a discussion of future challenges and alternatives. Out of these discussions came the future guidelines that enabled the brand teams to creatively search for new growth opportunities.

The case also describes the very real challenges, in times of change and future uncertainty, to align the leadership team. Here, the veterans had a different perspective on strategic choices than newer members—hired from the outside—evidenced. Clearly strong leadership, as provided by the new (externally sourced) president, was critical in bringing the two groups together.

While not explicitly discussed, imagine the cultural issues the organization must have faced in making the changes outlined. Since many brand managers felt frustrated with current practices, they were more willing to embrace the changes outlined. As with other case studies, communication was critical. The Executive Summit that began the transformational change effort involved "all department heads" that had previously not been engaged in prior strategic planning efforts. As Mr. O'Brien writes, this resulted in "… a number of surprising outcomes, specifically market changes and players that had not been considered before were now given central focus." More fundamentally, it began the process of engaging the entire organization in exploring new growth opportunities.

Finally, not everything went smoothly. Brand themes were challenged by the new strategic plan effort. While it "liberated thinking," it was also threatening to those vested in past decisions and processes. The key seemed to be constant leadership emphasizing the need to search for new solutions as well as the immediate impacts of the change: instead of days spent in Power-Point presentations, plan reviews took less than three hours.

To summarize, several questions must be answered in beginning a transformational change effort comparable to this case study:

1. What are the "unfiltered" views of the external environment that challenge existing orthodoxies and strategic development processes, leading to the need for transformational change?
2. What are the structural barriers to change in the organization and how can these be overcome?
3. How will the entire organization, not just past leaders, be engaged in the effort?
4. Will leadership "stay the course" even in the face of challenges from vested stakeholders questioning the need for change?
5. What immediate gains can be identified from the transformational change, and how will different levels of the organization value such gains?

6. Will a flexible portfolio of initiatives, balancing short-term operating requirements with longer term growth opportunities, be developed through this process?
7. What flexibility is built into plan execution so the organization can respond to unforeseen changes in the external environment?

References

Christensen C. How will you measure your life? Harvard Business Review 2010 July–Aug.

Part V

Concluding Remarks

Conclusion

14

Jim Austin, Judith Bentkover, and Laurence Chait

Abstract

Healthcare systems around the world face difficult, uncertain futures. From caring for aging populations to managing ever-increasing costs, healthcare leaders are challenged to meet the ideals that make the healthcare field so uplifting. As argued throughout this book, to deal with future uncertainty, healthcare leaders must seek longer-term, transformative opportunities while balancing short-term requirements. They need to focus on external uncertainties, driving transformational initiatives to create new growth, while also molding the internal culture and structures to adapt to newly emerging strategic requirements.

As Woodrow Wilson said, “If you want to make enemies, try to change something.”

Transformative efforts are hard. They are emotionally challenging, testing even the most loyal, supportive teams. Analytically, what is the “algorithm” for major change? How to know if the effort spent—the direct and indirect costs—is worth the results? According to an April 2015 McKinsey study, “Today, just 26 percent of respondents say the transformations they’re most familiar with have been very or

J. Austin (✉)
Executive Master of Healthcare Leadership, Brown University, Providence, RI, USA
e-mail: james_austin@brown.edu

J. Bentkover
Executive Master of Healthcare Leadership, Brown University, Providence, RI, USA
e-mail: judith_bentkover@brown.edu

L. Chait
Executive Master of Healthcare Leadership, Brown University, Providence, RI, USA
e-mail: Lpchait-ca@chait.net

J. Austin et al. (eds.), *Leading Strategic Change in an Era of Healthcare Transformation*, Management for Professionals,
DOI 10.1007/978-3-319-30776-3_14

completely successful at both improving performance and equipping the organization to sustain improvements over time" (Jacquemont et al. 2015).

In this book we argue that healthcare leaders need to confront the need for transformation in their operations for three reasons:

- The struggle all major healthcare systems have with the "iron triangle"
- The impact of the Affordable Care Act
- The decline in confidence with medical providers

All Major Healthcare Systems Struggle with the "Iron Triangle": It seems to be an aphorism of healthcare that any effort to raise quality, expand access, and manage costs at best achieves two out of three. Thus, the iron triangle. Unfortunately, cost issues appear to be pushing the other two concerns aside as every major healthcare system struggles to contain rising costs driven by multiple factors, such as aging populations, technology costs, increasing drug prices, and inefficient delivery systems.

Worse, the cost/value equation in healthcare is increasingly problematic. As articulated by the Robert Wood Johnson Foundation, "Researchers at the Dartmouth Institute for Health Policy and Clinical Practice have found that patients who get more medical tests and treatments do not always receive better care or the care they need. It is well established that US healthcare is riddled with unnecessary, ineffective, and even harmful treatments" (Jaffe 2009). Incremental change will not fundamentally alter these dynamics.

The Impact of the Affordable Care Act: With the passage of the Affordable Care Act, change within the US healthcare system has dramatically increased. From accountable care organizations to nonprofit insurance funds; from US Centers for Medicare and Medicaid Services (CMS) experiments with "pay for outcomes" to increased rates of provider integrations—there seems to be a new impetus for change. Some of the most dramatic new initiatives are occurring at local levels: from Vermont's efforts to create a "state-wide, integrated care network," to leading hospitals challenging their past business models (Mt. Sinai 2015).

Unfortunately, at least in the USA, the real worry is that even with the ACA and the rise in healthcare delivery experiments, costs may not decline. While in the last several years healthcare costs across developed markets have moderated, the question is whether such effects are due to structural changes or primarily the effect of the economic downturn and its impact on individual decisions about whether or not to seek healthcare services (The Economist 2015). Should healthcare costs rebound to historical rates of increase, public entities across the globe will face evermore pressure to restrict access and/or new drug and technology introductions.

Fall in Confidence with Medical Providers: As one practicing physician wrote in the New York Times:

> Physicians used to be the pillars of any community. If you were smart and sincere and ambitious, the top of your class, there was nothing nobler you could aspire to become. Doctors possessed special knowledge. They were caring and smart, the best kind of people you

could know. Today, medicine is just another profession, and doctors have become like everybody else: insecure, discontented and anxious about the future (Jauhar 2011).

Healthcare is a fundamentally altruistic endeavor—caring for others, and helping others regain "health." Medical ethics, or the communal values and norms governing the provision of healthcare services, is based on four principles:

1. Autonomy: respecting patients' wishes
2. Justice: impartial and fair approach to treatment; the fair distribution of resources
3. Beneficence: to do good
4. Non-maleficence: to do no harm (Kamilla and Rai 2009)

It would seem terribly sad if in the struggle to "square" the urge to be fairly compensated, or the need to satisfy shareholders, medicine lost the trust of the public. But that seems to be happening. When US presidential candidates talk more about healthcare cost containment and possibly importing drugs from Canada due to pricing differentials—rather than the incredible innovations the US healthcare system has spawned—have we lost our way? Incremental change will not restore the faith in medicine.

This book then outlined in Chapters 3–5 the frameworks for driving transformational change, whether in a medical practice or a major tertiary care center. Such a journey is fundamentally about strategy or the development of "sustainable competitive impact." Not short term … but longer term. What do leaders in any healthcare context need to do to sustain their institutions facing an increasingly uncertain future? Good strategies do several things:

- They indicate what will be considered … and what will NOT be considered by the organization. They clearly articulate "trade-offs" as organizations get into trouble when they pursue the "undisciplined pursuit of more" (Collins 2009).
- They build from an "aspirational" part—the vision—to very practical trade-offs and priorities as guides for actions, budgets, and marketplace choices.
- They answer two fundamental questions:
  - Where to play?—What markets, geographies, customers, and capabilities are we going after?
  - How to win?—Why will those segments choose us? What is it that we do, offer that is different, better than alternatives available today and in the foreseeable future?

As Jack Welch explains, "Strategy is an approximate course of action that you frequently revisit and redefine, according to shifting market conditions. It is an iterative process" (Welch 2005). And at its heart, strategy is a *creative process*: looking out into an uncertain future and trying to determine the best path forward to achieve the organization's goals. Thus, in Chapters 3-5, this book covered four primary topics:

1. Mindset changes
2. The high-performing organization
3. The tools of scenario planning
4. Execution

Mindset Changes: Transformation demands new ways of thinking, a willingness to experiment. Unfortunately, the human mind is prone to certain "decision traps" that limit the ability to handle future uncertainty creatively. Undertaking a transformational effort demands a different set of skills, more importantly, a different way of thinking. Just as the manual of a Japanese bicycle instructed: "To assemble Japanese bicycle, you need peace of mind"—so healthcare leaders must challenge their mental models to lead transformative change. As outlined in Chapter 3, before beginning a major transformative effort, teams should step back and assess:

- **What is the problem?** Are we "framing" or understanding the issues behind the need or opportunities for change?
- **What data are we gathering?** Are we willing to look at disconfirming information or are we only acknowledging the data sources that support our existing points of view?
- **How are we deciding?** What are the decision rules and how do we surface all points of view … while not falling victim to "analysis paralysis"?

The High-Performing Organization: Organizations, big or small, that create and execute viable strategies exhibit several common characteristics:

- **Build from a Unique Vision**: What are the aspirational and yet practical reasons for undertaking the transformational efforts? Leaders struggle when all they do is explain "what" needs to be accomplished; motivation comes from all levels understanding and believing in the "why."
- **Engage the Organization**: Strategy formulation used to be the purview of senior leadership. Instructing from "on high," strategies were rolled out to the masses, a bit like the "white smoke" emanating from the Vatican with the election of a new Pope. Today, with rapidly evolving markets, shifting governmental priorities, exploding innovation, and newly emerging competitors—all levels of an organization should provide critical input on developing transformational strategies that build from the "outside-in." And through such engagement comes the support necessary to execute any strategy.
- **Embrace Culture**: While somewhat outside the normal strategy discussions, culture is crucial to developing realistic strategies … strategies that can be executed. Culture is simply the formal and informal rules organizations create to get things done.[1] The problem comes when the expressed or explicit culture—the reminders put up on walls, the employee handbook, etc.—diverge from the

[1] Private conversation with Dr. Mario Moussa, Wharton.

embedded or implicit culture. Organizations may say that they are all about serving patients … but when management is not around, how do employees act?

The Tool of Scenario Planning: As argued from our opening chapter, healthcare leaders need to undertake transformational change in their current operations to survive—ideally to lead—into the future. The problem is that future seems more and more uncertain. At the very time leaders need to be bold, to seek new solutions, the very ground ahead is increasingly unstable. What to do? The traditional tools for strategy development—SWOT, Porter's Five Forces, etc.—are great for more stable, certain times. But in times of uncertainty, one needs a different framework, specifically scenario planning. As outlined in Chapter 4, scenario planning does three things:

- **Starts in the future and works back**: Counterintuitively, by getting teams out of today and placing them in alternative futures, creativity dramatically increases. The idea is not to forecast, but to develop a reasonable range of possible futures that can expand thinking to yield options and alternatives.
- **Challenges existing initiatives**: From those futures, "stress test" current initiatives to see how well they perform across multiple futures, not just in the short term. As a result, organizations develop perspectives on where and how to transform for more than just short-term, tactical responses to changing environments.
- **Develops a portfolio of strategic options**.: Organizations must continue to operate in the short term. While longer term, transformational efforts sound great … what about reducing current operating costs so this year's budget can be achieved, for example? The need to balance short-, medium-, and longer-term initiatives lies at the heart of transformational change. It cannot be one or the other—only short-term tactical responses, nor primarily longer term, transformational initiatives. Organizations that are best prepared to achieve sustainable competitive impact do both: they meet their short-term requirements *and* they invest in longer term, transformational initiatives. Without the resources from evermore efficiently managed short-term, immediate priorities, one cannot afford longer term investments. Conversely, if organizations only focus on the incremental, in times of significant change—as typifies healthcare today—they risk being bypassed by more innovative, flexible players.

Execution: Most change initiatives fail. The reasons are many: unclear direction, changing priorities, resource constraints, market challenges, etc. To improve the odds for success, Chapter 5 concludes with the keys to execution, specifically:

- **Start early**: Begin implementation as the strategy is still being articulated; seek small "wins" or incremental efficiency gains in current operations to create momentum for implementation and to free up resources for the longer term transformational efforts soon to come.

- **Establish governance infrastructure**: Assign a strong implementation manager with clear responsibilities and reporting relationships to the senior team.
- **Articulate value propositions**: Communicate, communicate, communicate. As John Kotter indicates in his many articles and books on change (Kotter 2007), most change efforts fail for lack of communication. Again, it is not the "what" … but the "why" that leaders forget.
- **Agree unambiguous priorities**: Execution thrives on clarity. What are the key—no more than half a dozen—major initiatives at the highest level that must be accomplished to drive success? Groups struggle when there are too many initiatives leading to overload. Worse, the very initiatives articulated lack specificity. For example, while "improve patient satisfaction" sounds great … what does it mean? How will supporting groups know what to do or how to build their priorities from such an ambiguous directive?
- **Establish program principles**: "Metrics for success" sound easy, but are difficult to develop. They can either mushroom out of control (leading to analysis paralysis) or remain too abstract (producing good sound bites but no real impact). Worse, they can result in unintended consequences, especially when the priorities of one group conflict with those of another. The Danaher Corporation, known for its execution focus, employs "*… a process and set of rules that force the firm's subsidiaries to translate their strategic objectives (e.g., increase market share in the Asia-Pacific market) into operational objectives (e.g., increase the rate of new product introductions). In turn, that objective triggers a series of objectives for other parts of the organization*" (Power 2011).
- **Ensure leadership**: Is the leadership team "walking the talk"? Change is hard … and it becomes near impossible if leaders do not mirror the behaviors and the new ways of working that the transformational changes require. And it is not the expressed rules, but the embedded … the rules all parts of the organization utilize when management is not around.

Frameworks are important … but what real-world examples reinforce these theories? As that great American philosopher and pugilist, Mike Tyson, opined, "*Everyone has a plan 'til they get punched in the mouth.*"

Chapters 6-13 are eight individual case studies utilizing the ideas outlined in Chapters 3-5 and applied in a range of healthcare settings. Several themes emerge from these case studies:

- **Change is not linear**: In every case, leaders had to be flexible. While the goals from driving transformational change did not change, how they were ultimately executed did.
- **Listen**: In times of change, strong leaders may want to drive ahead, issuing orders and "leading from the front." Again, in almost every case study, leaders *listened*. They had to establish the rationale for change, and its urgency with a broad range of relevant stakeholders; the "how" was realized through an iterative process of engaged staff and senior management working together for clearly defined ends or goals.

- **Democracy is suboptimal**: While it may be emotionally satisfying knowing everyone supports the actions taken, this rarely occurs. In the military, they use the rough designation of 70 % being behind a decision; less, there may be too large a contingent undermining … seeking greater consensus is wasted time. In nearly every case, not everyone supported the change; but enough did to move ahead.
- **Bias for action**: There will always be challenges. There will always be too many priorities and issues to be resolved. Leaders focus and they continue to press forward. In each case, the leader or leading team forged ahead, even when it meant taking a step back to reevaluate, reform, and then push on. In the Coastal Medical case example found in Chapter 7, Chief Operating Officer Meryl Moss movingly explains:

> Mostly, we needed to be resilient. Change is so hard and we needed to find ways to support and renew each other. I believe that this is hardest of all. It is easy to be worn down. Motivating and sustaining this very important work comes in reminding everyone, every day, that our efforts change patient lives.

In summary, David Teece writes:

> The best firms are able to rapidly leverage opportunities and constantly renew their structure and resources. The competences that enable firms to do this are known as dynamic capabilities. A firm's dynamic capabilities rest on two pillars: (1) the vision and leadership skills of managers, and (2) the cohesion and flexibility of the organization as a whole. An organization's culture and values are much slower and more difficult to change than its structure or processes, and can hamstring even an excellent strategy if its leaders cannot show the way forward (Krupp and Schoemaker 2014).

Healthcare leaders must seek longer-term transformative opportunities while balancing short-term requirements. They need to focus on external uncertainties, driving transformational initiatives to create new growth, while also molding the internal culture and structures to adapt to newly emerging strategic requirements. Only in this way will healthcare organizations continue to meet the noble needs of humankind.

References

Collins J. How the mighty fall. New York: Harper-Collins; 2009. p. 20.

Jacquemont D, Maor D, Reich A How to beat the transformation odds. McKinsey Global Survey 2015 April. http://www.mckinsey.com/insights/organization/how_to_beat_the_transformation_odds. Accessed 10 Aug 2015.

Jaffe S. Health policy brief: key issues in health reform. Health Affairs 2009 Aug 20. http://www.healthaffairs.org/healthpolicybriefs/brief_pdfs/healthpolicybrief_10.pdf. Accessed 10 Aug 2015.

Jauhar S. Out of Camelot, knights in white coats lose way. New York Times 2011 Feb 1.

Kamilla KK, Rai GS. Principles of medical ethics. In: Rai GS, editor. Medical ethics and the elderly. 4th ed. London: Radcliff Publishing; 2009. p. 1–8.

Kotter J. Leading change: why transformation efforts fail. Harvard Business Review 2007 Jan.

Krupp S, Schoemaker PJH. Winning the long game. New York: PublicAffairs; 2014. p. ix.
Mt. Sinai Health System. 2015. http://www.mountsinaihealth.org/static_files/MSHL/Files/MSHS-Our-Beds-Campaign.pdf. Accessed 10 Aug 2015.
Power B. Get your operations in shape by focusing on process. Harvard Business Review 2011 Feb.
The Economist. The pause before fast-forward. The Economist 2015 Oct 10: 76.
Welch J. Winning. New York: Harper; 2005.

Index

A
Academic health center, 141, 146
Accountability in execution, 94, 97, 100, 101, 142, 171
Accountable Care Organization (ACO), 21, 63, 65, 94, 108, 109, 111, 117, 126, 194
Acquisition, 122, 123, 125
Active role models, 86
Adequate resourcing, 78, 82
Advisory Commission for Medical Dosimetry, 164
Affiliation, 2, 60, 123
Affordable Care Act (ACA), 21, 23, 48, 52, 62, 63, 68, 94, 122, 125, 126, 152, 163, 172, 178, 181, 194
Alignment, 37, 39, 43, 77, 85, 86, 94, 96–98, 121, 122, 124, 166
  and execution, 97
American Association of Labor Legislation (AALL), 16
American Association of Medical Dosimetrists (AAMD), 163–165
American College of Healthcare Executives (ACHE), 131
American College of Surgeons Commission on Cancer (CoC), 152, 153
American Health Information Management Association (AHIMA), 4, 172–173, 175–180
American Medical Association (AMA), 16
Arthur D. Little, Inc., 35
Ask Me, 81
Assumptions
  challenging assumptions, 133
  implicit, 41
ASTRO's Radiation Oncology Incident Learning System (RO-ILS), 165
At-risk reimbursement contracts, 94
Augusta Health, 32
Augusta Way, 32
Austria, 15
Autonomy, 111, 123, 185, 195
Avastin, 47

B
Bain & Company (Bain & Co.), 58
Balanced scorecard, 83, 84, 176
Barrier busting, 79
Barriers to change, 7, 8, 76, 78, 79, 116, 188
Baxter Healthcare, 84
Behavioral economics, 21, 33, 129, 131, 133, 140–142, 147, 154–156
Behavioral Health Consumer Survey, 145
Beneficence, 195
Bias for action, 87, 167, 179, 199
Blind men and the elephant, 120
Boston Consulting Group (BCG), 28–30
Brand planning, 181–189
Brand planning to embrace future uncertainties, 181
Brigham and Women's Hospital (BWH) in Boston, 94
Britain, 16
Brown University's Executive Master of Healthcare Leadership (EMHL) program, 111, 113
Buddy system, 81
Buprenorphine Integrated Care Project, 147
Butler, Peter, 41
BWH Heart and Vascular Center (HVC), 95, 96, 105

J. Austin et al. (eds.), *Leading Strategic Change in an Era of Healthcare Transformation*, Management for Professionals,
DOI 10.1007/978-3-319-30776-3

C
Cahill, Timothy P., 19
Cancer survivor, 151–157
Care coordination, 125, 140, 141, 143, 145
CareInSync, 125
Case review, 9, 73, 94, 105, 107, 156
Celebrate results, 78, 83, 84
Centers for Medicare and Medicaid Services (CMS), 2, 62, 108, 142, 194
Certificate of Need (CoN), 127
Changing the emergency department, 124, 131, 140
Chesapeake regional information system for our patients (CRISP), 145
Christensen, Clayton, 3, 187
Cisco Systems, Inc., 27
Clinical industry benchmarks, 131
Clinical integration, 96, 97, 142
Clinical outcome, 20, 97, 121, 140, 144
Clinical specialist, 121
Coastal medical, 4, 107–118, 199
Collins, Jim, 38, 67
Communication, 4, 9, 17, 31, 39, 66, 74, 76, 80, 81, 85, 96–98, 100, 107, 166, 170, 172, 174, 177, 180, 188, 198
Community-based initiatives, 146
Competency, 81, 179
Competitive Strategy, Porter, 28, 51
Complex Functional Relationships, 133
Consistency, Accuracy, Responsibility, and Excellence in Medical Imaging and Radiation Therapy (CARE), 162
Consolidation, 123, 125, 129
Consumer-focused ventures, 52
Continuing Medical Education (CME), 155
Convenience king, 121
Coordinated comprehensive primary and specialty care services, 141–142
Core/short-term strategic initiatives, 60, 88
Core team, 76, 79–81
Core value, 37, 39–41
Cote, David, 35
Countries
- Austria, 15
- Britain, 15
- Denmark, 15
- France, 15
- Germany, 15, 58
- Hungry, 15
- Netherlands, 15
- Norway, 15, 22
- Russia, 15
- Sweden, 15, 16, 22
- Switzerland, 15
- United States (US), 1, 20, 52, 56, 139, 152, 153, 162, 170, 194

Covey, Sean, 78, 84
Creative process, 195
Cultural frameworks, 23, 88, 188
Culture
- difficulties in changing, 74, 95, 173
- embedded, 38, 74
- explicit, 196
- frameworks, 23
- implicit, embedded, 197
- importance of, 74
- links to implementation, 82
- links to strategy, 82

D
Dartmouth Institute for Health Policy and Clinical Practice, 194
Dashboard, 96, 98–100, 143
Data sources, 145, 196
Decision making, 5, 98, 127, 146, 152, 170, 176, 185, 188
Decision rules, 196
Decision Strategies International, Inc., 7, 65
Decision traps
- biases, 32
- confirmation bias, 45
- decision-making, 32, 33
- frame bias, 83
- group-think, 33, 34, 45
- overcoming, 33
- overconfidence, 33, 34, 45

Decision tree, 120
Demographics, 54, 163
Denmark, 15
Diagnostic/treatment platform, 133
Difficulties in changing culture, 74, 95, 173
Divide and conquer, 78, 83
Door-to-provider time, 22
Dranove, David, 26, 57
Drug manufacturers, 20, 22, 47, 182, 194, 195
Drug pricing, 194

E
Efficiency, 11, 29, 96, 98, 101, 105, 106, 113, 122, 129, 143, 144, 154, 186, 197
Electronic medical record (EMR), 22, 62, 63, 73, 75, 78, 82, 115, 125, 126, 156
Emanuel, Ezekiel, 124
Embedded barriers, 79, 80

Emergency department (ED), 126
engagement meetings, 145, 146
Emotional commitment, 39, 82
Employees First, Patients Second, Nayar, 113
End-of-life discussions, 155
Engage the organization, 196
Ethics, 195
Evolving tools and focus, 7
Execution
accountability, 85
alignment, 57, 85
component, 22, 33, 49, 59, 102, 128
issues with, 85
link with strategy, 83
metrics, 83
roles/responsibilities, 43, 87
stakeholders, 37, 69
of strategic plans, 71
successful, 23
Existing initiatives, 197
Explicit culture, 196
Extrapolative forecasting, 29, 182, 183

F
Facebook, 154
Faculty Practice Plan (FPP), 141
Financial sustainability, 100
Five forces strategic framework, 7, 49–52, 68, 197
Flexibility, 27, 45, 69, 85, 94, 98, 105–107, 118, 123, 128–130, 132, 187, 189, 199
Focused team, 5, 141
Fontenot, Teri, 45
Forbes, Glenn S., 40
Fostering positive lifestyle change, 154
Frame blindness, 33
Framework, 52, 57, 64, 68, 106, 121, 127, 128, 134, 146, 173, 176, 179, 185, 188, 195, 197, 198
France, 15
Franklin, Ben, 87
Fried, David, 114
Functional outcome, 144

G
Gender-specific healthcare concerns, 153
Gender-specific survivorship, 153
Genentech, 47, 48
Germany, 15, 58
General Electric (GE), 26
Governance infrastructure, 72–76, 87, 198
Ground Hog Day, 175
Group-think, 5, 33, 34, 45, 80, 177
Growth assessment tools, 102
Growth opportunities, 7, 11, 52, 53, 131, 163, 177, 188, 189

H
Halfon, Neal, 2, 3
Hambrick, Donald C., 49, 54, 167
Hambrick's Strategy Diamond, 49, 54–57
Hamel, Gary, 29
Harvard Business Review (HBR), 39, 72
Health Care Advisory Board, 3
Healthcare Clinics at Walgreens, 122
Healthcare leader, 2–5, 7, 11, 17, 19, 20, 22, 23, 33, 35, 44, 48, 49, 51–54, 58, 65, 68–69, 73, 87–88, 134, 196, 199
Health-grades, 32
Health information exchange, 143
Health information management (HIM), 169–180
Health Information Technology for Economic and Clinical Health (HITECH) Act, 152, 170
Health Insurance Portability and Accountability Act of 1996 (HIPAA), 171
Herzlinger, Regina, 52
Highest global market capitalization, 26
High performance model (HPM), 6, 35, 36, 38, 39, 41, 43, 82, 111
alignment, 43
Holistic approach, 5, 30, 35–37
Honeywell, 35
Horizontal Clinical Units, 100
Howard University, 140, 141, 143, 147
Howard University Urban Health Initiative, 10, 139–148
How to change, 2, 4, 18, 21–22, 24, 112
How to Win, 54–56, 63, 64, 69, 120, 167, 195

I
IBM, 3, 72
Implementation during planning, 72, 87
Implementation failure, 8
Implementation manager (IM), 73, 75, 76, 80–83, 85, 87
Implementation team, 75, 76, 79, 82
Implicit culture, 197
Importance of culture, 38
Incremental change, 2, 3, 7, 19, 21, 23, 24, 26, 27, 32, 44, 63, 177, 182, 185, 187, 194, 195
Industry-definition, 52
Infrastructure, 19, 41, 48, 86, 93

Infrastructure, integration & innovation, 8, 73–76, 96
Innovation in healthcare, 52
Innovative Incentive Programs, 100
Inpatient bed platform, 133
Institute of Medicine (IOM), 151
Integrated master planning for healthcare institutions, 4, 59, 64, 83, 93, 94, 120
Integrated Multidisciplinary Service Line (IMSL), 93–106
  asset grid, 102
  scorecard, 102, 104
Integrator, 52, 122
Iron triangle, 18, 194
Issues with execution, 85

J
Javanmardian, Minoo, 125
Joint operating agreement, 123
Joint Review Committee on Education in Radiologic Technology (JRCERT), 164
Joint venture (JV), 56, 123
Justice, 139, 195

K
Kahneman, Daniel, 32
Kano model, 55
Kaplan, Robert S., 83
Kelly, Margo, 119
Kennedy, Dennis V., 119
Kenya, 17
Keys to trust, 81
Key success factor (KSF), 146, 175
Kleiner Perkins Caulfield and Byers (KPCB), 34
Kloss Strategic Advisors, 171
Kodak, 27
Kotter, John, 72, 74, 198
Kunen, James, 39
Kurose, Alan, 107, 108

L
Leadership, 7, 11, 26, 29, 32, 41, 72, 73, 76, 82, 83, 86–88, 94, 97–100, 102, 105, 106, 109–111, 113, 117, 118, 123, 124, 131, 140, 145–147, 156, 172, 175–177, 179–183, 187, 188, 196, 198, 199
Level 5 leadership, 146
Lifespan Healthcare System, 153
Links to implementation, 73, 82
Links to strategy, 29
Lohr, Steve, 48
Long-range vision, 127–128
Lucentis, 47, 48

M
Managers
  importance of, 147
  role in execution, 74
Mannix, Mary N., 32
Market segments, 54
Massachusetts, 10, 19, 94, 162–166
Massachusetts State Legislature, 165
Mayo, William, 40
Mayo Clinic, 39, 40, 55
McGookin, Edward, 108
McGrath, Rita, 27
McKinsey & Company, 29
Meadows, Donella H., 122
Medicaid, 16, 21, 48, 54, 60
Medical Dosimetry Certification Board (MDCB), 162, 164
Medical Dosimetry Licensure, 162, 165, 166
Medical ethics, 195
Medical record management, 172
Medicare, 2, 16, 48, 54, 55, 60, 62, 109, 115, 126, 146
Medicare Modernization Act (MMA), 152
Medication assisted therapy (MAT), 142, 146
Merck & Co., 77
Merger, 56, 81, 122, 123, 125
Mindset
  confirmation bias, 45
  decision trap, 33, 57, 196
  frame bias, 83
  group think, 5
  overcoming, 33, 60
  overconfidence, 34, 45, 83
Minute Clinics at CVS, 122
Mission, 170, 175, 176, 179
Moussa, Mario, 38, 87

N
National Center for Healthcare Leadership, 146
National Center for Quality Assurance (NCQA), 109
National Comprehensive Cancer Network (NCCN), 153–156
  guidelines, 153
Nayar, Vaneet, 77
Netherlands, 15
Net present value analysis, 65
1900s, 16, 39

1915, 16
1930s, 16
1960s, 16, 37
1965, 16
1970s, 27
Non-maleficence, 195
No regret moves, 134
Norton, David P., 83
Norway, 15, 22
Novo Nordisk, 3, 37

O
Obama, Barack, 16, 52, 124
Ongoing oversight, 72, 84–86
Operating efficiencies, 1, 123
Options/portfolios, 68
Overconfidence, 33

P
Palliative care, 155
Pareto, Vilfredo, 132
Patient experience score, 144–145
Patient satisfaction survey, 2, 23, 96, 98, 99, 105, 198
Pearlson, Judith, 126
Peer benchmarking analysis, 95
Performance value drivers, 55
Peripheral vision, 185
Per member per month (PMPM), 2, 19, 144
Pharmaceutical industry, 22, 37, 50, 54, 57, 182, 186
Pioneer Accountable Care Organization pilot program, 94
Population health, 2–4, 9, 21, 52, 59, 63, 64, 68, 77, 110, 122, 125, 134, 135, 156, 157, 169
Porter, Michael, 51
Porter's Five Forces, 7, 49, 51–52, 68, 179
Pragmatism, 82, 83
Price reductions, 62, 124, 142, 153, 155
Primary-care practice of the future, 23
Problem definition, 21, 27, 33, 109–112
Processes, resources, and organization (PRO), 41–43
  alignment, 43
Program principles, 72, 78–84, 88

R
Radical redesign, 21, 22, 65
Ramos, Laura, 67
R&D Leader, 121
Range of values, 132, 133
Registered Health Information Administrator (RHIA), 172
Registered Health Information Technician (RHIT), 172
Reliability, 81, 170
Retail market, 3
Return on investment (ROI), 37, 65
Risk, 28, 34, 62, 64, 66, 68, 83, 94, 110, 112, 113, 117, 119–135, 140, 148, 153, 155, 157, 169, 172, 177, 181, 184, 186, 187, 197
Robert Wood Johnson Foundation, 64, 194
Rohrbeck, René, 58
Roles/responsibilities in execution, 76, 87
Roosevelt, Theodore (Teddy Roosevelt), 16
Rumelt, Richard, 27
Rush University Medical Center (RUMC), 41
Russia, 15

S
Scenario planning
  framework, 57
  process of developing, 134
  STEEP factor, 69, 179
  steps to develop, 58
  strategic portfolio, 68, 69, 84, 176, 197
  stress test, 60, 63, 197
  trends, 58, 173, 175
  uncertainties, 58, 60, 61
  utilization, 173
  value of, 172
Scenarios of the future, 60, 61, 63, 135
Schoemaker, Paul J.H., 7, 34
Schwarz, Jan Oliver, 58
Scorecards/metrics of success, 78–84
Senior management, 28, 29, 44, 74–76, 82, 83, 85, 198
Shapiro Cardiovascular Center, 94
Shared infrastructure, 97
Shared medical appointment (SMA), 154–155
Sickness funds, 16
Silo, 5, 79, 93, 97, 105, 125, 126, 134, 155, 157, 171
Sixth force, 51
Social, Technological, Economic, Environmental, and Political (STEEP) forces
  economic, 60, 69, 173
  environmental, 60, 69, 173
  political, 60, 69, 173
  social, 60, 69, 173
  technological, 60, 69, 173

Stakeholder, 31, 32, 36–39, 41, 45, 84, 97, 98, 105, 116, 135, 140, 141, 145, 146, 163–166, 173, 176, 180
STAR model, 87
Strategic initiatives
  core, 31, 65
  new, 65
  wow, 65
Strategic planning frameworks and tools, 7, 35
Strategos, 29
Strategy
  alignment, 43
  building blocks, 30–35
  change, 2, 3, 22, 106
  competitive strategy, 44
  evolution of, 28, 186
  goals of, 146
  issues, 50
  key success factors, 173, 175
  no regret moves, 134
  option, 64, 179, 185, 197
  planning, 6, 32, 62, 184
  portfolio of initiative, 58, 65
  stakeholders, 41
  sustainable competitive impact, 26, 28, 71, 197
  tools, 2, 6
  traditional, 134, 141
Strengths, Weaknesses, Opportunities and Threats (SWOT), 7, 49, 50, 68, 97, 106, 173, 179, 183, 197
Stress-test strategic initiatives, 60, 63–64
Studer, Quint, 23
Subramanian, Siva, 125
Successful communication efforts, 80
Successful execution, 23, 86–87
Support platform, 133
Survivorship care, 10, 151–157
Sustained innovation, 97
Sweden, 15, 16, 22
Switzerland, 15
Systems thinking, 134

T

Technology-based ventures, 52
Teece, David, 199
Tele-behavioral health, 142, 143
Tele-health, 10, 125, 140–143, 145, 146
Telemedicine Patient Satisfaction Survey, 145
3-I strategic model, 96–97
Traditional market, 3, 123
Transformation, 3, 7, 9–11, 16, 21, 22, 28–30, 32, 35, 41–43, 52, 53, 62, 71, 72, 75, 86, 105, 108, 112, 117, 141, 142, 169, 171–173, 181–189, 194, 196
Transformational change, 1–5, 9, 11, 19, 23, 24, 27, 30, 34, 35, 65, 68, 85, 101, 102, 106, 108, 118, 134, 157, 162, 165, 167, 173, 176–180, 188, 197, 198
Transforming cancer survivorship care, 151–157
Transforming the delivery of care, 20, 120
Transitioning workforces, 88
Triple-aim, 94
Two-way communication, 78, 80, 81, 85
Tyson, Mike, 198

U

Unambiguous priorities, 72, 88, 198
Uncertainty, 2, 5–7, 9, 11, 26–28, 32, 35, 44, 45, 49, 58, 60, 61, 64, 68, 71, 83, 85, 86, 119–135, 156, 167, 174, 176, 188, 196, 197
Unique differentiators, 55
United States (US), 108, 152, 153, 162, 170, 194
365-Urgent Care Clinic, 114

V

Value differentiators, 55
Value maximization, 122
Values
  core, 36, 38–40, 45, 76, 78
  ethics, 195
  range, 133
Value to the enterprise, 77
Value to the individual, 77
Value to the team, 77
Vertical/disease-based collaborative centers, 100
Vision
  aspirational, 37–39, 78, 86
  shared, 39, 78
  value of, 166
Visionary thinking, 6, 7, 49

W

Walmart, 26
Wayfinding, 124, 127, 129
Web of complexity, 78

Welch, Jack, 195
What to change, 4, 18–21, 23
When to change, 4, 5, 18, 23, 24
Where to play, 54–56, 64, 120, 167, 195
Why change, 4, 18–19, 23
Wilson, Woodrow, 193
Women's Cancer Screening Program, 152
Women's Hospital, 45, 105
Women's Medicine Collaborative, 153
World War I, 16
Wow/longer-term strategic initiatives, 186

Z
Ziskind, Andrew, 132
Zook, Chris, 54

The manufacturer's authorised representative in the EU is Springer Nature Customer Service Centre GmbH, Europaplatz 3, 69115 Heidelberg, Germany. If you have any concerns regarding our products, please contact ProductSafety@springernature.com

Printed and bound by CPI Group (UK) Ltd, Croydon, CR0 4YY
30/09/2026
02225571-0001